A Topical Scripture Reference Companion
for Personal and Spiritual Growth

SCRIPTURES
by Your Side

Compiled by
Richard Robles

**SIGNATURE
MEDIA**

26   25   24   23   22   21   1   2   3   4   5   6   7

SCRIPTURES BY YOUR SIDE

Published by:
Signature Media, llc
4770 Eureka Ave. Yorba Linda, CA 92885
www.Signature.pub

Library of Congress Cataloging-in-Publication Data:
ISBN: 978-1-954966-11-6   Paperback
E-book available exclusively on Kindle at www.Amazon.com

BISAC Category:
BIB008040   BIBLES / Multiple Translations / Reference
REL006700   RELIGION / Biblical Studies / Bible Study Guides

Printed in the United States

Contents

FOREWORD

Life is full of what my brother Tim Storey calls, "Life Interruptions." Whether you are a mother, father, business owner, or minister, if there is anything you can be sure of it's that life will throw you curve-balls. In those situations, it's the Word of God that is a 'lamp unto your feet' and will lead you through the darkness.

It's rare to find a book that has been designed to help believers at every part of their journey of faith than this book. Why? Because it was designed to help empower you when you will need it most. By providing you with God's Word it equips you to find your own words to pray to your specific situation. Not only that, it's meant to be always kept by your side. Like a great sword that cuts through fear and doubt let scripture be your ultimate weapon in your fight against your mountain.

Paige Junaeus

INTRODUCTION

I have been a believer for many years. In that time, I have seen God do some amazing things both in my life and in the lives of others. Those amazing things happened through praying God's Word. Scripture tells us that God's word is powerful. In fact, it's the most powerful force in the universe—it created existence itself. It's also a double-edged sword, able to cut through "soul and spirit, joint and marrow." Scripture is a weapon, a weapon that advances the goodness of God in a broken world. When you discover how to use it and keep it by your side, your life will change forever.

MY STORY

Since the early nineties, I have followed the Lord. During that time, I always had an interest in prayer. I would attend prayer meetings regularly at my church and practiced prayer daily in my personal life. Shortly after I moved to Orange County, California, I felt the Lord call me to volunteer as a prayer phone operator at Trinity Broadcasting Network. A few times a week, I'd answer phone calls from people all over America who needed prayer. As I heard their stories and troubles, my heart would go out to them. Sometimes, I would struggle to find the right words to say. Even so, I would just start to pray by faith. Somehow, the Holy Spirit would always lead me and give me the right words. Almost always, they would be words in the form of scripture. Eventually, I started bringing my Bible to my shifts. As people told me their prayer requests, I'd look up a scripture that addressed what they were going through and then prayed God's Word over their life. As time went on, something amazing began to happen—many people's situations would improve or even change! As they gave me feedback and praise reports, I would be amazed at how God would show up and meet their needs in miraculous ways! From then on, I was hooked! The power of praying God's word became a cornerstone of my faith and pillar of truth in my life. Every day I filled myself with God's word. When I felt down, God's word picked me up. When I felt weak, God's word would give me strength. When I felt timid, God's word gave me confidence and courage! The more I read and meditated, the more transformed my life became. Then one day, I noticed that one of the leaders at my home church's intercessory prayer team had started a prayer booth outside in front of the church. The idea was simple. Before and after service, church members (also people walking or driving by)x that wanted prayer could go up to the prayer booth and receive prayer. I immediately signed up to volunteer! As I began to serve alongside my prayer leader, I noticed that he would write down every prayer request he received in a notebook that he kept right beside him. Eventually I asked to borrow his log. As I read through each one, I was able to distill those thousands of prayer requests into a hundred and forty topics. From there I chose a topic and looked up scriptures pertaining to that topic in every translation. When a certain Scripture translation really seemed to "hit the spot" I wrote it down. In the end, that alphabetical list of prayer topics contained two thousand individual scriptures that spoke to over a hundred situations. This book is the culmination of that journey. For years I had gone to different bookstores in search of resources to help me apply scripture to prayer. While there are many scripture-based books out there, most of them only had a handful of topics or wrote out the prayers for you. In the end, it was the Holy Spirit who inspired me to take action. If I couldn't find a book designed to help me pray my own prayers with scripture, maybe I should be the one to make it happen. Now here we are!

MY HOPE

Why am I telling you this story? Because I want this book to bless you. From one believer to another, I wrote this book so that you might be built up and empowered, not by my words, by God's words! Just like when God used His word at the beginning of the world to speak light into existence, I want you to be equipped to speak God's divine light in your life. For God's word is living and active. Hebrews 4:12 says the Word is "sharper than a double-edged sword!" Ephesians 6:17 says it's "the sword of the Spirit, which is the Word of God!" The word of God is a weapon? Yes! It's a weapon that has the "divine power to demolish strongholds." Paul explains to us in 2 Corinthians 10:4. When we speak God's Word, it "does not return empty or void," Isaiah 55:11. See? You're starting to see God's Word in action already! God's Word is powerful! It has the power to transform your life. To bring "life and death in the power of the tongue!" Those that love God's word "shall see its fruit" Proverbs 18:21. It will help you speak to your biggest mountains! When you stand on God's word, what you say "will be done for him" Mark 11:23. For "his angels, you mighty ones who do his bidding" obey "the voice of his word" Psalms 103:20! The only thing left is for you to use it, to build your life with it on it, and to carry God's word by your side.

HOW IS THIS BOOK DESIGNED

I designed the book to be a resource in every area of your life. Each topic is a culmination of real-world prayers and needs. Every scripture has been used to bring healing, renewal, and divine intervention to real people's situations! Every scripture translation has been chosen to speak to the right spot. All of it assembled to build you and your faith. "Consequently, faith comes from hearing the message, and the message is heard through the word about Christ" Romans 10:17. There you have it! I hope this resource blesses you as much as it has blessed my life. I hope God's word empowers you as much as it has empowered me. I hope it encourages you and enables you to speak with power to every situation you encounter. Finally, I hope it will help keep scripture by your side at all times! God bless you.

ABUNDANCE

Deuteronomy 8: 18 (NIV)
18 But remember the Lord your God, for it is he who gives you the ability to produce wealth, and so confirms his covenant, which he swore to your ancestors, as it is today.

Deuteronomy 28: 2, 5, 8 (HCSB)
2 All these blessings will come and overtake you, because you obey the Lord your God: 5 Your bas-ket and kneading bowl will be blessed. 8 The Lord will grant you a blessing on your storehouses and on everything you do; He will bless you in the land the Lord your God is giving you.

2 Chronicles 25: 9 (NLT)
9 Amaziah asked the man of God, "But what about all that silver I paid to hire the army of Israel?" The man of God replied, "The Lord is able to give you much more than this!"

Psalms 36: 7 - 8 (AMP)
7 How precious is Your steadfast love, O God! The children of men take refuge and put their trust under the shadow of Your wings. 8 They relish and feast on the abundance of Your house; and You cause them to drink of the stream of Your pleasures.

Psalms 37: 16 (GNT)
16 The little that a good person owns is worth more than the wealth of all the wicked.

Psalms 92: 13 - 14 (NKJV)
13 Those who are planted in the house of the Lord Shall flourish in the courts of our God. 14 They shall still bear fruit in old age; They shall be fresh and flourishing,

Psalms 112: 1 - 3 (NKJV)
1 Praise the Lord! Blessed is the man who fears the Lord, Who delights greatly in His command-ments. 2 His descendants will be mighty on earth; The generation of the upright will be blessed. 3 Wealth and riches will be in his house, And his righteousness endures forever.

Proverbs 3: 9 - 10 (NKJV)
9 Honor the Lord with your possessions, And with the firstfruits of all your increase; 10 So your barns will be filled with plenty, And your vats will overflow with new wine.

Proverbs 8: 12, 18 - 19 (HCSB)
12 I, Wisdom, share a home with shrewdness and have knowledge and discretion. 18 With me are riches and honor, lasting wealth and righteousness. 19 My fruit is better than solid gold, and my har-vest than pure silver.

Proverbs 10: 4 (HCSB)
4 Idle hands make one poor, but diligent hands bring riches.

Proverbs 10: 22 (NLT)
22 The blessing of the Lord makes a person rich, and he adds no sorrow with it.

Proverbs 11: 25 (NIV)
25 A generous person will prosper; whoever refreshes others will be refreshed.

Proverbs 11: 28 (NKJV)
28 He who trusts in his riches will fall, But the righteous will flourish like foliage.

Ecclesiastes 5: 19 (WEB)
19 Every man also to whom God has given riches and wealth, and has given him power to eat of it, and to take his portion, and to rejoice in his labor—this is the gift of God.

Joel 2: 26 (ESV)
26 "You shall eat in plenty and be satisfied, and praise the name of the Lord your God, who has dealt wondrously with you. And my people shall never again be put to shame.

Malachi 3: 10 - 11 (NASB)
10 Bring the whole tithe into the storehouse, so that there may be food in My house, and test Me now in this," says the Lord of hosts, "if I will not open for you the windows of heaven and pour out for you a blessing until it overflows. 11 Then I will rebuke the devourer for you, so that it will not destroy the fruits of the ground; nor will your vine in the field cast its grapes," says the Lord of hosts.

Luke 6: 38 (NIVUK)
38 Give, and it will be given to you. A good measure, pressed down, shaken together and running over, will be poured into your lap. For with the measure you use, it will be measured to you.'

Luke 15: 29, 31 (NIVUK)
29 But he answered his father, "Look! All these years I've been slaving for you and never disobeyed your orders. Yet you never gave me even a young goat so I could celebrate with my friends.

Romans 10: 12 (NET)
12 For there is no distinction between the Jew and the Greek, for the same Lord is Lord of all, who richly blesses all who call on him.

2 Corinthians 9: 6 - 8 (HCSB)
6 Remember this: The person who sows sparingly will also reap sparingly, and the person who sows generously will also reap generously. 7 Each person should do as he has decided in his heart—not reluctantly or out of necessity, for God loves a cheerful giver. 8 And God is able to make every grace overflow to you, so that in every way, always having everything you need, you may excel in every good work.

ACCOMMODATE

Leviticus 23: 22 (NLT)
22 "When you harvest the crops of your land, do not harvest the grain along the edges of your fields, and do not pick up what the harvesters drop. Leave it for the poor and the foreigners living among you. I am the Lord your God."

Psalms 41: 1 - 2 (NKJV)
1 Blessed is he who considers the poor; The Lord will deliver him in time of trouble. 2 The Lord will preserve him and keep him alive, And he will be blessed on the earth; You will not deliver him to the will of his enemies.

Psalms 112: 5, 9 (CEV)
5 Life will go well for those who freely lend and are honest in business. 9 They will always be remem-bered and greatly praised, because they were kind and freely gave to the poor.

Proverbs 22: 9 (CEV)
9 The Lord blesses everyone who freely gives food to the poor.

Isaiah 58: 7 - 11 (NLT)

7 Share your food with the hungry, and give shelter to the homeless. Give clothes to those who need them, and do not hide from relatives who need your help. 8 "Then your salvation will come like the dawn, and your wounds will quickly heal. Your godliness will lead you forward, and the glory of the Lord will protect you from behind. 9 Then when you call, the Lord will answer. 'Yes, I am here,' he will quickly reply. "Remove the heavy yoke of oppression. Stop pointing your finger and spreading vicious rumors! 10 Feed the hungry, and help those in trouble. Then your light will shine out from the dark-ness, and the darkness around you will be as bright as noon. 11 The Lord will guide you continually, giving you water when you are dry and restoring your strength. You will be like a well-watered garden, like an ever-flowing spring.

Matthew 5: 41 - 42 (MEV)

41 And whoever compels you to go a mile, go with him two. 42 Give to him who asks you, and from him who would borrow from you do not turn away.

Matthew 6: 1 - 4 (WEB)

"Be careful that you don't do your charitable giving before men, to be seen by them, or else you have no reward from your Father who is in heaven. 2 Therefore when you do merciful deeds, don't sound a trumpet before yourself, as the hypocrites do in the synagogues and in the streets, that they may get glory from men. Most certainly I tell you, they have received their reward. 3 But when you do merciful deeds, don't let your left hand know what your right hand does, 4 so that your merciful deeds may be in secret, then your Father who sees in secret will reward you openly.

Matthew 25: 34 - 40 (ESV)

34 Then the King will say to those on his right, 'Come, you who are blessed by my Father, inherit the kingdom prepared for you from the foundation of the world. 35 For I was hungry and you gave me food, I was thirsty and you gave me drink, I was a stranger and you welcomed me, 36 I was naked and you clothed me, I was sick and you visited me, I was in prison and you came to me.' 37 Then the righteous will answer him, saying, 'Lord, when did we see you hungry and feed you, or thirsty and give you drink? 38 And when did we see you a stranger and welcome you, or naked and clothe you? 39 And when did we see you sick or in prison and visit you?' 40 And the King will answer them, 'Truly, I say to you, as you did it to one of the least of these my brothers, you did it to me.'

Luke 16: 10 - 13 (NIVUK)

10 'Whoever can be trusted with very little can also be trusted with much, and whoever is dishonest with very little will also be dishonest with much. 11 So if you have not been trustworthy in handling worldly wealth, who will trust you with true riches? 12 And if you have not been trustworthy with someone else's property, who will give you property of your own? 13 'No one can serve two masters. Either you will hate the one and love the other, or you will be devoted to the one and despise the other. You cannot serve both God and Money.'

Acts 20: 35 (ESV)
35 In all things I have shown you that by working hard in this way we must help the weak and remem-ber the words of the Lord Jesus, how he himself said, 'It is more blessed to give than to receive.'"

Romans 12: 9, 13 (NKJV)
9 Let love be without hypocrisy. Abhor what is evil. Cling to what is good. 13 distributing to the needs of the saints, given to hospitality.

2 Corinthians 8: 9, 12 - 14 (MEV)
9 For you know the grace of our Lord Jesus Christ, that though He was rich, yet for your sakes He became poor, that through His poverty you might be rich. 12 For if there is a willing mind first, the gift is accepted according to what a man possesses and not according to what he does not possess. 13 I do not mean that other men have relief, and you be burdened, 14 but for equality, that your abun - dance now at this time may supply their need, and their abundance may supply your need— that there may be equality.

Ephesians 4: 32 (NIV)
32 Be kind and compassionate to one another, forgiving each other, just as in Christ God forgave you.

Hebrews 13: 2 (NKJV)
2 Do not forget to entertain strangers, for by so doing some have unwittingly entertained angels.

James 2: 15 - 16 (ISV)
15 Suppose a brother or sister does not have any clothes or daily food 16 and one of you tells them, "Go in peace! Stay warm and eat heartily." If you do not provide for their bodily needs, what good does it do?

1 Peter 4: 9 - 10 (NIV)
9 Offer hospitality to one another without grumbling. 10 Each of you should use whatever gift you have received to serve others, as faithful stewards of God's grace in its various forms.

ADDICTION

Psalms 91: 2, 3, 4, 11, 15 (NKJV)
2 I will say of the Lord, "He is my refuge and my fortress; My God, in Him I will trust." 3 Surely He shall deliver you from the snare of the fowler And from the perilous pestilence. 4 He shall cover you with His feathers, And under His wings you shall take refuge; His truth shall be your shield and buckler. 11 For He shall give His angels charge over you, To keep you in all your ways. 15 He shall call upon Me, and I will answer him; I will be with him in trouble; I will deliver him and hon-or him.

Psalms 107:14, 19, 20 (NKJV)
14 He brought them out of darkness and the shadow of death, And broke their chains in pieces. 19 Then they cried out to the Lord in their trouble, And He saved them out of their distresses. 20 He sent His word and healed them, And delivered them from their destructions.

Matthew 6:13 (DRA)
13 And lead us not into temptation. But deliver us from evil. Amen.

Matthew 11: 29, 30 (WEB)

29 Take my yoke upon you, and learn from me, for I am gentle and humble in heart; and you will find rest for your souls. 30 For my yoke is easy, and my burden is light."

John 10:10 (NIV)

10 The thief comes only to steal and kill and destroy; I have come that they may have life, and have it to the full.

Romans 7: 15 - 20 (ESV)

15 For I do not understand my own actions. For I do not do what I want, but I do the very thing I hate. 16 Now if I do what I do not want, I agree with the law, that it is good. 17 So now it is no longer I who do it, but sin that dwells within me. 18 For I know that nothing good dwells in me, that is, in my flesh. For I have the desire to do what is right, but not the ability to carry it out. 19 For I do not do the good I want, but the evil I do not want is what I keep on doing. 20 Now if I do what I do not want, it is no longer I who do it, but sin that dwells within me.

Romans 8: 2 (NKJV)

2 For the law of the Spirit of life in Christ Jesus has made me free from the law of sin and death.

1 Corinthians 6:12 (RSV)

12 "All things are lawful for me," but not all things are helpful. "All things are lawful for me," but I will not be enslaved by anything.

1 Corinthians 10:13 (WEB)

13 No temptation has taken you except what is common to man. God is faithful, who will not allow you to be tempted above what you are able, but will with the temptation also make the way of escape, that you may be able to endure it.

2 Corinthians 6:14 (WEB)

14 Don't be unequally yoked with unbelievers, for what fellowship have righteousness and iniquity? Or what fellowship has light with darkness?

James 4:7 - 8 (NKJV)

7 Therefore submit to God. Resist the devil and he will flee from you. 8 Draw near to God and He will draw near to you. Cleanse your hands, you sinners; and purify your hearts, you double-minded.

1 Peter 5: 8 - 11 (WEB)

8 Be sober and self-controlled. Be watchful. Your adversary, the devil, walks around like a roaring lion, seeking whom he may devour. 9 Withstand him steadfast in your faith, knowing that your broth - ers who are in the world are undergoing the same sufferings. 10 But may the God of all grace, who called you to his eternal glory by Christ Jesus, after you have suffered a little while, perfect, establish, strengthen, and settle you. 11 To him be the glory and the power forever and ever. Amen.

2 Peter 1:3 (NIV)

3 His divine power has given us everything we need for a godly life through our knowledge of him who called us by his own glory and goodness.

ADULTERY

Leviticus 18: 20 (NASB)

20 You shall not have intercourse with your neighbor's wife, to be defiled with her.

Proverbs 5: 15 - 21 (NIV)
15 Drink water from your own cistern, running water from your own well. 16 Should your springs over-flow in the streets, your streams of water in the public squares? 17 Let them be yours alone, never to be shared with strangers. 18 May your fountain be blessed, and may you rejoice in the wife of your youth. 19 A loving doe, a graceful deer— may her breasts satisfy you always, may you ever be intoxicated with her love. 20 Why, my son, be intoxicated with another man's wife? Why embrace the bosom of a wayward woman? 21 For your ways are in full view of the Lord, and he examines all your paths.

Proverbs 6: 24 - 29 (NIV)
24 keeping you from your neighbor's wife, from the smooth talk of a wayward woman. 25 Do not lust in your heart after her beauty or let her captivate you with her eyes. 26 For a prostitute can be had for a loaf of bread, but another man's wife preys on your very life. 27 Can a man scoop fire into his lap without his clothes being burned? 28 Can a man walk on hot coals without his feet being scorched? 29 So is he who sleeps with another man's wife; no one who touches her will go unpunished.

Matthew 5: 28 (WEB)
28 but I tell you that everyone who gazes at a woman to lust after her has committed adultery with her already in his heart.

Matthew 15: 19 (ESV)
19 For out of the heart come evil thoughts, murder, adultery, sexual immorality, theft, false witness, slander.

Mark 10: 11 - 12 (HCSB)
11 And He said to them, "Whoever divorces his wife and marries another commits adultery against her. 12 Also, if she divorces her husband and marries another, she commits adultery."

Romans 7: 1 - 3 (NET)
1 Or do you not know, brothers and sisters (for I am speaking to those who know the law), that the law is lord over a person as long as he lives? 2 For a married woman is bound by law to her husband as long as he lives, but if her husband dies, she is released from the law of the marriage. 3 So then, if she is joined to another man while her husband is alive, she will be called an adulteress. But if her husband dies, she is free from that law, and if she is joined to another man, she is not an adulteress.

1 Corinthians 6: 15 (NKJV)
15 Do you not know that your bodies are members of Christ? Shall I then take the members of Christ and make them members of a harlot? Certainly not!

1 Corinthians 10: 13 (NIV)
13 No temptation has overtaken you except what is common to mankind. And God is faithful; he will not let you be tempted beyond what you can bear. But when you are tempted, he will also provide a way out so that you can endure it.

Galatians 5: 19 (WEB)
19 Now the deeds of the flesh are obvious, which are: adultery, sexual immorality, uncleanness, lust-fulness,

1 Thessalonians 4: 3 - 5 (NKJV)
3 For this is the will of God, your sanctification: that you should abstain from sexual immorality; 4 that each of you should know how to possess his own vessel in sanctification and honor, 5 not in passion of lust, like the Gentiles who do not know God;

ANGELS

Genesis 24: 40 (NKJV)
40 But he said to me, 'The Lord, before whom I walk, will send His angel with you and prosper your way; and you shall take a wife for my son from my family and from my father's house.

Genesis 32: 1 (NKJV)
32 So Jacob went on his way, and the angels of God met him.

Exodus 23: 20 (NKJV)
20 "Behold, I send an Angel before you to keep you in the way and to bring you into the place which I have prepared.

2 Kings 6: 16 - 17 (NASB)
16 So he answered, "Do not fear, for those who are with us are more than those who are with them." 17 Then Elisha prayed and said, "O Lord, I pray, open his eyes that he may see." And the Lord opened the servant's eyes and he saw; and behold, the mountain was full of horses and chariots of fire all around Elisha.

Psalms 34: 7 (NIV)
7 The angel of the Lord encamps around those who fear him, and he delivers them.

Psalms 35: 4 - 6 (NKJV)
4 Let those be put to shame and brought to dishonor Who seek after my life; Let those be turned back and brought to confusion Who plot my hurt. 5 Let them be like chaff before the wind, And let the an-gel of the Lord chase them. 6 Let their way be dark and slippery, And let the angel of the Lord pursue them.

Psalms 103: 20 - 21 (NASB)
20 Bless the Lord, you His angels, Mighty in strength, who perform His word, Obeying the voice of His word! 21 Bless the Lord, all you His hosts, You who serve Him, doing His will.

Psalms 104: 3 - 4 (ESV)
3 He lays the beams of his chambers on the waters; he makes the clouds his chariot; he rides on the wings of the wind; 4 he makes his messengers winds, his ministers a flaming fire.

Daniel 10: 12 - 13 (NKJV)
12 Then he said to me, "Do not fear, Daniel, for from the first day that you set your heart to under-stand, and to humble yourself before your God, your words were heard; and I have come because of your words. 13 But the prince of the kingdom of Persia withstood me twenty-one days; and behold, Michael, one of the chief princes, came to help me, for I had been left alone there with the kings of Persia.

Galatians 1: 8 (NKJV)
8 But even if we, or an angel from heaven, preach any other gospel to you than what we have preached to you, let him be accursed.

Hebrews 1: 7, 14 (AMP)
7 Referring to the angels He says, [God] Who makes His angels winds and His ministering servants flames of fire; 14 Are not the angels all ministering spirits (servants) sent out in the service [of God for the assistance] of those who are to inherit salvation?

Hebrews 13: 2 (NKJV)
2 Do not forget to entertain strangers, for by so doing some have unwittingly entertained angels.

ANGER

Proverbs 14:17 (GNT)
17 People with a hot temper do foolish things; wiser people remain calm.

Proverbs 15: 1 (NKJV)
15 A soft answer turns away wrath, But a harsh word stirs up anger.

Proverbs 15: 18 (NIV)
18 A hot-tempered person stirs up conflict, but the one who is patient calms a quarrel.

Proverbs 16: 32 (HCSB)
32 Patience is better than power, and controlling one's temper, than capturing a city.

Proverbs 21: 9, 19 (NKJV)
9 Better to dwell in a corner of a housetop, Than in a house shared with a contentious woman. 19 Better to dwell in the wilderness, Than with a contentious and angry woman.

Ecclesiastes 7: 9 (HCSB)
9 Don't let your spirit rush to be angry, for anger abides in the heart of fools.

Matthew 5: 22 (NCV)
22 But I tell you, if you are angry with a brother or sister,[a] you will be judged. If you say bad things to a brother or sister, you will be judged by the council. And if you call someone a fool, you will be in danger of the fire of hell.

Galatians 5: 22 - 23 (WEB)
22 But the fruit of the Spirit is love, joy, peace, patience, kindness, goodness, faith, 23 gentleness, and self-control. Against such things there is no law.

Ephesians 4: 26 - 27 (NKJV)
26 "Be angry, and do not sin": do not let the sun go down on your wrath, 27 nor give place to the devil.

Ephesians 4: 31 - 32 (NET)
31 You must put away all bitterness, anger, wrath, quarreling, and slanderous talk—indeed all malice. 32 Instead, be kind to one another, compassionate, forgiving one another, just as God in Christ also forgave you.

Phillipians 4: 8 (NLT)
8 And now, dear brothers and sisters, one final thing. Fix your thoughts on what is true, and honor-able, and right, and pure, and lovely, and admirable. Think about things that are excellent and worthy of praise.

Colossians 3:8 (HCSB)
8 But now you must also put away all the following: anger, wrath, malice, slander, and filthy language from your mouth.

Colossians 3:21 (HCSB)
21 Fathers, do not exasperate your children, so they won't become discouraged.

2 Timothy 2: 24 (NKJV)
24 And a servant of the Lord must not quarrel but be gentle to all, able to teach, patient,

James 1: 19 - 20 (HCSB)
19 My dearly loved brothers, understand this: Everyone must be quick to hear, slow to speak, and slow to anger, 20 for man's anger does not accomplish God's righteousness.

ANGUISH

Joshua 1:9 (NET)
9 I repeat, be strong and brave! Don't be afraid and don't panic, for I, the Lord your God, am with you in all you do."

2 Samuel 22:7 (NKJV)
7 In my distress I called upon the Lord, And cried out to my God; He heard my voice from His temple, And my cry entered His ears.

Psalms 4:1 (NKJV)
Hear me when I call, O God of my righteousness! You have relieved me in my distress; Have mercy on me, and hear my prayer.

Psalms 27:14 (NKJV)
14 Wait on the Lord; Be of good courage, And He shall strengthen your heart; Wait, I say, on the Lord!

Psalms 30: 5, 11 (HCSB)
5 For His anger lasts only a moment, but His favor, a lifetime. Weeping may spend the night, but there is joy in the morning. 11 You turned my lament into dancing; You removed my sackcloth and clothed me with gladness,

Psalms 32:7 (NKJV)
7 You are my hiding place; You shall preserve me from trouble; You shall surround me with songs of deliverance.

Psalms 46: 1 - 5 (NIV)
God is our refuge and strength, an ever-present help in trouble. Therefore we will not fear, though the earth give way and the mountains fall into the heart of the sea, though its waters roar and foam and the mountains quake with their surging.[c] 4 There is a river whose streams make glad the city of God, the holy place where the Most High dwells. 5 God is within her, she will not fall; God will help her at break of day.

Psalms 55: 17 - 18 (NKJV)
17 Evening and morning and at noon I will pray, and cry aloud, And He shall hear my voice. 18 He has redeemed my soul in peace from the battle that was against me, For there were many against me.

Psalms 91: 15 (NKJV)
15 He shall call upon Me, and I will answer him; I will be with him in trouble; I will deliver him and hon-or him.

Psalms 107: 9 (NKJV)
9 For He satisfies the longing soul, And fills the hungry soul with goodness.

Isaiah 26: 3 (ESV)
3 You keep him in perfect peace whose mind is stayed on you, because he trusts in you.

Isaiah 40: 29 - 31 (NET)
29 He gives strength to those who are tired; to the ones who lack power, he gives renewed energy 30 Even youths get tired and weary; even strong young men clumsily stumble. 31 But those who wait for the Lord's help find renewed strength; they rise up as if they had eagles' wings, they run without growing weary, they walk without getting tired.

Isaiah 41: 10 (NIV)
10 So do not fear, for I am with you do not be dismayed, for I am your God. I will strengthen you and help you; I will uphold you with my righteous right hand.

Matthew 11: 28 (WEB)
28 "Come to me, all you who labor and are heavily burdened, and I will give you rest.

Romans 12: 12 (NET)
12 Rejoice in hope, endure in suffering, persist in prayer.

Philippians 4: 6 - 8 (HCSB)
6 Don't worry about anything, but in everything, through prayer and petition with thanksgiving, let your requests be made known to God. 7 And the peace of God, which surpasses every thought, will guard your hearts and minds in Christ Jesus. 8 Finally brothers, whatever is true, whatever is honorable, whatever is just, whatever is pure, what-ever is lovely, whatever is commendable—if there is any moral excellence and if there is any praise— dwell on these things.

2 Timothy 1: 7 (NKJV)
7 For God has not given us a spirit of fear, but of power and of love and of a sound mind.

1 Peter 5: 6 - 9 (NET)
6 And God will exalt you in due time, if you humble yourselves under his mighty hand 7 by casting all your cares on him because he cares for you. 8 Be sober and alert. Your enemy the devil, like a roar-ing lion, is on the prowl looking for someone to devour. 9 Resist him, strong in your faith, because you know that your brothers and sisters throughout the world are enduring the same kinds of suffering.

1 John 4: 4 (WEB)
4 You are of God, little children, and have overcome them; because greater is he who is in you than he who is in the world.

ANSWERED PRAYER

Psalms 20: 1 - 6 (RSV)
1 The Lord answer you in the day of trouble! The name of the God of Jacob protect you! 6 Now I know that the Lord will help his anointed; he will answer him from his holy heaven with mighty victo-ries by his right hand.

Psalms 21: 2 (NIV)
2 You have granted him his heart's desire and have not withheld the request of his lips.

Psalms 34: 4 (NET)
4 I sought the Lord's help and he answered me; he delivered me from all my fears.

Psalms 37: 4-5 (NKJV)
4 Delight yourself also in the Lord, And He shall give you the desires of your heart. 5 Commit your way to the Lord, Trust also in Him, And He shall bring it to pass.

Psalms 65: 5 (NIV)
5 You answer us with awesome and righteous deeds, God our Savior, the hope of all the ends of the earth and of the farthest seas,

Psalms 86:7 (NIV)
7 When I am in distress, I call to you, because you answer me.

Psalms 91: 15 (NLT)
5 When they call on me, I will answer; I will be with them in trouble. I will rescue and honor them.

Psalms 138:3 (NKJV)
3 In the day when I cried out, You answered me, And made me bold with strength in my soul.

Psalms 145: 18 - 19 (NLT)
18 The Lord is close to all who call on him, yes, to all who call on him in truth. 19 He grants the desires of those who fear him; he hears their cries for help and rescues them.

Proverbs 10: 24 (NKJV)
The fear of the wicked will come upon him, And the desire of the righteous will be granted.

Isaiah 38: 14 - 16 (CEV)
14 I cry like a swallow; I mourn like a dove. My eyes are red from looking to you, Lord. I am terribly abused. Please come and help me.[a] 15 There's nothing I can say in answer to you, since you are the one who has done this to me. My life has turned sour; I will limp until I die. 16 Your words and your deeds bring life to everyone, including me. Please make me healthy and strong again.

Isaiah 65: 24 (NLT)
24 I will answer them before they even call to me. While they are still talking about their needs, I will go ahead and answer their prayers!

Jeremiah 29: 12 (WEB)
12 You shall call on me, and you shall go and pray to me, and I will listen to you.

Jeremiah 33: 3 (GNT)
3 "Call to me, and I will answer you; I will tell you wonderful and marvelous things that you know nothing about.

Matthew 18: 19 - 20 (CEV)
19 I promise that when any two of you on earth agree about something you are praying for, my Father in heaven will do it for you. 20 Whenever two or three of you come together in my name, I am there with you.

Matthew 21: 22 (WEB)
22 All things, whatever you ask in prayer, believing, you will receive."

Matthew 6: 6 (MEV)
6 But you, when you pray, enter your closet, and when you have shut your door, pray to your Father who is in

secret. And your Father who sees in secret will reward you openly.

Matthew 7: 7 - 8 (WEB)

7 "Ask, and it will be given you. Seek, and you will find. Knock, and it will be opened for you. 8 For everyone who asks receives. He who seeks finds. To him who knocks it will be opened.

Mark 11: 24 - 25 (HCSB)

24 Therefore I tell you, all the things you pray and ask for—believe that you have received them, and you will have them. 25 And whenever you stand praying, if you have anything against anyone, forgive him, so that your Father in heaven will also forgive you your wrongdoing. 25 "And whenever you stand praying, if you have anything against anyone, forgive him, that your Fa-ther in heaven may also forgive you your trespasses.

John 14: 13 - 14 (NCV)

13 And if you ask for anything in my name, I will do it for you so that the Father's glory will be shown through the Son. 14 If you ask me for anything in my name, I will do it.

John 15: 7 (WEB)

7 If you remain in me, and my words remain in you, you will ask whatever you desire, and it will be done for you.

John 16: 23 - 24 (HCSB)

23 In that day you will not ask Me anything. "I assure you: Anything you ask the Father in My name, He will give you. 24 Until now you have asked for nothing in My name. Ask and you will receive, so that your joy may be complete.

Hebrews 4: 16 (TLB)

16 So let us come boldly to the very throne of God and stay there to receive his mercy and to find grace to help us in our times of need.

1 John 3: 22 - 23 (WEB)

22 and whatever we ask, we receive from him, because we keep his commandments and do the things that are pleasing in his sight. 23 This is his commandment, that we should believe in the name of his Son, Jesus Christ, and love one another, even as he commanded.

ASK

Psalms 50:15 (NIV)

15 and call on me in the day of trouble; I will deliver you, and you will honor me."

Psalms 81:7 (NIV)

7 In your distress you called and I rescued you, I answered you out of a thundercloud; I tested you at the waters of Meribah.

Psalms 91:15 (NKJV)

15 He shall call upon Me, and I will answer him; I will be with him in trouble; I will deliver him and hon-or him.

Psalms 145:19 (NIV)

19 He fulfills the desires of those who fear him; he hears their cry and saves them.

Jeremiah 29:12 (NIV)

12 Then you will call on me and come and pray to me, and I will listen to you.

Jeremiah 33:3 (NIV)

3 'Call to me and I will answer you and tell you great and unsearchable things you do not know.'

Matthew 18:19 (WEB)

19 Again, assuredly I tell you, that if two of you will agree on earth concerning anything that they will ask, it will be done for them by my Father who is in heaven.

Matthew 7: 7 - 11 (WEB)

7 "Ask, and it will be given you. Seek, and you will find. Knock, and it will be opened for you. 8 For everyone who asks receives. He who seeks finds. To him who knocks it will be opened. 9 Or who is there among you, who, if his son asks him for bread, will give him a stone? 10 Or if he asks for a fish, who will give him a serpent? 11 If you then, being evil, know how to give good gifts to your children, how much more will your Father who is in heaven give good things to those who ask him!

Mark 11:23 - 24 (NET)

23 I tell you the truth, if someone says to this mountain, 'Be lifted up and thrown into the sea,' and does not doubt in his heart but believes that what he says will happen, it will be done for him. 24 For this reason I tell you, whatever you pray and ask for, believe that you have received it, and it will be yours.

John 14: 13 - 14 (NIV)

13 And I will do whatever you ask in my name, so that the Father may be glorified in the Son. 14 You may ask me for anything in my name, and I will do it.

John 15:7 (NIV)

7 If you remain in me and my words remain in you, ask whatever you wish, and it will be done for you.

Ephesians 3:20 (WEB)

20 Now to him who is able to do exceedingly abundantly above all that we ask or think, according to the power that works in us,

Philippians 4:6 (HCSB)

6 Don't worry about anything, but in everything, through prayer and petition with thanksgiving, let your requests be made known to God.

James 4:2 - 3 (GNT)

2 You want things, but you cannot have them, so you are ready to kill; you strongly desire things, but you cannot get them, so you quarrel and fight. You do not have what you want because you do not ask God for it. 3 And when you ask, you do not receive it, because your motives are bad; you ask for things to use for your own pleasures.

1 John 5: 14 - 15 (ESV)

14 And this is the confidence that we have toward him, that if we ask anything according to his will he hears us. 15 And if we know that he hears us in whatever we ask, we know that we have the requests that we have asked of him.

AUTHORITY

Psalms 18: 29 (NET)

29 Indeed, with your help I can charge against an army; by my God's power I can jump over a wall.

Psalms 18: 30 (NIV)
30 As for God, his way is perfect: The Lord's word is flawless; he shields all who take refuge in him.

Proverbs 18: 21 (NKJV)
21 Death and life are in the power of the tongue, And those who love it will eat its fruit.

Psalms 68: 35 (NASB)
35 O God, You are awesome from Your sanctuary. The God of Israel Himself gives strength and pow-er to the people. Blessed be God!

Proverbs 24: 5 (NIV)
5 The wise prevail through great power, and those who have knowledge muster their strength.

Matthew 28: 18 (WEB)
18 Jesus came to them and spoke to them, saying, "All authority has been given to me in heaven and on earth.

Luke 9: 1 - 2 (WEB)
1 He called the twelve together, and gave them power and authority over all demons, and to cure diseases. 2 He sent them out to preach God's Kingdom and to heal the sick.

Luke 10: 19 (NOG)
19 I have given you the authority to trample snakes and scorpions and to destroy the enemy's power. Nothing will hurt you.

John 1: 3 (NKJV)
3 All things were made through Him, and without Him nothing was made that was made.

Acts 4: 19 - 20, 29 (WEB)
19 But Peter and John answered them, "Whether it is right in the sight of God to listen to you rather than to God, judge for yourselves, 20 for we can't help telling the things which we saw and heard." 29 Now, Lord, look at their threats, and grant to your servants to speak your word with all boldness,

1 Corinthians 2: 4 - 5 (NCV)
4 My teaching and preaching were not with words of human wisdom that persuade people but with proof of the power that the Spirit gives. 5 This was so that your faith would be in God's power and not in human wisdom.

Ephesians 1: 19, 21 (AMP)
19 And [so that you can know and understand] what is the immeasurable and unlimited and surpass-ing greatness of His power in and for us who believe, as demonstrated in the working of His mighty strength, 21 Far above all rule and authority and power and dominion and every name that is named [above every title that can be conferred], not only in this age and in this world, but also in the age and the world which are to come.

Ephesians 3: 20 (WEB)
20 Now to him who is able to do exceedingly abundantly above all that we ask or think, according to the power that works in us,

Ephesians 6: 10, 12 (NKJV)
10 Finally, my brethren, be strong in the Lord and in the power of His might. 12 For we do not wrestle against flesh and blood, but against

principalities, against powers, against the rulers of the darkness of this age, against spiritual hosts of wickedness in the heavenly places.

Colossians 1: 16 - 17 (WEB)

16 For by him all things were created, in the heavens and on the earth, things visible and things invis-ible, whether thrones or dominions or principalities or powers; all things have been created through him, and for him. 17 He is before all things, and in him all things are held together.

2 Timothy 1: 7 (NKJV)

7 For God has not given us a spirit of fear, but of power and of love and of a sound mind.

1 Peter 3: 22 (GNT)

22 who has gone to heaven and is at the right side of God, ruling over all angels and heavenly au-thorities and powers.

Barren
Genesis 18: 14 (HCSB)

14 Is anything impossible for the Lord? At the appointed time I will come back to you, and in about a year she will have a son."

Genesis 20: 17 (NCV)

17 Then Abraham prayed to God, and God healed Abimelech, his wife, and his servant girls so they could have children.

Genesis 25: 21 (NIV)

21 Isaac prayed to the Lord on behalf of his wife, because she was childless. The Lord answered his prayer, and his wife Rebekah became pregnant.

Genesis 30: 22 (MEV)

22 Then God remembered Rachel, and God listened to her and opened her womb.

Exodus 23: 26 (NIV)

26 and none will miscarry or be barren in your land. I will give you a full life span.

Deuteronomy 7: 14 (ESV)

14 You shall be blessed above all peoples. There shall not be male or female barren among you or among your livestock.

1 Samuel 1: 10 - 11, 17 (NIV)

10 In her deep anguish Hannah prayed to the Lord, weeping bitterly. 11 And she made a vow, saying, "Lord Almighty, if you will only look on your servant's misery and remember me, and not forget your servant but give her a son, then I will give him to the Lord for all the days of his life, and no razor will ever be used on his head." 17 Eli answered, "Go in peace, and may the God of Israel grant you what you have asked of him."

Psalms 113: 9 (HCSB)

9 He gives the childless woman a household, making her the joyful mother of children. Hallelujah!

Psalms 127: 3 (NASB)

3 Behold, children are a gift of the Lord, The fruit of the womb is a reward.

Psalms 139: 13 (NASB)

13 For You formed my inward parts; You wove me in my mother's womb.

Luke 1: 36 - 37 (HCSB)
36 And consider your relative Elizabeth—even she has conceived a son in her old age, and this is the sixth month for her who was called childless. 37 For nothing will be impossible with God."

Ephesians 2: 10 (NIVUK)
10 For we are God's handiwork, created in Christ Jesus to do good works, which God prepared in advance for us to do.

BELIEVE

Psalms 119: 49 - 50 (NIV)
49 Remember your word to your servant, for you have given me hope. 50 My comfort in my suffering is this: Your promise preserves my life.

Matthew 9: 20, 22 (NKJV)
20 And suddenly, a woman who had a flow of blood for twelve years came from behind and touched the hem of His garment. 22 But Jesus turned around, and when He saw her He said, "Be of good cheer, daughter; your faith has made you well." And the woman was made well from that hour.

Matthew 9: 28 - 29 (WEB)
28 When he had come into the house, the blind men came to him. Jesus said to them, "Do you be - lieve that I am able to do this?" They told him, "Yes, Lord." 29 Then he touched their eyes, saying, "According to your faith be it done to you."

Matthew 15: 28 (WEB)
28 Then Jesus answered her, "Woman, great is your faith! Be it done to you

even as you desire." And her daughter was healed from that hour.

Matthew 17: 20 (WEB)
20 He said to them, "Because of your unbelief. For most certainly I tell you, if you have faith as a grain of mustard seed, you will tell this mountain, 'Move from here to there,' and it will move; and nothing will be impossible for you.

Matthew 21: 22 (WEB)
22 All things, whatever you ask in prayer, believing, you will receive."

Mark 5: 35 - 36 (HCSB)
35 While He was still speaking, people came from the synagogue leader's house and said, "Your daughter is dead. Why bother the Teacher anymore?" 36 But when Jesus overheard what was said, He told the synagogue leader, "Don't be afraid. Only believe."

Mark 9: 23 - 24 (NIV)
23 "'If you can'?" said Jesus. "Everything is possible for one who believes." 24 Immediately the boy's father exclaimed, "I do believe; help me overcome my unbelief!"

Mark 11: 22 - 24 (NIVUK)
22 'Have faith in God,' Jesus answered. 23 'Truly I tell you, if anyone says to this mountain, "Go, throw yourself into the sea," and does not doubt in their heart but believes that what they say will happen, it will be done for them. 24 Therefore I tell you, whatever you ask for in prayer, believe that you have received it, and it will be yours.

Mark 16: 17 - 18 (NIV)
17 And these signs will accompany those who believe: In my name they

will drive out demons; they will speak in new tongues; 18 they will pick up snakes with their hands; and when they drink deadly poison, it will not hurt them at all; they will place their hands on sick people, and they will get well."

John 1: 12 (NCV)
12 But to all who did accept him and believe in him he gave the right to become children of God.

John 20: 29 (NCV)
29 Then Jesus told him, "You believe because you see me. Those who believe without seeing me will be truly blessed."

Acts 16: 31 (NIV)
31 They replied, "Believe in the Lord Jesus, and you will be saved—you and your household."

Romans 15: 13 (NKJV)
13 Now may the God of hope fill you with all joy and peace in believing, that you may abound in hope by the power of the Holy Spirit.

2 Corinthians 4: 13 (NKJV)
13 And since we have the same spirit of faith, according to what is written, "I believed and therefore I spoke,"[a] we also believe and therefore speak,

2 Corinthians 5: 7 (EXB)
7 We ·live [walk] by ·what we believe [faith], not by ·what we can see [sight].

Galatians 3: 6 (NIV)
6 So also Abraham "believed God, and it was credited to him as righteousness."

Ephesians 1: 18 - 21 (HCSB)
18 I pray that the perception of your mind[a] may be enlightened so you may know what is the hope of His calling, what are the glorious riches of His inheritance among the saints, 19 and what is the im - measurable greatness of His power to us who believe, according to the working of His vast strength. 20 He demonstrated this power in the Messiah by raising Him from the dead and seating Him at His right hand in the heavens— 21 far above every ruler and authority, power and dominion, and every title given,[b] not only in this age but also in the one to come.

Hebrews 11: 1 - 3, 6 (NLV)
1 Now faith is being sure we will get what we hope for. It is being sure of what we cannot see. 2 God was pleased with the men who had faith who lived long ago. 3 Through faith we understand that the world was made by the Word of God. Things we see were made from what could not be seen. 6 A man cannot please God unless he has faith. Anyone who comes to God must believe that He is. That one must also know that God gives what is promised to the one who keeps on looking for Him.

James 1: 5 - 6 (NIV)
5 If any of you lacks wisdom, you should ask God, who gives generously to all without finding fault, and it will be given to you. 6 But when you ask, you must believe and not doubt, because the one who doubts is like a wave of the sea, blown and tossed by the wind.

1 Peter 2: 6 (AMP)
6 For thus it stands in Scripture: Behold, I am laying in Zion a chosen (honored), precious chief Cor-nerstone, and he who believes in Him [who adheres to, trusts in, and relies on Him] shall never be disappointed or put to shame.

BLESSINGS

Genesis 26: 12 (NKJV)
12 Then Isaac sowed in that land, and reaped in the same year a hundredfold; and the Lord blessed him.

Deuteronomy 28: 1 - 14 (HCSB)
1 "Now if you faithfully obey the Lord your God and are careful to follow all His commands I am giving you today, the Lord your God will put you far above all the nations of the earth. 2 All these blessings will come and overtake you, because you obey the Lord your God: 3 You will be blessed in the city and blessed in the country. 4 Your descendants[a] will be blessed, and your land's produce, and the offspring of your livestock, including the young of your herds and the newborn of your flocks. 5 Your basket and kneading bowl will be blessed. 6 You will be blessed when you come in and blessed when you go out. 7 "The Lord will cause the enemies who rise up against you to be defeated before you. They will march out against you from one direction but flee from you in seven directions. 8 The Lord will grant you a blessing on your storehouses and on everything you do;[b] He will bless you in the land the Lord your God is giving you. 9 The Lord will establish you as His holy people, as He swore to you, if you obey the commands of the Lord your God and walk in His ways. 10 Then all the peoples of the earth will see that you are called by Yahweh's name, and they will stand in awe of you. 11 The Lord will make you prosper abundantly with children,[c] the offspring of your livestock, and your land's produce in the land the Lord swore to your fathers to give you. 12 The Lord will open for you His abundant storehouse, the sky, to give your land rain in its season and to bless all the work of your hands. You will lend to many nations, but you will not borrow. 13 The Lord will make you the head and not the tail; you will only move upward and never downward if you listen to the Lord your God's commands I am giving you today and are careful to follow them. 14 Do not turn aside to the right or the left from all the things I am commanding you today, and do not go after other gods to wor-ship them.

Genesis 28: 15 (NIV)
15 I am with you and will watch over you wherever you go, and I will bring you back to this land. I will not leave you until I have done what I have promised you."

Deuteronomy 30: 9 - 10 (NKJV)
9 The Lord your God will make you abound in all the work of your hand, in the fruit of your body, in the increase of your livestock, and in the produce of your land for good. For the Lord will again rejoice over you for good as He rejoiced over your fathers, 10 if you obey the voice of the Lord your God, to keep His commandments and His

statutes which are written in this Book of the Law, and if you turn to the Lord your God with all your heart and with all your soul.

Psalms 1: 3 (NKJV)
3 He shall be like a tree Planted by the rivers of water, That brings forth its fruit in its season, Whose leaf also shall not wither; And whatever he does shall prosper.

Psalms 23: 6 (NKJV)
6 Surely goodness and mercy shall follow me All the days of my life; And I will dwell in the house of the Lord Forever.

Psalms 30: 11 (NKJV)
11 You have turned for me my mourning into dancing; You have put off my sackcloth and clothed me with gladness,

Psalms 34: 10 (NET)
10 Even young lions sometimes lack food and are hungry, but those who seek the Lord lack no good thing.

Psalms 37: 4 - 5 (NKJV)
4 Delight yourself also in the Lord, And He shall give you the desires of your heart. 5 Commit your way to the Lord, Trust also in Him, And He shall bring it to pass.

Psalms 84: 11 (NKJV)
11 For the Lord God is a sun and shield; The Lord will give grace and glory; No good thing will He withhold From those who walk uprightly.

Psalms 85: 12 (NKJV)
12 Yes, the Lord will give what is good; And our land will yield its increase.

Psalms 91: 1 - 16 (NKJV)
1 He who dwells in the secret place of the Most High Shall abide under the shadow of the Almighty. 2 I will say of the Lord, "He is my refuge and my fortress; My God, in Him I will trust." 3 Surely He shall deliver you from the snare of the fowler[a] And from the perilous pestilence. 4 He shall cover you with His feathers, And under His wings you shall take refuge; His truth shall be your shield and buckler. 5 You shall not be afraid of the terror by night, Nor of the arrow that flies by day, 6 Nor of the pestilence that walks in darkness, Nor of the destruction that lays waste at noonday. 7 A thousand may fall at your side, And ten thousand at your right hand; But it shall not come near you. 8 Only with your eyes shall you look, And see the reward of the wicked. 9 Because you have made the Lord, who is my ref-uge, Even the Most High, your dwelling place, 10 No evil shall befall you, Nor shall any plague come near your dwelling; 11 For He shall give His angels charge over you, To keep you in all your ways. 12 In their hands they shall bear you up, Lest you dash your foot against a stone. 13 You shall tread upon the lion and the cobra, The young lion and the serpent you shall trample underfoot. 14 "Because he has set his love upon Me, therefore I will deliver him; I will set him on high, because he has known My name. 15 He shall call upon Me, and I will answer him; I will be with him in trouble; I will deliver him and honor him. 16 With long life I will satisfy him, And show him My salvation."

Psalms 104: 14 - 15 (NIV)
14 He makes grass grow for the cattle, and plants for people to

cultivate— bringing forth food from the earth: 15 wine that gladdens human hearts, oil to make their faces shine, and bread that sustains their hearts.

Psalms 113: 7 (NIV)
7 He raises the poor from the dust and lifts the needy from the ash heap;

Psalms 115: 13 - 15 (NKJV)
13 He will bless those who fear the Lord, Both small and great. 14 May the Lord give you increase more and more, You and your children. 15 May you be blessed by the Lord, Who made heaven and earth.

Psalms 128: 1 - 2 (NLT)
1 How joyful are those who fear the Lord— all who follow his ways! 2 You will enjoy the fruit of your labor. How joyful and prosperous you will be!

Psalms 145: 16 (NIV)
16 You open your hand and satisfy the desires of every living thing.

Proverbs 11: 25 (NET)
25 A generous person will be enriched, and the one who provides water for others will himself be satisfied.

Proverbs 15: 6 (WEB)
6 In the house of the righteous is much treasure, but the income of the wicked brings trouble.

Proverbs 22: 4 (NKJV)
4 By humility and the fear of the Lord Are riches and honor and life.

Proverbs 28: 25 (AMP)
25 He who is of a greedy spirit stirs up strife, but he who puts his trust in the Lord shall be enriched and blessed.

Proverbs 3: 3 - 4 (HCSB)
3 Never let loyalty and faithfulness leave you. Tie them around your neck; write them on the tablet of your heart. 4 Then you will find favor and high regard in the sight of God and man.

Proverbs 8: 12, 17 - 19, 21 (NIV)
12 "I, wisdom, dwell together with prudence; I possess knowledge and discretion. 17 I love those who love me, and those who seek me find me. 18 With me are riches and honor, enduring wealth and prosperity. 19 My fruit is better than fine gold; what I yield surpasses choice silver. 21 bestowing a rich inheritance on those who love me and making their treasuries full.

Ecclesiastes 5: 18 - 20 (GNT)
18 Here is what I have found out: the best thing we can do is eat and drink and enjoy what we have worked for during the short life that God has given us; this is our fate. 19 If God gives us wealth and property and lets us enjoy them, we should be grateful and enjoy what we have worked for. It is a gift from God. 20 Since God has allowed us to be happy, we will not worry too much about how short life is.

Malachi 3: 10 (GNT)
10 Bring the full amount of your tithes to the Temple, so that there will be plenty of food there. Put me to the test and you will see that I will open the windows of heaven and pour out on you in abundance all kinds of good things.

Luke 12: 32 (HCSB)
32 Don't be afraid, little flock, because your Father delights to give you the kingdom.

John 10: 10 (HCSB)
10 A thief comes only to steal and to kill and to destroy. I have come so that they may have life and have it in abundance.

Romans 8: 32 (WEB)
32 He who didn't spare his own Son, but delivered him up for us all, how would he not also with him freely give us all things?

Ephesians 6: 8 (ESV)
8 knowing that whatever good anyone does, this he will receive back from the Lord, whether he is a bondservant or is free.

1 Timothy 6: 17 (NKJV)
17 Command those who are rich in this present age not to be haughty, nor to trust in uncertain riches but in the living God, who gives us richly all things to enjoy.

2 Peter 1: 3 (NIV)
3 His divine power has given us everything we need for a godly life through our knowledge of him who called us by his own glory and goodness.

Revelation 1: 3 (NIV)
3 Blessed is the one who reads aloud the words of this prophecy, and blessed are those who hear it and take to heart what is written in it, because the time is near.

BOLDNESS

Joshua 1: 7 (NIV)
7 "Be strong and very courageous. Be careful to obey all the law my servant Moses gave you; do not turn from it to the right or to the left, that you may be successful wherever you go.

1 Samuel 17: 45 - 47 (NIV)
45 David said to the Philistine, "You come against me with sword and spear and javelin, but I come against you in the name of the Lord Almighty, the God of the armies of Israel, whom you have defied. 46 This day the Lord will deliver you into my hands, and I'll strike you down and cut off your head. This very day I will give the carcasses of the Philistine army to the birds and the wild animals, and the whole world will know that there is a God in Israel. 47 All those gathered here will know that it is not by sword or spear that the Lord saves; for the battle is the Lord's, and he will give all of you into our hands."

Proverbs 28: 1 (NLT)
1 The wicked run away when no one is chasing them, but the godly are as bold as lions.

Isaiah 50: 7 (NCV)
7 The Lord God helps me, so I will not be ashamed. I will be determined, and I know I will not be dis-graced.

Jeremiah 12: 5 (NASB)
5 "If you have run with footmen and they have tired you out, Then how can you compete with horses? If you fall down in a land of peace, How will you do in the thicket of the Jordan?

Daniel 3: 17 - 18 (NASB)
17 If it be so, our God whom we serve is able to deliver us from the furnace of blazing fire; and He will deliver us out of your hand, O king. 18 But even

if He does not, let it be known to you, O king, that we are not going to serve your gods or worship the golden image that you have set up."

Acts 1: 8 (NIV)
8 But you will receive power when the Holy Spirit comes on you; and you will be my witnesses in Jerusalem, and in all Judea and Samaria, and to the ends of the earth."

Acts 4: 13 - 14 (NKJV)
13 Now when they saw the boldness of Peter and John, and perceived that they were uneducated and untrained men, they marveled. And they realized that they had been with Jesus. 14 And seeing the man who had been healed standing with them, they could say nothing against it.

Acts 4: 29 - 31 (HCSB)
29 And now, Lord, consider their threats, and grant that Your slaves may speak Your message with complete boldness, 30 while You stretch out Your hand for healing, signs, and wonders to be per-formed through the name of Your holy Servant Jesus." 31 When they had prayed, the place where they were assembled was shaken, and they were all filled with the Holy Spirit and began to speak God's message with boldness.

Ephesians 6: 19 - 20 (HCSB)
19 Pray also for me, that the message may be given to me when I open my mouth to make known with boldness the mystery of the gospel. 20 For this I am an ambassador in chains. Pray that I might be bold enough in Him to speak as I should.

Hebrews 4: 16 (HCSB)
16 Therefore let us approach the throne of grace with boldness, so that we may receive mercy and find grace to help us at the proper time.

Hebrews 13: 6 (NKJV)
6 So we may boldly say: "The Lord is my helper; I will not fear. What can man do to me?"

1 John 4: 17 (ASV)
17 Herein is love made perfect with us, that we may have boldness in the day of judgment; because as he is, even so are we in this world.

BROKEN HEARTED

Psalms 4: 1 (WEB)
1 Answer me when I call, God of my righteousness. Give me relief from my distress. Have mercy on me, and hear my prayer.

Psalms 6: 7 - 9 (NKJV)
7 My eye wastes away because of grief; It grows old because of all my enemies. 8 Depart from me, all you workers of iniquity; For the Lord has heard the voice of my weeping. 9 The Lord has heard my supplication; The Lord will receive my prayer.

Psalms 30: 11 - 12 (NKJV)
11 You have turned for me my mourning into dancing; You have put off my sackcloth and clothed me with gladness, 12 To the end that my glory may sing praise to You and not be silent. O Lord my God, I will give thanks to You forever.

Psalms 34: 18 (NKJV)
18 The Lord is near to those who have a broken heart, and saves such as have a contrite spirit.

Psalms 42: 11 (NKJV)
11 Why are you cast down, O my soul? And why are you disquieted within me? Hope in God; For I shall yet praise Him, The help of my countenance and my God.

Psalms 119: 28 (NKJV)
28 My soul melts from heaviness; Strengthen me according to Your word.

Psalms 126: 5 - 6 (HCSB)
5 Those who sow in tears will reap with shouts of joy. 6 Though one goes along weeping, carrying the bag of seed, he will surely come back with shouts of joy, carrying his sheaves.

Psalms 147: 3 (NET)
3 He heals the brokenhearted, and bandages their wounds.

Isaiah 26: 3 (ESV)
3 You keep him in perfect peace whose mind is stayed on you, because he trusts in you.

Isaiah 61: 1 - 2 (MEV)
1 The Spirit of the Lord God is upon me because the Lord has anointed me to preach good news to the poor; He has sent me to heal the broken-hearted, to proclaim liberty to the captives, and the opening of the prison to those who are bound; 2 to proclaim the acceptable year of the Lord and the day of vengeance of our God; to comfort all who mourn,

Jeremiah 31: 25 (ESV)
25 For I will satisfy the weary soul, and every languishing soul I will replenish."

Matthew 11: 28 - 29 (WEB)
28 "Come to me, all you who labor and are heavily burdened, and I will give you rest. 29 Take my yoke upon you, and learn from me, for I am gentle and humble in heart; and you will find rest for your souls.

Matthew 5: 4 (MEV)
4 Blessed are those who mourn, for they shall be comforted.

John 11: 33 (GNT)
33 Jesus saw her weeping, and he saw how the people with her were weeping also; his heart was touched, and he was deeply moved.

CAPTIVES

Genesis 39: 21 (NET)
21 But the Lord was with Joseph and showed him kindness. He granted him favor in the sight of the prison warden.

Job 42: 10 (AMP)
10 And the Lord turned the captivity of Job and restored his fortunes, when he prayed for his friends; also the Lord gave Job twice as much as he had before.

Psalms 69: 33 (GNT)
33 The Lord listens to those in need and does not forget his people in prison.

Psalms 107: 14 (NLT)
14 He led them from the darkness and deepest gloom; he snapped their chains.

Psalms 126: 4 - 5 (AMP)
4 Turn to freedom our captivity and restore our fortunes, O Lord, as the

streams in the South (the Negeb) [are restored by the torrents]. 5 They who sow in tears shall reap in joy and singing.

Psalms 146: 7 (GW)

7 He brings about justice for those who are oppressed. He gives food to those who are hungry. The Lord sets prisoners free.

Isaiah 49: 24 - 25 (ESV)

24 Can the prey be taken from the mighty, or the captives of a tyrant be rescued? 25 For thus says the Lord: "Even the captives of the mighty shall be taken, and the prey of the tyrant be rescued, for I will contend with those who contend with you, and I will save your children.

Isaiah 61: 1 - 2 (MEV)

1 The Spirit of the Lord God is upon me because the Lord has anointed me to preach good news to the poor; He has sent me to heal the broken-hearted, to proclaim liberty to the captives, and the opening of the prison to those who are bound; 2 to proclaim the acceptable year of the Lord and the day of vengeance of our God; to comfort all who mourn,

Jeremiah 30: 16 - 17 (NET)

16 But all who destroyed you will be destroyed. All your enemies will go into exile. Those who plundered you will be plundered. I will cause those who pillaged you to be pillaged. 17 Yes, I will re-store you to health. I will heal your wounds. I, the Lord, affirm it! For you have been called an outcast, Zion, whom no one cares for.

Matthew 25: 36, 39, 40 (WEB)

36 I was naked and you clothed me. I was sick and you visited me. I was in prison and you came to me.' 39 When did we see you sick or in prison and come to you?' 40 "The King will answer them, 'Most certainly I tell you, because you did it to one of the least of these my brothers, you did it to me.'

Hebrews 13: 3 (NET)

3 Remember those in prison as though you were in prison with them, and those ill-treated as though you too felt their torment.

CHANGE HEART

Deuteronomy 30: 6 (AMP)

6 "And the Lord your God will circumcise your heart and the hearts of your descendants [that is, He will remove the desire to sin from your heart], so that you will love the Lord your God with all your heart and all your soul, so that you may live [as a recipient of His blessing].

1 Samuel 10: 9 - 10, 26 (NCV)

9 When Saul turned to leave Samuel, God changed Saul's heart. All these signs came true that day. 10 When Saul and his servant arrived at Gibeah, Saul met a group of prophets. The Spirit of God rushed upon him, and he prophesied with the prophets. 26 Saul also went to his home in Gibeah. God touched the hearts of certain brave men who went along with him.

Psalms 19: 14 (HCSB)

14 May the words of my mouth and the meditation of my heart be acceptable to You, Lord, my rock and my Redeemer.

Psalms 51: 10 (WEB)
10 Create in me a clean heart, O God. Renew a right spirit within me.

Psalms 94: 12 (NET)
12 How blessed is the one whom you instruct, O Lord, the one whom you teach from your law

Psalms 139: 23 - 24 (NKJV)
23 Search me, O God, and know my heart; Try me, and know my anxieties; 24 And see if there is any wicked way in me, And lead me in the way everlasting.

Psalms 141: 5 (NCV)
5 If a good person punished me, that would be kind. If he corrected me, that would be like perfumed oil on my head. I shouldn't refuse it. But I pray against those who do evil.

Proverbs 1: 23 (NLT)
23 Come and listen to my counsel. I'll share my heart with you and make you wise.

Proverbs 3: 11 - 12 (NKJV)
11 My son, do not despise the chastening of the Lord, Nor detest His correction; 12 For whom the Lord loves He corrects, Just as a father the son in whom he delights.

Proverbs 21: 1 (NLT)
1 The king's heart is like a stream of water directed by the Lord; he guides it wherever he pleases.

Jeremiah 10: 24 (ESV)
24 Correct me, O Lord, but in justice; not in your anger, lest you bring me to nothing.

Ezekiel 36: 26 - 27 (NKJV)
26 I will give you a new heart and put a new spirit within you; I will take the heart of stone out of your flesh and give you a heart of flesh. 27 I will put My Spirit within you and cause you to walk in My stat-utes, and you will keep My judgments and do them.

Acts 16: 14 (NKJV)
14 Now a certain woman named Lydia heard us. She was a seller of purple from the city of Thyatira, who worshiped God. The Lord opened her heart to heed the things spoken by Paul.

2 Timothy 3: 16 (MEV)
16 All Scripture is inspired by God and is profitable for teaching, for reproof, for correction, and for instruction in righteousness,

CHILDREN

Deuteronomy 30: 6 (AMP)
6 And the Lord your God will circumcise your hearts and the hearts of your descendants, to love the Lord your God with all your [mind and] heart and with all your being, that you may live.

Psalms 37: 25 - 26 (NIV)
25 I was young and now I am old, yet I have never seen the righteous forsaken or their children beg-ging bread. 26 They are always generous and lend freely; their children will be a blessing.

Psalms 72: 4 (WEB)
4 He will judge the poor of the people. He will save the children of the needy, and will break the op-pressor in pieces.

Psalms 90: 16 (NKJV)
16 Let Your work appear to Your servants, And Your glory to their children.

Psalms 102: 28 (NCV)
28 Our children will live in your presence, and their children will remain with you.

Psalms 127: 3 - 5 (NIV)
3 Children are a heritage from the Lord, offspring a reward from him. 4 Like arrows in the hands of a warrior are children born in one's youth. 5 Blessed is the man whose quiver is full of them. They will not be put to shame when they contend with their opponents in court.

Psalms 128: 1, 3 (NIV)
1 Blessed are all who fear the Lord, who walk in obedience to him. 3 Your wife will be like a fruitful vine within your house; your children will be like olive shoots around your table.

Psalms 144: 12 (GNT)
12 May our sons in their youth be like plants that grow up strong. May our daughters be like stately columns which adorn the corners of a palace.

Proverbs 14: 26 (HCSB)
26 In the fear of the Lord one has strong confidence and his children have a refuge.

Proverbs 17: 2, 6 (NET)
2 A servant who acts wisely will rule over an heir who behaves shamefully, and will share the inheri-tance along with the relatives. 6 Grandchildren are like a crown to the elderly, and the glory of children is their parents.

Proverbs 23: 24 (WEB)
24 The father of the righteous has great joy. Whoever fathers a wise child delights in him.

Isaiah 43: 5 - 6 (ERV)
5 "So don't be afraid, because I am with you. I will gather your children and bring them to you. I will gather them from the east and from the west. 6 I will tell the north: Give my people to me. I will tell the south: Don't keep my people in prison. Bring my sons and daughters to me from the faraway places.

Jeremiah 46: 27 (ESV)
27 But fear not, O Jacob my servant, nor be dismayed, O Israel, for behold, I will save you from far away, and your offspring from the land of their captivity. Jacob shall return and have quiet and ease, and none shall make him afraid.

Matthew 18: 10 (WEB)
10 See that you don't despise one of these little ones, for I tell you that in heaven their angels always see the face of my Father who is in heaven.

Matthew 19: 14 (WEB)
14 But Jesus said, "Allow the little children, and don't forbid them to come to me; for the Kingdom of Heaven belongs to ones like these."

Mark 9: 37 (NIVUK)
37 'Whoever welcomes one of these little children in my name welcomes me; and whoever welcomes me does not welcome me but the one who sent me.'

Acts 16: 31 (NCV)
31 They said to him, "Believe in the Lord Jesus and you will be saved—you and all the people in your house."

Acts 2: 38 - 39 (NCV)
38 Peter said to them, "Change your hearts and lives and be baptized, each one of you, in the name of Jesus Christ for the forgiveness of your sins. And you will receive the gift of the Holy Spirit. 39 This promise is for you, for your children, and for all who are far away. It is for everyone the Lord our God calls to himself."

1 Corinthians 7: 14 (NIVUK)
14 For the unbelieving husband has been sanctified through his wife, and the unbelieving wife has been sanctified through her believing husband. Otherwise your children would be unclean, but as it is, they are holy.

CHILDREN OF GOD

Matthew 5: 9 (NIV)
9 Blessed are the peacemakers, for they will be called children of God.

John 1: 12 - 13 (CEV)
12 Yet some people accepted him and put their faith in him. So he gave them the right to be the children of God. 13 They were not God's children by nature or because of any human desires. God himself was the one who made them his children.

John 10: 14 - 15, 28 (CEV)
14 I am the good shepherd. I know my sheep, and they know me. 15 Just as the Father knows me, I know the Father, and I give up my life for my sheep. 28 and I give them eternal life, so that they will never be lost. No one can snatch them out of my hand.

Romans 8: 14 - 17 (NKJV)
14 For as many as are led by the Spirit of God, these are sons of God. 15 For you did not receive the spirit of bondage again to fear, but you received the Spirit of adoption by whom we cry out, "Abba, Father." 16 The Spirit Himself bears witness with our spirit that we are children of God, 17 and if chil-dren, then heirs—heirs of God and joint heirs with Christ, if indeed we suffer with Him, that we may also be glorified together.

Galatians 3: 26 - 27 (NIV)
26 So in Christ Jesus you are all children of God through faith, 27 for all of you who were baptized into Christ have clothed yourselves with Christ.

Galatians 4: 6 - 7 (NIV)
6 Because you are his sons, God sent the Spirit of his Son into our hearts, the Spirit who calls out, "Abba, Father." 7 So you are no longer a slave, but God's child; and since you are his child, God has made you also an heir.

Ephesians 2: 19 (NIV)
19 Consequently, you are no longer foreigners and strangers, but fellow citizens with God's people and also members of his household,

Ephesians 5: 1 (NKJV)
1 Therefore be imitators of God as dear children.

1 John 3: 1 - 2 (NIVUK)
3 See what great love the Father has lavished on us, that we should be called children of God! And that is what we are! The reason the world does not know us is that it did not know him. 2 Dear friends, now we are children of God, and what we will be has not yet

been made known. But we know that when Christ appears, we shall be like him, for we shall see him as he is.

1 John 4: 4 (GNT)

4 But you belong to God, my children, and have defeated the false prophets, because the Spirit who is in you is more powerful than the spirit in those who belong to the world.

CLOSE TO GOD

Psalms 139: 7 - 10 (NKJV)

7 Where can I go from Your Spirit? Or where can I flee from Your presence? 8 If I ascend into heaven, You are there; If I make my bed in hell, behold, You are there. 9 If I take the wings of the morning, And dwell in the uttermost parts of the sea, 10 Even there Your hand shall lead me, And Your right hand shall hold me.

Psalms 145: 18 - 19 (NKJV)

18 The Lord is near to all who call upon Him, To all who call upon Him in truth. 19 He will fulfill the desire of those who fear Him; He also will hear their cry and save them.

Psalms 55: 17 (NKJV)

17 Evening and morning and at noon I will pray, and cry aloud, And He shall hear my voice.

Psalms 65: 4 (HCSB)

4 How happy is the one You choose and bring near to live in Your courts! We will be satisfied with the goodness of Your house, the holiness of Your temple.

Proverbs 24: 12 (NLT)

12 Don't excuse yourself by saying, "Look, we didn't know." For God understands all hearts, and he sees you. He who guards your soul knows you knew. He will repay all people as their actions de-serve.

Proverbs 8: 17 (NKJV)

17 I love those who love me, And those who seek me diligently will find me.

Isaiah 30: 21 (MEV)

21 Your ears shall hear a word behind you, saying, "This is the way, walk in it," whenever you turn to the right hand and when you turn to the left.

Isaiah 55: 6 (CEV)

6 Turn to the Lord!He can still be found.Call out to God! He is near.

Isaiah 57: 15 (NIV)

15 For this is what the high and exalted One says—he who lives forever, whose name is holy: "I live in a high and holy place, but also with the one who is contrite and lowly in spirit,to revive the spirit of the lowly and to revive the heart of the contrite.

Jeremiah 23: 23 (RSV)

23 "Am I a God at hand, says the Lord, and not a God afar off?

Jeremiah 29: 13 (ESV)

13 You will seek me and find me, when you seek me with all your heart.

Matthew 6: 6, 18 (MEV)

6 But you, when you pray, enter your closet, and when you have shut your door, pray to your Father who is in secret. And your Father who sees in secret will reward you openly. 18 so

that you will not appear to men to be fasting, but to your Father who is in secret. And your Father who sees in secret will reward you openly.

Mark 9: 37 (NIVUK)
37 'Whoever welcomes one of these little children in my name welcomes me; and whoever welcomes me does not welcome me but the one who sent me.'

Luke 11: 9 - 13 (NKJV)
9 "So I say to you, ask, and it will be given to you; seek, and you will find; knock, and it will be opened to you. 10 For everyone who asks receives, and he who seeks finds, and to him who knocks it will be opened. 11 If a son asks for bread[a] from any father among you, will he give him a stone? Or if he asks for a fish, will he give him a serpent instead of a fish? 12 Or if he asks for an egg, will he offer him a scorpion? 13 If you then, being evil, know how to give good gifts to your children, how much more will your heavenly Father give the Holy Spirit to those who ask Him!"

Luke 12: 32 (HCSB)
32 Don't be afraid, little flock, because your Father delights to give you the kingdom.

John 14: 16 - 18, 20, 21 (HCSB)
16 And I will ask the Father, and He will give you another Counselor to be with you forever. 17 He is the Spirit of truth. The world is unable to receive Him because it doesn't see Him or know Him. But you do know Him, because He remains with you and will be in you. 18 I will not leave you as orphans; I am coming to you. 20 In

that day you will know that I am in My Father, you are in Me, and I am in you. 21 The one who has My commands and keeps them is the one who loves Me. And the one who loves Me will be loved by My Father. I also will love him and will reveal Myself to him."

Acts 17: 26 - 28 (NIV)
26 From one man he made all the nations, that they should inhabit the whole earth; and he marked out their appointed times in history and the boundaries of their lands. 27 God did this so that they would seek him and perhaps reach out for him and find him, though he is not far from any one of us. 28 'For in him we live and move and have our being.' As some of your own poets have said, 'We are his offspring.'

Romans 8: 26 - 27 (NKJV)
26 Likewise the Spirit also helps in our weaknesses. For we do not know what we should pray for as we ought, but the Spirit Himself makes intercession for us[a] with groanings which cannot be uttered. 27 Now He who searches the hearts knows what the mind of the Spirit is, because He makes intercession for the saints according to the will of God.

Ephesians 2: 13 (NKJV)
13 But now in Christ Jesus you who once were far off have been brought near by the blood of Christ.

James 4: 8 (CEV)
8 Come near to God, and he will come near to you. Clean up your lives, you sinners. Purify your hearts, you people who can't make up your mind.

COMING BACK TO GOD

1 Samuel 7: 3 (NLT)

3 Then Samuel said to all the people of Israel, "If you want to return to the Lord with all your hearts, get rid of your foreign gods and your images of Ashtoreth. Turn your hearts to the Lord and obey him alone; then he will rescue you from the Philistines."

2 Chronicles 7: 14 (NIV)

14 if my people, who are called by my name, will humble themselves and pray and seek my face and turn from their wicked ways, then I will hear from heaven, and I will forgive their sin and will heal their land.

Nehemiah 1: 9 (NASB)

9 but if you return to Me and keep My commandments and do them, though those of you who have been scattered were in the most remote part of the heavens, I will gather them from there and will bring them to the place where I have chosen to cause My name to dwell.

Psalms 107: 17 - 20 (NLT)

17 Some were fools; they rebelled and suffered for their sins. 18 They couldn't stand the thought of food, and they were knocking on death's door. 19 "Lord, help!" they cried in their trouble, and he saved them from their distress. 20 He sent out his word and healed them, snatching them from the door of death.

Isaiah 30: 15 (CEV)

15 The holy Lord God of Israel had told all of you, "I will keep you safe if you turn back to me and calm down. I will make you strong if you quietly trust me."

Isaiah 55: 6 - 7 (CEV)

6 Turn to the Lord! He can still be found. Call out to God! He is near. 7 Give up your crooked ways and your evil thoughts. Return to the Lord our God. He will be merciful and forgive your sins.

Jeremiah 6: 16 (NIV)

16 Stand at the crossroads and look; ask for the ancient paths, ask where the good way is, and walk in it, and you will find rest for your souls.

Hosea 14: 2, 4 (NIV)

2 Take words with you and return to the Lord. Say to him: "Forgive all our sins and receive us gra-ciously, that we may offer the fruit of our lips. 4 "I will heal their waywardness and love them freely, for my anger has turned away from them.

Malachi 3: 7 (NKJV)

7 Yet from the days of your fathers You have gone away from My ordinances And have not kept them. Return to Me, and I will return to you," Says the Lord of hosts.

Luke 15: 21 - 24 (WEB)

21 The son said to him, 'Father, I have sinned against heaven, and in your sight. I am no longer worthy to be called your son.' 22 "But the father said to his servants, 'Bring out the best robe, and put it on him. Put a ring on his hand, and shoes on his feet. 23 Bring the fattened calf, kill it, and let us eat, and celebrate; 24 for this, my son, was

dead, and is alive again. He was lost, and is found.' They began to celebrate.

James 4: 8 (ERV)
8 Come near to God and he will come near to you. You are sinners, so clean sin out of your lives. You are trying to follow God and the world at the same time. Make your thinking pure.

1 John 1: 9 - 10 (NIVUK)
9 If we confess our sins, he is faithful and just and will forgive us our sins and purify us from all unrighteousness. 10 If we claim we have not sinned, we make him out to be a liar and his word is not in us.

CONDEMNATION

Psalms 51: 1 - 2 (MEV)
1 Have mercy on me, O God, according to Your lovingkindness; according to the abundance of Your compassion, blot out my transgressions. 2 Wash me thoroughly from my iniquity, and cleanse me from my sin.

Psalms 91: 14 - 16 (NKJV)
14 Because he has set his love upon Me, therefore I will deliver him; I will set him on high, because he has known My name. 15 He shall call upon Me, and I will answer him; I will be with him in trouble; I will deliver him and honor him. 16 With long life I will satisfy him, And show him My salvation.

Psalms 94: 12 - 14 (NIRV)
12 Lord, blessed is the person you correct. Blessed is the person you teach from your law. 13 You give them rest from times of trouble, until a pit is dug

to trap sinners. 14 The Lord won't say no to his people. He will never desert those who belong to him.

Psalms 103: 2 - 3, 10 - 13 (NIV)
2 Praise the Lord, my soul, and forget not all his benefits— 3 who forgives all your sins and heals all your diseases, 10 he does not treat us as our sins deserve or repay us according to our iniquities. 11 For as high as the heavens are above the earth, so great is his love for those who fear him; 12 as far as the east is from the west, so far has he removed our transgressions from us. 13 As a father has compassion on his children, so the Lord has compassion on those who fear him;

Psalms 107: 17, 19 - 20 (MEV)
17 Some were fools because of their transgressions, and because of their iniquities they are afflicted. 19 Then they cried unto the Lord in their trouble, and He saved them out of their distress. 20 He sent His word and healed them and delivered them from their destruction.

Psalms 130: 3 - 4 (NKJV)
3 If You, Lord, should mark iniquities, O Lord, who could stand? 4 But there is forgiveness with You, That You may be feared.

Psalms 145: 14 (MEV)
14 The Lord upholds all who fall, and raises up all who are bowed down.

Matthew 5: 11 - 12 (HCSB)
11 "You are blessed when they insult and persecute you and falsely say every kind of evil against you because of Me. 12 Be glad and rejoice, because your reward is great in heaven. For that is

how they persecuted the prophets who were before you.

John 3: 36 (CEB)
36 Whoever believes in the Son has eternal life. Whoever doesn't believe in the Son won't see life, but the angry judgment of God remains on them.

Romans 5: 5 (ESV)
5 and hope does not put us to shame, because God's love has been poured into our hearts through the Holy Spirit who has been given to us.

Romans 8: 1 - 2 (NKJV)
1 There is therefore now no condemnation to those who are in Christ Jesus, who do not walk accord-ing to the flesh, but according to the Spirit. 2 For the law of the Spirit of life in Christ Jesus has made me free from the law of sin and death.

2 Corinthians 5: 19 - 21 (NET)
19 In other words, in Christ God was reconciling the world to himself, not counting people's trespass-es against them, and he has given us the message of reconciliation. 20 Therefore we are ambas-sadors for Christ, as though God were making His plea through us. We plead with you on Christ's behalf, "Be reconciled to God!" 21 God made the one who did not know sin to be sin for us, so that in him we would become the righteousness of God.

1 Thessalonians 5: 9 (GW)
9 It was not God's intention that we experience his anger but that we obtain salvation through our Lord Jesus Christ.

1 Timothy 3: 1, 6 (GNT)
1 This is a true saying: If a man is eager to be a church leader, he desires an excellent work. 6 He must be mature in the faith, so that he will not swell up with pride and be condemned, as the Devil was.

Hebrews 4: 16 (WEB)
16 Let us therefore draw near with boldness to the throne of grace, that we may receive mercy, and may find grace for help in time of need.

Hebrews 8: 12 (HCSB)
12 For I will be merciful to their wrongdoing, and I will never again remember their sins.

James 1: 5 (AMP)
5 If any of you is deficient in wisdom, let him ask of the giving God [Who gives] to everyone liberally and ungrudgingly, without reproaching or faultfinding, and it will be given him.

James 1: 21 (NIV)
21 Therefore, get rid of all moral filth and the evil that is so prevalent and humbly accept the word planted in you, which can save you.

1 Peter 4: 14 - 16 (NKJV)
14 If you are reproached for the name of Christ, blessed are you, for the Spirit of glory and of God rests upon you. On their part He is blasphemed, but on your part He is glorified. 15 But let none of you suffer as a murderer, a thief, an evildoer, or as a busybody in other people's matters. 16 Yet if anyone suffers as a Christian, let him not be ashamed, but let him glorify God in this matter.

1 John 1: 8 - 9 (NIVUK)
8 If we claim to be without sin, we deceive ourselves and the truth is not in

us. 9 If we confess our sins, he is faithful and just and will forgive us our sins and purify us from all unrighteousness.

1 John 3: 19 - 20 (NCV)
19 This is the way we know that we belong to the way of truth. When our hearts make us feel guilty, we can still have peace before God. God is greater than our hearts, and he knows everything.

CONFUSION

Psalms 19: 14 (NKJV)
14 Let the words of my mouth and the meditation of my heart Be acceptable in Your sight, O Lord, my strength and my Redeemer.

Psalms 26: 2 - 3 (CEB)
2 Examine me, Lord; put me to the test! Purify my mind and my heart. 3 Because your faithful love is right in front of me — I walk in your truth!

Psalms 104: 34 (NIV)
34 May my meditation be pleasing to him, as I rejoice in the Lord.

Proverbs 3: 5 - 6 (MEV)
5 Trust in the Lord with all your heart, and lean not on your own understanding; 6 in all your ways acknowledge Him, and He will direct your paths.

Proverbs 4: 23 (CEV)
32 Carefully guard your thoughts because they are the source of true life.

Proverbs 23: 30, 32 - 33 (NIV)
30 Those who linger over wine, who go to sample bowls of mixed wine.

32 In the end it bites like a snake and poisons like a viper. 33 Your eyes will see strange sights, and your mind will imagine con-fusing things.

Isaiah 26: 3 (ESV)
3 You keep him in perfect peace whose mind is stayed on you, because he trusts in you.

Romans 8: 5 - 6 (WEB)
5 For those who live according to the flesh set their minds on the things of the flesh, but those who live according to the Spirit, the things of the Spirit. 6 For the mind of the flesh is death, but the mind of the Spirit is life and peace;

Romans 12: 2 (NKJV)
2 And do not be conformed to this world, but be transformed by the renewing of your mind, that you may prove what is that good and acceptable and perfect will of God.

1 Corinthians 14: 33 (WEB)
33 for God is not a God of confusion, but of peace. As in all the assemblies of the saints,

2 Timothy 1: 7 (NKJV)
7 For God has not given us a spirit of fear, but of power and of love and of a sound mind.

James 3: 16 - 17 (WEB)
16 For where jealousy and selfish ambition are, there is confusion and every evil deed. 17 But the wisdom that is from above is first pure, then peaceful, gentle, reasonable, full of mercy and good fruits, without partiality, and without hypocrisy.

COURAGE

Joshua 1: 7 (NIV)
7 Be strong and very courageous. Be careful to obey all the law my servant Moses gave you; do not turn from it to the right or to the left, that you may be successful wherever you go.

1 Samuel 17: 45 - 47 (NIV)
45 David said to the Philistine, "You come against me with sword and spear and javelin, but I come against you in the name of the Lord Almighty, the God of the armies of Israel, whom you have defied. 46 This day the Lord will deliver you into my hands, and I'll strike you down and cut off your head. This very day I will give the carcasses of the Philistine army to the birds and the wild animals, and the whole world will know that there is a God in Israel. 47 All those gathered here will know that it is not by sword or spear that the Lord saves; for the battle is the Lord's, and he will give all of you into our hands."

2 Kings 6: 16 - 17 (NASB)
16 So he answered, "Do not fear, for those who are with us are more than those who are with them." 17 Then Elisha prayed and said, "O Lord, I pray, open his eyes that he may see." And the Lord opened the servant's eyes and he saw; and behold, the mountain was full of horses and chariots of fire all around Elisha.

Nehemiah 8: 10 (ESV)
10 Then he said to them, "Go your way. Eat the fat and drink sweet wine and send portions to anyone who has nothing ready, for this day is holy to our Lord. And do not be grieved, for the joy of the Lord is your strength."

Psalms 27: 1 - 2, 14 (HCSB)
1 The Lord is my light and my salvation— whom should I fear? The Lord is the stronghold of my life— of whom should I be afraid? 2 When evildoers came against me to devour my flesh, my foes and my enemies stumbled and fell. 14 Wait for the Lord; be strong and courageous. Wait for the Lord.

Psalms 145: 14 (NKJV)
14 The Lord upholds all who fall, And raises up all who are bowed down.

Proverbs 8: 12, 14 (AMP)
12 I, Wisdom [from God], make prudence my dwelling, and I find out knowledge and discretion. 14 I have counsel and sound knowledge, I have understanding, I have might and power.

Proverbs 28: 1 (GNT)
1 The wicked run when no one is chasing them, but an honest person is as brave as a lion.

Isaiah 40: 29 - 31 (NET)
29 He gives strength to those who are tired; to the ones who lack power, he gives renewed energy. 30 Even youths get tired and weary; even strong young men clumsily stumble. 31 But those who wait for the Lord's help find renewed strength; they rise up as if they had eagles' wings, they run without growing weary, they walk without getting tired.

Isaiah 41: 10 - 13 (ESV)
10 fear not, for I am with you; be not dismayed, for I am your God; I will strengthen you, I will help you, I will

uphold you with my righteous right hand. 11 Behold, all who are incensed against you shall be put to shame and confounded; those who strive against you shall be as nothing and shall perish. 12 You shall seek those who contend with you, but you shall not find them; those who war against you shall be as nothing at all. 13 For I, the Lord your God, hold your right hand; it is I who say to you, "Fear not, I am the one who helps you."

Isaiah 43: 1 - 2 (NKJV)
1 But now, thus says the Lord, who created you, O Jacob, And He who formed you, O Israel: "Fear not, for I have redeemed you; I have called you by your name; You are Mine. 2 When you pass through the waters, I will be with you; And through the rivers, they shall not overflow you. When you walk through the fire, you shall not be burned, Nor shall the flame scorch you.

Isaiah 50: 7 - 9 (NASB)
7 For the Lord God helps Me, Therefore, I am not disgraced; Therefore, I have set My face like flint, And I know that I will not be ashamed. 8 He who vindicates Me is near; Who will contend with Me? Let us stand up to each other; Who has a case against Me? Let him draw near to Me. 9 Behold, the Lord God helps Me; Who is he who condemns Me? Behold, they will all wear out like a garment; The moth will eat them.

Jeremiah 12: 5 (NASB)
5 "If you have run with footmen and they have tired you out, Then how can you compete with horses? If you fall down in a land of peace, How will you do in the [a]thicket of the Jordan?

Daniel 3: 17 - 18 (NASB)
17 If it be so, our God whom we serve is able to deliver us from the furnace of blazing fire; and He will deliver us out of your hand, O king. 18 But even if He does not, let it be known to you, O king, that we are not going to serve your gods or worship the golden image that you have set up."

Acts 1: 8 (NIV)
8 But you will receive power when the Holy Spirit comes on you; and you will be my witnesses in Jerusalem, and in all Judea and Samaria, and to the ends of the earth."

Acts 4: 29 - 31 (ESV)
29 And now, Lord, look upon their threats and grant to your servants[a] to continue to speak your word with all boldness, 30 while you stretch out your hand to heal, and signs and wonders are per - formed through the name of your holy servant Jesus." 31 And when they had prayed, the place in which they were gathered together was shaken, and they were all filled with the Holy Spirit and con-tinued to speak the word of God with boldness.

Ephesians 6: 10 - 18 (WEB)
10 Finally, be strong in the Lord, and in the strength of his might. 11 Put on the whole armor of God, that you may be able to stand against the wiles of the devil. 12 For our wrestling is not against flesh and blood, but against the principalities, against the powers, against the world's rulers of the darkness of this age, and against the spiritual forces of wickedness in the heavenly places. 13 Therefore put on the whole armor of God, that you may be able to withstand in the evil

day, and, having done all, to stand. 14 Stand therefore, having the utility belt of truth buckled around your waist, and having put on the breastplate of righteousness, 15 and having fitted your feet with the preparation of the Good News of peace; 16 above all, taking up the shield of faith, with which you will be able to quench all the fiery darts of the evil one. 17 And take the helmet of salvation, and the sword of the Spirit, which is the word[a] of God; 18 with all prayer and requests, praying at all times in the Spirit, and being watchful to this end in all perseverance and requests for all the saints:

Hebrews 4: 16 (WEB)
16 Let us therefore draw near with boldness to the throne of grace, that we may receive mercy, and may find grace for help in time of need. ,

1 John 4: 17 (ASV)
17 Herein is love made perfect with us, that we may have boldness in the day of judgment; because as he is, even so are we in this world.

COURT

Proverbs 31: 8 - 9 (NIV)
8 Speak up for those who cannot speak for themselves, for the rights of all who are destitute. 9 Speak up and judge fairly; defend the rights of the poor and needy.

Proverbs 25: 8 - 9 (AMP)
8 Rush not forth soon to quarrel [before magistrates or elsewhere], lest you know not what to do in the end when your neighbor has put you to shame. 9

Argue your cause with your neighbor himself; discover not and disclose not another's secret,

Zechariah 8: 16 - 17 (GW)
16 You must do these things: Speak the truth to each other. Give correct and fair verdicts for peace in your courts. 17 Don't even think of doing evil to each other. Don't enjoy false testimony. I hate all these things, declares the Lord.

Matthew 5: 25, 40 (GNT)
25 "If someone brings a lawsuit against you and takes you to court, settle the dispute while there is time, before you get to court. Once you are there, you will be turned over to the judge, who will hand you over to the police, and you will be put in jail. 40 And if someone takes you to court to sue you for your shirt, let him have your coat as well.

Matthew 10: 18, 20 (GW)
18 Because of me you will even be brought in front of governors and kings to testify to them and to everyone in the world. 20 Indeed, you're not the ones who will be speaking. The Spirit of your Father will be speaking through you.

Romans 13: 1 - 3 (NIV)
1 Let everyone be subject to the governing authorities, for there is no authority except that which God has established. The authorities that exist have been established by God. 2 Consequently, whoever rebels against the authority is rebelling against what God has instituted, and those who do so will bring judgment on themselves. 3 For rulers hold no terror for those who do right, but for those who do wrong.

Do you want to be free from fear of the one in authority? Then do what is right and you will be commended.

1 Corinthians 6: 1 - 5 (HCSB)

1 If any of you has a legal dispute against another, do you dare go to court before the unrighteous, and not before the saints? 2 Or don't you know that the saints will judge the world? And if the world is judged by you, are you unworthy to judge the smallest cases? 3 Don't you know that we will judge angels—not to mention ordinary matters? 4 So if you have cases pertaining to this life, do you select those who have no standing in the church to judge? 5 I say this to your shame! Can it be that there is not one wise person among you who is able to arbitrate between his brothers?

2 Corinthians 13: 1 (NIV)

1 This will be my third visit to you. "Every matter must be established by the testimony of two or three witnesses."

CRYING OUT

Exodus 3: 7 (NIV)

7 The Lord said, "I have indeed seen the misery of my people in Egypt. I have heard them crying out because of their slave drivers, and I am concerned about their suffering.

2 Chronicles 14: 11 - 12 (AMP)

11 Asa cried to the Lord his God, O Lord, there is none besides You to help, and it makes no differ-ence to You whether the one You help is mighty or powerless. Help us, O Lord our God! For we rely on You, and we go against this multitude in Your name. O Lord, You are our God; let no man prevail against You! 12 So the Lord smote the Ethiopians before Asa and Judah, and the Ethiopians fled.

Psalms 5: 1 - 2 (NIV)

1 Listen to my words, Lord, consider my lament. 2 Hear my cry for help, my King and my God, for to you I pray.

Psalms 17: 1 (NET)

1 Lord, consider my just cause! Pay attention to my cry for help! Listen to the prayer I sincerely offer!

Psalms 22: 24 (NLT)

24 For he has not ignored or belittled the suffering of the needy. He has not turned his back on them, but has listened to their cries for help.

Psalms 34: 4, 6 (NKJV)

4 I sought the Lord, and He heard me, And delivered me from all my fears. 6 This poor man cried out, and the Lord heard him, And saved him out of all his troubles.

Psalms 50: 15 (HCSB)

15 Call on Me in a day of trouble; I will rescue you, and you will honor Me."

Psalms 55: 17 - 18 (NKJV)

17 Evening and morning and at noon I will pray, and cry aloud, And He shall hear my voice. 18 He has redeemed my soul in peace from the battle that was against me, For there were many against me.

Psalms 57: 2 - 3 (NKJV)

2 I will cry out to God Most High, To God who performs all things for me. 3 He shall send from heav-en

and save me; He reproaches the one who would swallow me up. Selah God shall send forth His mercy and His truth.

Psalms 91: 15 (NKJV)
15 He shall call upon Me, and I will answer him; I will be with him in trouble; I will deliver him and hon-or him.

Psalms 138: 3 (NKJV)
3 In the day when I cried out, You answered me, And made me bold with strength in my soul.

Psalms 143: 1 (NIV)
1 Lord, hear my prayer, listen to my cry for mercy; in your faithfulness and righteousness come to my relief.

Psalms 145: 18 (NET)
18 The Lord is near all who cry out to him, all who cry out to him sincerely.

Isaiah 30: 19, 21 (AMP)
19 O people who dwell in Zion at Jerusalem, you will weep no more. He will surely be gracious to you at the sound of your cry; when He hears it, He will answer you. 21 And your ears will hear a word behind you, saying, This is the way; walk in it, when you turn to the right hand and when you turn to the left.

Isaiah 38: 14 - 16 (NCV)
14 I cried like a bird and moaned like a dove. My eyes became tired as I looked to the heavens. Lord, I have troubles. Please help me." 15 What can I say? The Lord told me what would happen and then made it happen. I have had these troubles

in my soul, so now I will be humble all my life. 16 Lord, because of you, people live. Because of you, my spirit also lives; you made me well and let me live.

Jeremiah 33: 3 (GNT)
3 "Call to me, and I will answer you; I will tell you wonderful and marvelous things that you know noth-ing about.

Matthew 7: 7 - 10 (WEB)
7 "Ask, and it will be given you. Seek, and you will find. Knock, and it will be opened for you. 8 For everyone who asks receives. He who seeks finds. To him who knocks it will be opened. 9 Or who is there among you who, if his son asks him for bread, will give him a stone? 10 Or if he asks for a fish, who will give him a serpent?

Matthew 9: 27 - 30 (NIV)
27 As Jesus went on from there, two blind men followed him, calling out, "Have mercy on us, Son of David!" 28 When he had gone indoors, the blind men came to him, and he asked them, "Do you believe that I am able to do this?" "Yes, Lord," they replied. 29 Then he touched their eyes and said, "According to your faith let it be done to you"; 30 and their sight was restored. Jesus warned them sternly, "See that no one knows about this."

Luke 18: 6 - 8 (GNT)
6 And the Lord continued, "Listen to what that corrupt judge said. 7 Now, will God not judge in favor of his own people who cry to him day and night for help? Will he be slow to help them? 8 I tell you, he will judge in their favor and do it quickly. But will the Son

of Man find faith on earth when he comes?"

Luke 18: 38 - 39, 41 - 42 (GNT)
38 He cried out, "Jesus! Son of David! Have mercy on me!" 39 The people in front scolded him and told him to be quiet. But he shouted even more loudly, "Son of David! Have mercy on me!" 41 "What do you want me to do for you?" "Sir," he answered, "I want to see again." 42 Jesus said to him, "Then see! Your faith has made you well."

James 5: 16 (TLB)
16 Admit your faults to one another and pray for each other so that you may be healed. The earnest prayer of a righteous man has great power and wonderful results.

DEATH

2 Samuel 12: 22 - 23 (GW)
22 David answered, "As long as the child was alive, I fasted and cried. I thought, 'Who knows? The Lord may be gracious to me and let the child live.' 23 But why should I fast now that he's dead? Can I bring him back? Someday I'll go to him, but he won't come back to me."

Psalms 116: 15 (HCSB)
15 The death of His faithful ones is valuable in the Lord's sight.

Psalms 49: 8 - 9, 15 (NLT)
8 Redemption does not come so easily, for no one can ever pay enough 9 to live forever and never see the grave. 15 But as for me, God will redeem my life.

He will snatch me from the power of the grave.

Proverbs 14: 27, 32 (NLT)
27 Fear of the Lord is a life-giving fountain; it offers escape from the snares of death. 32 The wicked are crushed by disaster, but the godly have a refuge when they die.

Ecclesiastes 9: 4 - 6 (NLT)
4 There is hope only for the living. As they say, "It's better to be a live dog than a dead lion!" 5 The liv - ing at least know they will die, but the dead know nothing. They have no further reward, nor are they remembered. 6 Whatever they did in their lifetime—loving, hating, envying—is all long gone. They no longer play a part in anything here on earth.

Ecclesiastes 12: 7 (NLT)
7 For then the dust will return to the earth, and the spirit will return to God who gave it.

John 14: 16 - 19 (WEB)
16 I will pray to the Father, and he will give you another Counselor,[a] that he may be with you forev-er,— 17 the Spirit of truth, whom the world can't receive; for it doesn't see him, neither knows him. You know him, for he lives with you, and will be in you. 18 I will not leave you orphans. I will come to you. 19 Yet a little while, and the world will see me no more; but you will see me. Because I live, you will live also.

John 14: 2 - 3 (WEB)
2 In my Father's house are many homes. If it weren't so, I would have told you. I am going to prepare a place for you.

3 If I go and prepare a place for you, I will come again, and will receive you to myself; that where I am, you may be there also.

John 8: 51 (MEV)
51 Truly, truly I say to you, if anyone keeps My word, he shall never see death.

2 Corinthians 5: 8 - 10 (NLT)
8 Yes, we are fully confident, and we would rather be away from these earthly bodies, for then we will be at home with the Lord. 9 So whether we are here in this body or away from this body, our goal is to please him. 10 For we must all stand before Christ to be judged. We will each receive whatever we deserve for the good or evil we have done in this earthly body.

1 Thessalonians 4: 13 - 14 (NIV)
13 Brothers and sisters, we do not want you to be uninformed about those who sleep in death, so that you do not grieve like the rest of mankind, who have no hope. 14 For we believe that Jesus died and rose again, and so we believe that God will bring with Jesus those who have fallen asleep in him.

1 Thessalonians 5: 10 - 11 (NIV)
10 He died for us so that, whether we are awake or asleep, we may live together with him. 11 There-fore encourage one another and build each other up, just as in fact you are doing.

Hebrews 9: 27 (NKJV)
27 And as it is appointed for men to die once, but after this the judgment,

DEATH OF CHILD

Samuel 12: 22 - 23 (GW)
22 David answered, "As long as the child was alive, I fasted and cried. I thought, 'Who knows? The Lord may be gracious to me and let the child live.' 23 But why should I fast now that he's dead? Can I bring him back? Someday I'll go to him, but he won't come back to me."

Acts 2: 39 (NKJV)
39 For the promise is to you and to your children, and to all who are afar off, as many as the Lord our God will call."

DELIVERER

2 Samuel 22: 17 - 18 (NKJV)
17 "He sent from above, He took me, He drew me out of many waters. 18 He delivered me from my strong enemy, From those who hated me; For they were too strong for me.

Psalms 18: 18 - 19 (GNT)
18 When I was in trouble, they attacked me, but the Lord protected me. 19 He helped me out of dan-ger; he saved me because he was pleased with me.

Psalms 34: 17, 19 (NKJV)
17 The righteous cry out, and the Lord hears, And delivers them out of all their troubles. 19 Many are the afflictions of the righteous, But the Lord delivers him out of them all.

Psalms 34: 7 (NIV)
7 The angel of the Lord encamps around those who fear him, and he delivers them.

Psalms 37: 40 (NKJV)

40 And the Lord shall help them and deliver them; He shall deliver them from the wicked, And save them, Because they trust in Him.

Psalms 50: 15 (WEB)

15 Call on me in the day of trouble. I will deliver you, and you will honor me.

Psalms 55: 17 - 18 (WEB)

17 Evening, morning, and at noon, I will cry out in distress. He will hear my voice. 18 He has re-deemed my soul in peace from the battle that was against me, although there are many who oppose me.

Psalms 91: 3, 14 - 15 (NKJV)

3 Surely He shall deliver you from the snare of the fowler And from the perilous pestilence. 14 "Be-cause he has set his love upon Me, therefore I will deliver him; I will set him on high, because he has known My name. 15 He shall call upon Me, and I will answer him; I will be with him in trouble; I will deliver him and honor him.

Psalms 107: 20, 28 - 29 (NKJV)

20 He sent His word and healed them, And delivered them from their destructions. 28 Then they cry out to the Lord in their trouble, And He brings them out of their distresses. 29 He calms the storm, So that its waves are still.

Psalms 108: 13 (NKJV)

13 Through God we will do valiantly, For it is He who shall tread down our enemies.

Isaiah 46: 4 (NIV)

4 Even to your old age and gray hairs I am he, I am he who will sustain you. I have made you and I will carry you; I will sustain you and I will rescue you.

Daniel 3: 17 - 30 (NIVUK)

17 If we are thrown into the blazing furnace, the God we serve is able to deliver us from it, and he will deliver us from Your Majesty's hand. 18 But even if he does not, we want you to know, Your Majesty, that we will not serve your gods or worship the image of gold you have set up.' 19 Then Nebuchadnezzar was furious with Shadrach, Meshach and Abednego, and his attitude towards them changed. He ordered the furnace to be heated seven times hotter than usual 20 and commanded some of the strongest soldiers in his army to tie up Shadrach, Meshach and Abednego and throw them into the blazing furnace. 21 So these men, wearing their robes, trousers, turbans and other clothes, were bound and thrown into the blazing furnace. 22 The king's command was so urgent and the furnace so hot that the flames of the fire killed the soldiers who took up Shadrach, Meshach and Abednego, 23 and these three men, firmly tied, fell into the blazing furnace. 24 Then King Nebuchadnezzar leaped to his feet in amazement and asked his advisors, 'Weren't there three men that we tied up and threw into the fire?' They replied, 'Certainly, Your Majesty.' 25 He said, 'Look! I see four men walking around in the fire, unbound and unharmed, and the fourth looks like a son of the gods.' 26 Nebuchadnezzar then approached the opening of the blazing furnace

and shouted, 'Shadrach, Meshach and Abednego, servants of the Most High God, come out! Come here!' So Shadrach, Meshach and Abednego came out of the fire, 27 and the satraps, prefects, governors and royal advisors crowded around them. They saw that the fire had not harmed their bodies, nor was a hair of their heads singed; their robes were not scorched, and there was no smell of fire on them. 28 Then Nebuchadnezzar said, 'Praise be to the God of Shadrach, Meshach and Abednego, who has sent his angel and rescued his servants! They trusted in him and defied the king's command and were willing to give up their lives rather than serve or worship any god except their own God. 29 Therefore I decree that the people of any nation or language who say anything against the God of Shadrach, Meshach and Abednego be cut into pieces and their houses be turned into piles of rubble, for no other god can save in this way.' 30 Then the king promoted Shadrach, Meshach and Abednego in the province of Babylon.

Malachi 4: 2 (HCSB)
2 But for you who fear My name, the sun of righteousness will rise with healing in its wings, and you will go out and playfully jump like calves from the stall.

1 Corinthians 10: 13 (NIV)
13 No temptation has overtaken you except what is common to mankind. And God is faithful; he will not let you be tempted beyond what you can bear. But when you are tempted, he will also provide a way out so that you can endure it.

2 Timothy 3: 11 (NET)
11 as well as the persecutions and sufferings that happened to me in Antioch, in Iconium, and in Lystra. I endured these persecutions and the Lord delivered me from them all.

Romans 8: 2 (NKJV)
2 For the law of the Spirit of life in Christ Jesus has made me free from the law of sin and death.

DISCIPLES

Matthew 9: 37 - 38 (WEB)
37 Then he said to his disciples, "The harvest indeed is plentiful, but the laborers are few. 38 Pray therefore that the Lord of the harvest will send out laborers into his harvest."

Matthew 10: 1 (HCSB)
1 Summoning His 12 disciples, He gave them authority over unclean spirits, to drive them out and to heal every disease and sickness.

Matthew 21: 20 - 22 (WEB)
20 When the disciples saw it, they marveled, saying, "How did the fig tree immediately wither away?" 21 Jesus answered them, "Most certainly I tell you, if you have faith, and don't doubt, you will not only do what was done to the fig tree, but even if you told this mountain, 'Be taken up and cast into the sea,' it would be done. 22 All things, whatever you ask in prayer, believing, you will receive."

Matthew 28: 18 - 20 (WEB)
18 Jesus came to them and spoke to them, saying, "All authority has been

given to me in heaven and on earth. 19 Go and make disciples of all nations, baptizing them in the name of the Father and of the Son and of the Holy Spirit, 20 teaching them to observe all things that I commanded you. Behold, I am with you always, even to the end of the age." Amen.

Mark 11: 22 - 24 (NKJV)
22 So Jesus answered and said to them, "Have faith in God. 23 For assuredly, I say to you, whoev-er says to this mountain, 'Be removed and be cast into the sea,' and does not doubt in his heart, but believes that those things he says will be done, he will have whatever he says. 24 Therefore I say to you, whatever things you ask when you pray, believe that you receive them, and you will have them.

Luke 10: 17, 19 (WEB)
17 The seventy returned with joy, saying, "Lord, even the demons are subject to us in your name!" 19 Behold, I give you authority to tread on serpents and scorpions, and over all the power of the ene-my. Nothing will in any way hurt you.

Luke 6: 40 (HCSB)
40 A disciple is not above his teacher, but everyone who is fully trained will be like his teacher.

Luke 14: 26 - 27 (WEB)
26 "If anyone comes to me, and doesn't disregard[a] his own father, mother, wife, children, brothers, and sisters, yes, and his own life also, he can't be my disciple. 27 Whoever doesn't bear his own cross, and come after me, can't be my disciple.

John 8: 31 - 32 (WEB)
31 Jesus therefore said to those Jews who had believed him, "If you remain in my word, then you are truly my disciples. 32 You will know the truth, and the truth will make you free."

John 10: 27 (NCV)
27 My sheep listen to my voice; I know them, and they follow me.

John 12: 26 (WEB)
26 If anyone serves me, let him follow me. Where I am, there my servant will also be. If anyone serves me, the Father will honor him.

John 13: 13 - 14 (NCV)
13 You call me 'Teacher' and 'Lord,' and you are right, because that is what I am. 14 If I, your Lord and Teacher, have washed your feet, you also should wash each other's feet.

John 15: 5, 7 - 9 (NET)
5 "I am the vine; you are the branches. The one who remains in me—and I in him—bears much fruit, because apart from me you can accomplish nothing. 7 If you remain in me and my words remain in you, ask whatever you want, and it will be done for you. 8 My Father is honored by this, that you bear much fruit and show that you are my disciples. 9 "Just as the Father has loved me, I have also loved you; remain in my love.

2 Peter 2: 9 (WEB)
9 the Lord knows how to deliver the godly out of temptation and to keep the unrighteous under pun-ishment for the day of judgment;

DISCOURAGED

Joshua 1: 9 (HCSB)
9 Haven't I commanded you: be strong and courageous? Do not be afraid or discouraged, for the Lord your God is with you wherever you go.

Psalms 37: 3 - 7 (NKJV)
3 Trust in the Lord, and do good; Dwell in the land, and feed on His faithfulness. 4 Delight yourself also in the Lord, And He shall give you the desires of your heart. 5 Commit your way to the Lord, Trust also in Him, And He shall bring it to pass. 6 He shall bring forth your righteousness as the light, And your justice as the noonday. 7 Rest in the Lord, and wait patiently for Him; Do not fret because of him who prospers in his way, Because of the man who brings wicked schemes to pass.

Psalms 138: 7 - 8 (AMP)
7 Though I walk in the midst of trouble, You will revive me; You will stretch forth Your hand against the wrath of my enemies, and Your right hand will save me. 8 The Lord will perfect that which concerns me; Your mercy and loving-kindness, O Lord, endure forever—forsake not the works of Your own hands.

Psalms 27: 1 - 6, 14 (NET)
1 The Lord delivers and vindicates me! I fear no one! The Lord protects my life! I am afraid of no one! 2 When evil men attack me to devour my flesh, when my adversaries and enemies attack me, they stumble and fall. 3 Even when an army is deployed against me, I do not fear. Even when war is immi-nent, I remain confident. 4 I have asked the Lord for one thing— this is what I desire! I want to live in the Lord's house all the days of my life, so I can gaze at the splendor of the Lord and contemplate in his temple. 5 He will surely give me shelter in the day of danger; he will hide me in his home; he will place me on an inaccessible rocky summit. 6 Now I will triumph over my enemies who surround me! I will offer sacrifices in his dwelling place and shout for joy! I will sing praises to the Lord! 14 Rely on the Lord! Be strong and confident! Rely on the Lord!

Psalms 30: 5 (NKJV)
5 For His anger is but for a moment, His favor is for life; Weeping may endure for a night, But joy comes in the morning.

Psalms 31: 23 - 24 (HCSB)
23 Love the Lord, all His faithful ones. The Lord protects the loyal, but fully repays the arrogant. 24 Be strong and courageous, all you who put your hope in the Lord.

Psalms 34: 10 (NCV)
10 Even lions may get weak and hungry, but those who look to the Lord will have every good thing.

Psalms 34: 17 (NCV)
17 The Lord hears good people when they cry out to him, and he saves them from all their troubles.

Isaiah 26: 3 (ESV)
3 You keep him in perfect peace whose mind is stayed on you, because he trusts in you.

Isaiah 40: 31 (HCSB)
31 but those who trust in the Lord will renew their strength; they will soar on wings like eagles; they will run and not grow weary; they will walk and not faint.

Isaiah 41: 10 (NIV)
10 So do not fear, for I am with you do not be dismayed, for I am your God. I will strengthen you and help you; I will uphold you with my righteous right hand.

Joel 2: 26 (NIV)
26 You will have plenty to eat, until you are full, and you will praise the name of the Lord your God, who has worked wonders for you; never again will my people be shamed.

Malachi 4: 2 - 3 (NLT)
2 "But for you who fear my name, the Sun of Righteousness will rise with healing in his wings. And you will go free, leaping with joy like calves let out to pasture. 3 On the day when I act, you will tread upon the wicked as if they were dust under your feet," says the Lord of Heaven's Armies.

Matthew 5: 6 (WEB)
6 Blessed are those who hunger and thirst after righteousness, for they shall be filled.

Luke 18: 1 (HCSB)
1 He then told them a parable on the need for them to pray always and not become discouraged:

Galatians 6: 9 (NKJV)
9 And let us not grow weary while doing good, for in due season we shall reap if we do not lose heart.

Hebrews 10: 35 - 37 (GNT)
35 Do not lose your courage, then, because it brings with it a great reward. 36 You need to be patient, in order to do the will of God and receive what he promises. 37 For, as the scripture says, "Just a little while longer, and he who is coming will come; he will not delay.

Phillipians 4: 6 - 8 (NKJV)
6 Be anxious for nothing, but in everything by prayer and supplication, with thanksgiving, let your requests be made known to God; 7 and the peace of God, which surpasses all understanding, will guard your hearts and minds through Christ Jesus. 8 Finally, brethren, whatever things are true, what - ever things are noble, whatever things are just, whatever things are pure, whatever things are lovely, whatever things are of good report, if there is any virtue and if there is anything praiseworthy—medi-tate on these things.

Phillipians 4: 12 - 13 (NKJV)
12 I know how to be abased, and I know how to abound. Everywhere and in all things I have learned both to be full and to be hungry, both to abound and to suffer need. 13 I can do all things through Christ who strengthens me.

1 Peter 5: 6 - 8 (NKJV)
6 Therefore humble yourselves under the mighty hand of God, that He may exalt you in due time, 7 casting all your care upon Him, for He cares for you. 8 Be sober, be vigilant; because your adversary the devil walks about like a roaring lion, seeking whom he may devour.

DISTRESSED

Genesis 28: 15 (NIV)
15 I am with you and will watch over you wherever you go, and I will bring you back to this land. I will not leave you until I have done what I have promised you."

2 Samuel 22: 7 (NKJV)
7 In my distress I called upon the Lord, And cried out to my God; He heard my voice from His temple, And my cry entered His ears.

2 Chronicles 33: 12 - 13 (AMP)
12 When he was in affliction, he besought the Lord his God and humbled himself greatly before the God of his fathers. 13 He prayed to Him, and God, entreated by him, heard his supplication and brought him again to Jerusalem to his kingdom. Then Manasseh knew that the Lord is God.

Psalms 4: 1 (NKJV)
1 Hear me when I call, O God of my righteousness! You have relieved me in my distress; Have mercy on me, and hear my prayer.

Psalms 6: 7 - 9 (NKJV)
7 My eye wastes away because of grief; It grows old because of all my enemies. 8 Depart from me, all you workers of iniquity; For the Lord has heard the voice of my weeping. 9 The Lord has heard my supplication; The Lord will receive my prayer.

Psalms 12: 5 (NKJV)
5 "For the oppression of the poor, for the sighing of the needy, Now I will

arise," says the Lord; "I will set him in the safety for which he yearns."

Psalms 20: 1 (NET)
1 May the Lord answer you when you are in trouble; may the God of Jacob make you secure!

Psalms 22: 24 (HCSB)
24 For He has not despised or detested the torment of the afflicted. He did not hide His face from him but listened when he cried to Him for help.

Psalms 30: 11 - 12 (NLT)
11 You have turned my mourning into joyful dancing. You have taken away my clothes of mourning and clothed me with joy, 12 that I might sing praises to you and not be silent. O Lord my God, I will give you thanks forever!

Psalms 37: 24 (HCSB)
24 Though he falls, he will not be overwhelmed, because the Lord holds his hand.

Psalms 55: 17 - 18 (WEB)
17 Evening, morning, and at noon, I will cry out in distress. He will hear my voice. 18 He has re-deemed my soul in peace from the battle that was against me, although there are many who oppose me.

Psalms 55: 22 (NET)
22 Throw your burden upon the Lord, and he will sustain you. He will never allow the godly to be up-ended.

Psalms 121: 1 - 8 (NKJV)
1 I will lift up my eyes to the hills— From whence comes my help? 2 My help comes from the Lord, Who made heaven and earth. 3 He will

not allow your foot to be moved; He who keeps you will not slumber. 4 Behold, He who keeps Israel Shall neither slumber nor sleep. 5 The Lord is your keeper; The Lord is your shade at your right hand. 6 The sun shall not strike you by day, Nor the moon by night. 7 The Lord shall preserve you from all evil; He shall preserve your soul. 8 The Lord shall pre-serve your going out and your coming in From this time forth, and even forevermore.

Psalms 126: 5 - 6 (WEB)
5 Those who sow in tears will reap in joy. 6 He who goes out weeping, carrying seed for sowing, will certainly come again with joy, carrying his sheaves.

Psalms 138: 7 - 8 (WEB)
7 Though I walk in the middle of trouble, you will revive me. You will stretch out your hand against the wrath of my enemies. Your right hand will save me. 8 Yahweh will fulfill that which concerns me; your loving kindness, Yahweh, endures forever. Don't forsake the works of your own hands.

Isaiah 26: 3 (ESV)
3 You keep him in perfect peace whose mind is stayed on you, because he trusts in you.

Isaiah 42: 16 (HCSB)
16 I will lead the blind by a way they did not know; I will guide them on paths they have not known. I will turn darkness to light in front of them and rough places into level ground. This is what I will do for them, and I will not forsake them.

Jeremiah 12: 5 (NASB)
5 If you have run with footmen and they have tired you out, Then how can you compete with horses? If you fall down in a land of peace, How will you do in the thicket of the Jordan?

Nahum 1: 7 (HCSB)
7 The Lord is good, a stronghold in a day of distress; He cares for those who take refuge in Him.

Matthew 11: 28 - 29 (WEB)
28 "Come to me, all you who labor and are heavily burdened, and I will give you rest. 29 Take my yoke upon you, and learn from me, for I am gentle and humble in heart; and you will find rest for your souls.

Matthew 6: 34 (GW)
34 So don't ever worry about tomorrow. After all, tomorrow will worry about itself. Each day has enough trouble of its own.

John 14: 18 (WEB)
18 I will not leave you orphans. I will come to you.

2 Corinthians 1: 3 - 4 (NKJV)
3 Blessed be the God and Father of our Lord Jesus Christ, the Father of mercies and God of all comfort, 4 who comforts us in all our tribulation, that we may be able to comfort those who are in any trouble, with the comfort with which we ourselves are comforted by God.

2 Corinthians 4: 8 - 9 (NKJV)
8 We are hard-pressed on every side, yet not crushed; we are perplexed, but not in despair; 9 perse-cuted, but not forsaken; struck down, but not destroyed—

James 3: 16 - 17 (TLB)
16 For wherever there is jealousy or selfish ambition, there will be disorder and every other kind of evil. 17 But the wisdom that comes from heaven is first of all pure and full of quiet gentleness. Then it is peace-loving and courteous. It allows discussion and is willing to yield to others; it is full of mercy and good deeds. It is wholehearted and straightforward and sincere.

1 Peter 3: 14 (GW)
14 But even if you suffer for doing what God approves, you are blessed. Don't be afraid of those who want to harm you. Don't get upset.

1 Peter 5: 6 - 10 (HCSB)
6 Humble yourselves, therefore, under the mighty hand of God, so that He may exalt you at the proper time, 7 casting all your care on Him, because He cares about you. 8 Be serious! Be alert! Your adversary the Devil is prowling around like a roaring lion, looking for anyone he can devour. 9 Resist him and be firm in the faith, knowing that the same sufferings are being experienced by your fellow believers throughout the world. 10 Now the God of all grace, who called you to His eternal glory in Christ Jesus, will personally restore, establish, strengthen, and support you after you have suffered a little.

DIVORCE

Genesis 2: 24 (WEB)
24 Therefore a man will leave his father and his mother, and will join with his wife, and they will be one flesh.

Malachi 2: 15 - 16 (NLT)
15 Didn't the Lord make you one with your wife? In body and spirit you are his. And what does he want? Godly children from your union. So guard your heart; remain loyal to the wife of your youth. 16 "For I hate divorce!" says the Lord, the God of Israel. "To divorce your wife is to overwhelm her with cruelty," says the Lord of Heaven's Armies. "So guard your heart; do not be unfaithful to your wife."

Matthew 19: 4 - 8 (NLT)
4 "Haven't you read the Scriptures?" Jesus replied. "They record that from the beginning 'God made them male and female.'" 5 And he said, "'This explains why a man leaves his father and mother and is joined to his wife, and the two are united into one.' 6 Since they are no longer two but one, let no one split apart what God has joined together." 7 "Then why did Moses say in the law that a man could give his wife a written notice of divorce and send her away?" they asked. 8 Jesus replied, "Moses permitted divorce only as a concession to your hard hearts, but it was not what God had originally intended.

Mark 10: 4 - 9, 11 - 12 (ESV)
4 They said, "Moses allowed a man to write a certificate of divorce and to send her away." 5 And Jesus said to them, "Because of your hardness of heart he wrote you this commandment. 6 But from the beginning of creation, 'God made them male and female.' 7 'Therefore a man shall leave his father and mother and hold fast to his wife, 8 and the two shall become one flesh.' So they are no longer two but

one flesh. 9 What therefore God has joined together, let not man separate." 11 And he said to them, "Whoever divorces his wife and marries another commits adultery against her, 12 and if she divorces her husband and marries another, she commits adultery."
Luke 16: 18 (AMP)

Luke 16: 18 (AMP)

4 They said, "Moses allowed a man to write a certificate of divorce and to send her away." 5 And Jesus said to them, "Because of your hardness of heart he wrote you this commandment. 6 But from the beginning of creation, 'God made them male and female.' 7 'Therefore a man shall leave his father and mother and hold fast to his wife, 8 and the two shall become one flesh.' So they are no longer two but one flesh. 9 What therefore God has joined together, let not man separate." 11 And he said to them, "Whoever divorces his wife and marries another commits adultery against her, 12 and if she divorces her husband and marries another, she commits adultery."

Romans 7: 1 - 3 (NIV)

1 Do you not know, brothers and sisters—for I am speaking to those who know the law—that the law has authority over someone only as long as that person lives? 2 For example, by law a married wom-an is bound to her husband as long as he is alive, but if her husband dies, she is released from the law that binds her to him. 3 So then, if she has sexual relations with another man while her husband is still alive, she is called an adulteress. But if her husband dies, she is released from that law and is not an adulteress if she marries another man.

1 Corinthians 7: 10 - 16 (NIV)

10 To the married I give this command (not I, but the Lord): A wife must not separate from her hus-band. 11 But if she does, she must remain unmarried or else be reconciled to her husband. And a husband must not divorce his wife. 12 To the rest I say this (I, not the Lord): If any brother has a wife who is not a believer and she is willing to live with him, he must not divorce her. 13 And if a woman has a husband who is not a believer and he is willing to live with her, she must not divorce him. 14 For the unbelieving husband has been sanctified through his wife, and the unbelieving wife has been sanctified through her believing husband. Otherwise your children would be unclean, but as it is, they are holy. 15 But if the unbeliever leaves, let it be so. The brother or the sister is not bound in such circumstances; God has called us to live in peace. 16 How do you know, wife, whether you will save your husband? Or, how do you know, husband, whether you will save your wife?

EMPOWER

1 Samuel 17: 45 - 47 (NIV)

45 David said to the Philistine, "You come against me with sword and spear and javelin, but I come against you in the name of the Lord Almighty, the God of the armies of Israel, whom you have defied. 46 This day the Lord will deliver you into my hands, and I'll strike you down and cut off your head. This very day I will give the carcasses of the Philistine army to the birds and the wild animals, and the whole world will

know that there is a God in Israel. 47 All those gathered here will know that it is not by sword or spear that the Lord saves; for the battle is the Lord's, and he will give all of you into our hands."

Psalms 18: 29, 32 - 34, 39 (NKJV)

29 For by You I can run against a troop, By my God I can leap over a wall. 32 It is God who arms me with strength, And makes my way perfect. 33 He makes my feet like the feet of deer, And sets me on my high places. 34 He teaches my hands to make war, So that my arms can bend a bow of bronze. 39 For You have armed me with strength for the battle; You have subdued under me those who rose up against me.

Proverbs 28: 1 (CEB)

1 The wicked run away even though no one pursues them, but the righteous are as confident as a lion.

Isaiah 40: 29 - 31 (NET)

29 He gives strength to those who are tired; to the ones who lack power, he gives renewed energy 30 Even youths get tired and weary; even strong young men clumsily stumble. 31 But those who wait for the Lord's help find renewed strength; they rise up as if they had eagles' wings, they run without growing weary, they walk without getting tired.

Psalms 68: 35 (NLT)

35 God is awesome in his sanctuary. The God of Israel gives power and strength to his people. Praise be to God!

Jeremiah 12: 5 (GNT)

5 The Lord said, "Jeremiah, if you get tired racing against people, how can you race against horses? If you can't even stand up in open country, how will you manage in the jungle by the Jordan?

Matthew 18: 18 (NIV)

18 "Truly I tell you, whatever you bind on earth will be bound in heaven, and whatever you loose on earth will be loosed in heaven.

Luke 10: 19 (WEB)

19 Behold, I give you authority to tread on serpents and scorpions, and over all the power of the ene-my. Nothing will in any way hurt you.

Luke 12: 12 (MEV)

12 For the Holy Spirit will teach you at that time what you should say.

Acts 1: 8 (WEB)

8 But you will receive power when the Holy Spirit has come upon you. You will be witnesses to me in Jerusalem, in all Judea and Samaria, and to the uttermost parts of the earth.

2 Corinthians 12: 9 - 10 (NKJV)

9 And He said to me, "My grace is sufficient for you, for My strength is made perfect in weakness." Therefore most gladly I will rather boast in my infirmities, that the power of Christ may rest upon me. 10 Therefore I take pleasure in infirmities, in reproaches, in needs, in persecutions, in distresses, for Christ's sake. For when I am weak, then I am strong.

Ephesians 1: 18 - 20 (GNT)

18 I ask that your minds may be opened to see his light, so that you will know what is the hope to which he has called you, how rich are the wonderful

blessings he promises his people, 19 and how very great is his power at work in us who believe. This power working in us is the same as the mighty strength 20 which he used when he raised Christ from death and seated him at his right side in the heavenly world.

Ephesians 3: 16 - 17, 20 (NCV)
16 I ask the Father in his great glory to give you the power to be strong inwardly through his Spirit. 17 I pray that Christ will live in your hearts by faith and that your life will be strong in love and be built on love. 20 With God's power working in us, God can do much, much more than anything we can ask or imagine.

Ephesians 6: 10 - 18 (GNT)
10 Finally, build up your strength in union with the Lord and by means of his mighty power. 11 Put on all the armor that God gives you, so that you will be able to stand up against the Devil's evil tricks. 12 For we are not fighting against human beings but against the wicked spiritual forces in the heavenly world, the rulers, authorities, and cosmic powers of this dark age. 13 So put on God's armor now! Then when the evil day comes, you will be able to resist the enemy's attacks; and after fighting to the end, you will still hold your ground. 14 So stand ready, with truth as a belt tight around your waist, with righteousness as your breastplate, 15 and as your shoes the readiness to announce the Good News of peace. 16 At all times carry faith as a shield; for with it you will be able to put out all the burning arrows shot by the Evil One. 17 And accept salvation as a helmet, and the word of God as the sword which the Spirit gives you. 18 Do all this in prayer, asking for God's help. Pray on every occasion, as the Spirit leads. For this reason keep alert and never give up; pray always for all God's people.

Colossians 2: 9 -10, 15 (NCV)
9 All of God lives fully in Christ (even when Christ was on earth), 10 and you have a full and true life in Christ, who is ruler over all rulers and powers. 15 God stripped the spiritual rulers and powers of their authority. With the cross, he won the victory and showed the world that they were powerless.

2 Timothy 1: 7 (NKJV)
7 For God has not given us a spirit of fear, but of power and of love and of a sound mind.

Hebrews 4: 16 (HCSB)
16 Therefore let us approach the throne of grace with boldness, so that we may receive mercy and find grace to help us at the proper time.

ENCOURAGE

Deuteronomy 20:4 (HCSB)
4 For the Lord your God is the One who goes with you to fight for you against your enemies to give you victory.'

Joshua 1: 9 (GNT)
9 Remember that I have commanded you to be determined and confident! Do not be afraid or dis-couraged, for I, the Lord your God, am with you wherever you go.

Psalms 5: 12 (NIV)
12 Surely, Lord, you bless the righteous; you surround them with your favor as with a shield.

Psalms 30: 4 - 5 (NKJV)
4 Sing praise to the Lord, you saints of His, And give thanks at the remembrance of His holy name. 5 For His anger is but for a moment, His favor is for life; Weeping may endure for a night, But joy comes in the morning.

Psalms 31: 23 (AMP)
23 O love the Lord, all you His saints! The Lord preserves the faithful, and plentifully pays back him who deals haughtily.

Psalms 34: 10 (NIV)
10 The lions may grow weak and hungry, but those who seek the Lord lack no good thing.

Psalms 34: 18 - 19 (GNT)
18 The Lord is near to those who are discouraged; he saves those who have lost all hope. 19 Good people suffer many troubles, but the Lord saves them from them all;

Psalms 37: 23 - 24 (GNT)
23 The Lord guides us in the way we should go and protects those who please him. 24 If they fall, they will not stay down, because the Lord will help them up.

Psalms 37: 3 - 5 (NIV)
3 Trust in the Lord and do good; dwell in the land and enjoy safe pasture. 4 Take delight in the Lord, and he will give you the desires of your heart. 5 Commit your way to the Lord; trust in him and he will do this:

Psalms 46: 1 - 3, 5 (HCSB)
1 God is our refuge and strength, a helper who is always found in times of trouble. 2 Therefore we will not be afraid, though the earth trembles and the mountains topple into the depths of the seas, 3 though its waters roar and foam and the mountains quake with its turmoil. Selah 5 God is within her; she will not be toppled. God will help her when the morning dawns.

Psalms 91: 1 - 16 (MEV)
1 He who dwells in the shelter of the Most High shall abide under the shadow of the Almighty. 2 I will say of the Lord, "He is my refuge and my fortress, my God in whom I trust." 3 Surely He shall deliver you from the snare of the hunter and from the deadly pestilence. 4 He shall cover you with His feath-ers, and under His wings you shall find protection; His faithfulness shall be your shield and wall. 5 You shall not be afraid of the terror by night, nor of the arrow that flies by day; 6 nor of the pestilence that pursues in darkness, nor of the destruction that strikes at noonday. 7 A thousand may fall at your side and ten thousand at your right hand, but it shall not come near you. 8 Only with your eyes shall you behold and see the reward of the wicked. 9 Because you have made the Lord, who is my refuge, even the Most High, your dwelling, 10 there shall be no evil befall you, neither shall any plague come near your tent; 11 for He shall give His angels charge over you to guard you in all your ways. 12 They shall bear you up in their hands, lest you strike your foot against a stone. 13 You shall tread upon the lion and adder; the young lion and the serpent you shall trample underfoot.

14 Because he has set his love upon Me, therefore I will deliver him; I will set him on high, because he has known My name. 15 He shall call upon Me, and I will answer him; I will be with him in trouble, and I will deliver him and honor him. 16 With long life I will satisfy him and show him My salvation.

Psalms 103: 1 - 5 (NKJV)
1 Bless the Lord, O my soul; And all that is within me, bless His holy name! 2 Bless the Lord, O my soul, And forget not all His benefits: 3 Who forgives all your iniquities, Who heals all your diseases, 4 Who redeems your life from destruction, Who crowns you with lovingkindness and tender mercies, 5 Who satisfies your mouth with good things, So that your youth is renewed like the eagle's.

Psalms 138: 3, 7 - 8 (NIV)
3 When I called, you answered me; you greatly emboldened me. 7 Though I walk in the midst of trou-ble, you preserve my life. You stretch out your hand against the anger of my foes; with your right hand you save me. 8 The Lord will vindicate me; your love, Lord, endures forever— do not abandon the works of your hands.

Psalms 145: 14, 18 - 19 (NKJV)
14 The Lord upholds all who fall, And raises up all who are bowed down. 18 To all who call upon Him in truth. 19 He will fulfill the desire of those who fear Him; He also will hear their cry and save them.

Proverbs 16: 3 (NCV)
3 Depend on the Lord in whatever you do, and your plans will succeed.

Proverbs 23: 17 - 18 (NCV)
17 Don't envy sinners, but always respect the Lord. 18 Then you will have hope for the future, and your wishes will come true.

Ecclesiastes 9: 7 (NKJV)
7 Go, eat your bread with joy, And drink your wine with a merry heart; For God has already accepted your works.

Isaiah 41: 10 (HCSB)
10 Do not fear, for I am with you; do not be afraid, for I am your God. I will strengthen you; I will help you; I will hold on to you with My righteous right hand.

Isaiah 46: 11 (NIV)
11 From the east I summon a bird of prey; from a far-off land, a man to fulfill my purpose. What I have said, that I will bring about; what I have planned, that I will do.

Jeremiah 12: 5 (NIV)
12 "If you have raced with men on foot and they have worn you out, how can you compete with hors-es? If you stumble in safe country, how will you manage in the thickets by the Jordan?

Habakkuk 2: 2 - 3 (GW)
2 Then the Lord answered me, "Write the vision. Make it clear on tablets so that anyone can read it quickly. 3 The vision will still happen at the appointed time. It hurries toward its goal. It won't be a lie. If it's delayed, wait for it. It will certainly happen. It won't be late.

Zechariah 4: 7 (GNT)
7 Obstacles as great as mountains will disappear before you. You will rebuild

the Temple, and as you put the last stone in place, the people will shout, 'Beautiful, beautiful!'"

Matthew 7: 7 - 10 (WEB)

7 "Ask, and it will be given you. Seek, and you will find. Knock, and it will be opened for you. 8 For everyone who asks receives. He who seeks finds. To him who knocks it will be opened. 9 Or who is there among you who, if his son asks him for bread, will give him a stone? 10 Or if he asks for a fish, who will give him a serpent?

Matthew 8: 25 - 26 (NKJV)

25 Then His disciples came to Him and awoke Him, saying, "Lord, save us! We are perishing!" 26 But He said to them, "Why are you fearful, O you of little faith?" Then He arose and rebuked the winds and the sea, and there was a great calm.

Matthew 11: 29 - 30 (NIV)

29 Take my yoke upon you and learn from me, for I am gentle and humble in heart, and you will find rest for your souls. 30 For my yoke is easy and my burden is light.

Matthew 14: 29 - 31 (GW)

29 Jesus said, "Come!" So Peter got out of the boat and walked on the water toward Jesus. 30 But when he noticed how strong the wind was, he became afraid and started to sink. He shouted, "Lord, save me!" 31 Immediately, Jesus reached out, caught hold of him, and said, "You have so little faith! Why did you doubt?"

Luke 18: 1 (WEB)

1 He also spoke a parable to them that they must always pray, and not give up,

1 Corinthians 15: 57 - 58 (HCSB)

57 But thanks be to God, who gives us the victory through our Lord Jesus Christ! 58 Therefore, my dear brothers, be steadfast, immovable, always excelling in the Lord's work, knowing that your labor in the Lord is not in vain.

2 Corinthians 2: 14 (WEB)

14 Now thanks be to God, who always leads us in triumph in Christ, and reveals through us the sweet aroma of his knowledge in every place.

Galatians 6: 9 (HCSB)

9 So we must not get tired of doing good, for we will reap at the proper time if we don't give up.

2 Timothy 1: 7 - 9 (NKJV)

7 For God has not given us a spirit of fear, but of power and of love and of a sound mind. 8 There-fore do not be ashamed of the testimony of our Lord, nor of me His prisoner, but share with me in the sufferings for the gospel according to the power of God, 9 who has saved us and called us with a holy calling, not according to our works, but according to His own purpose and grace which was given to us in Christ Jesus before time began,

Hebrews 10: 35 - 37 (GNT)

35 Do not lose your courage, then, because it brings with it a great reward. 36 You need to be patient, in order to do the will of God and receive what he promises. 37 For, as the scripture says, "Just a little while longer, and he who is coming will come; he will not delay.

ENEMY

Deuteronomy 20: 4 (HCSB)
4 For the Lord your God is the One who goes with you to fight for you against your enemies to give you victory.

Deuteronomy 28: 7 (NKJV)
7 "The Lord will cause your enemies who rise against you to be defeated before your face; they shall come out against you one way and flee before you seven ways.

2 Kings 17: 38 - 39 (NIV)
38 Do not forget the covenant I have made with you, and do not worship other gods. 39 Rather, wor-ship the Lord your God; it is he who will deliver you from the hand of all your enemies.

Psalms 60: 12 (NKJV)
12 Through God we will do valiantly, For it is He who shall tread down our enemies.

Psalms 91: 3, 5 - 13 (NKJV)
3 Surely He shall deliver you from the snare of the fowler And from the perilous pestilence. 5 You shall not be afraid of the terror by night, Nor of the arrow that flies by day, 6 Nor of the pestilence that walks in darkness, Nor of the destruction that lays waste at noonday. 7 A thousand may fall at your side, And ten thousand at your right hand; But it shall not come near you. 8 Only with your eyes shall you look, And see the reward of the wicked. 9 Because you have made the Lord, who is my refuge, Even the Most High, your dwelling place, 10 No evil shall befall you, Nor shall any plague come near your dwelling; 11 For He shall give His angels charge over you, To keep you in all your ways. 12 In their hands they shall bear you up, Lest you dash your foot against a stone. 13 You shall tread upon the lion and the cobra, The young lion and the serpent you shall trample underfoot.

Psalms 97: 10 (NIRV)
10 Let those who love the Lord hate evil. He guards the lives of those who are faithful to him. He saves them from the power of sinful people.

Proverbs 3: 25 - 26 (NIV)
25 Have no fear of sudden disaster or of the ruin that overtakes the wicked, 26 for the Lord will be at your side and will keep your foot from being snared.

Proverbs 16: 7 (GW)
7 When a person's ways are pleasing to the Lord, he makes even his enemies to be at peace with him.

Isaiah 41: 11 - 12 (NKJV)
11 Behold, all those who were incensed against you Shall be ashamed and disgraced; They shall be as nothing, And those who strive with you shall perish. 12 You shall seek them and not find them— Those who contended with you. Those who war against you Shall be as nothing, As a nonexistent thing.

Isaiah 54: 15, 17 (NKJV)
15 Indeed they shall surely assemble, but not because of Me. Whoever assembles against you shall fall for your sake. 17 No weapon formed against you shall prosper, And every tongue which rises against you in judgment You shall condemn. This is the heritage of the servants of the Lord, And their righteousness is from Me," Says the Lord.

Mark 16: 17 - 18 (WEB)

17 These signs will accompany those who believe: in my name they will cast out demons; they will speak with new languages; 18 they will take up serpents; and if they drink any deadly thing, it will in no way hurt them; they will lay hands on the sick, and they will recover."

Luke 1: 71, 74 (GW)

71 He promised to save us from our enemies and from the power of all who hate us. 74 He promised to rescue us from our enemies' power so that we could serve him without fear

Luke 10: 17 - 20 (GW)

17 The 70 disciples came back very happy. They said, "Lord, even demons obey us when we use the power and authority of your name!" 18 Jesus said to them, "I watched Satan fall from heaven like lightning. 19 I have given you the authority to trample snakes and scorpions and to destroy the enemy's power. Nothing will hurt you. 20 However, don't be happy that evil spirits obey you. Be happy that your names are written in heaven.

2 Corinthians 6: 14 - 15 (MEV)

14 Do not be unequally yoked together with unbelievers. For what fellowship has righteousness with unrighteousness? What communion has light with darkness? 15 What agreement has Christ with Belial? Or what part has he who believes with an unbeliever?

Ephesians 6: 10 - 18 (NIV)

10 Finally, be strong in the Lord and in his mighty power. 11 Put on the full armor of God, so that you can take your stand against the devil's schemes. 12 For our struggle is not against flesh and blood, but against the rulers, against the authorities, against the powers of this dark world and against the spiritual forces of evil in the heavenly realms. 13 Therefore put on the full armor of God, so that when the day of evil comes, you may be able to stand your ground, and after you have done everything, to stand. 14 Stand firm then, with the belt of truth buckled around your waist, with the breastplate of righteousness in place, 15 and with your feet fitted with the readiness that comes from the gospel of peace. 16 In addition to all this, take up the shield of faith, with which you can extinguish all the flam-ing arrows of the evil one. 17 Take the helmet of salvation and the sword of the Spirit, which is the word of God. 18 And pray in the Spirit on all occasions with all kinds of prayers and requests. With this in mind, be alert and always keep on praying for all the Lord's people.

James 4: 7 - 8 (ASV)

7 Be subject therefore unto God; but resist the devil, and he will flee from you. 8 Draw nigh to God, and he will draw nigh to you.

1 Peter 5: 8 - 9 (ASV)

8 Be sober, be watchful: your adversary the devil, as a roaring lion, walketh about, seeking whom he may devour, 9 whom withstand stedfast in your faith, knowing that the same sufferings are accom-plished in your brethren who are in the world.

1 John 3: 8 (WEB)

8 He who sins is of the devil, for the devil has been sinning from the

beginning. To this end the Son of God was revealed: that he might destroy the works of the devil.

1 John 4: 1 - 6 (NCV)
1 My dear friends, many false prophets have gone out into the world. So do not believe every spirit, but test the spirits to see if they are from God. 2 This is how you can know God's Spirit: Every spir-it who confesses that Jesus Christ came to earth as a human is from God. 3 And every spirit who refuses to say this about Jesus is not from God. It is the spirit of the enemy of Christ, which you have heard is coming, and now he is already in the world. 4 My dear children, you belong to God and have defeated them; because God's Spirit, who is in you, is greater than the devil, who is in the world. 5 And they belong to the world, so what they say is from the world, and the world listens to them. 6 But we belong to God, and those who know God listen to us. But those who are not from God do not listen to us. That is how we know the Spirit that is true and the spirit that is false.

Revelation 12: 10 - 11 (TLB)
10 Then I heard a loud voice shouting across the heavens, "It has happened at last! God's salvation and the power and the rule, and the authority of his Christ are finally here; for the Accuser of our brothers has been thrown down from heaven onto earth—he accused them day and night before our God. 11 They defeated him by the blood of the Lamb and by their testimony; for they did not love their lives but laid them down for him.

ETERNAL LIFE

Psalms 37: 18 (NLT)
18 Day by day the Lord takes care of the innocent, and they will receive an inheritance that lasts for-ever.

Psalms 49: 8 - 9, 15 (NLT)
8 Redemption does not come so easily, for no one can ever pay enough 9 to live forever and never see the grave. 15 But as for me, God will redeem my life. He will snatch me from the power of the grave.

Psalms 116: 15 (HCSB)
15 The death of His faithful ones is valuable in the Lord's sight.

Proverbs 14: 27, 32 (NLT)
27 Fear of the Lord is a life-giving fountain; it offers escape from the snares of death. 32 The wicked are crushed by disaster, but the godly have a refuge when they die.

John 11: 25 - 26 (WEB)
25 Jesus said to her, "I am the resurrection and the life. He who believes in me will still live, even if he dies. 26 Whoever lives and believes in me will never die. Do you believe this?

John 14: 16, 17, 19 (WEB)
16 I will pray to the Father, and he will give you another Counselor,[a] that he may be with you forev-er,— 17 the Spirit of truth, whom the world can't receive; for it doesn't see him, neither knows him. You know him, for he lives with you, and will be in you. 19 Yet a little while, and the world will see me no more; but you will see me. Because I live, you will live also.

John 14: 2 - 3 (WEB)
2 In my Father's house are many homes. If it weren't so, I would have told you. I am going to prepare a place for you. 3 If I go and prepare a place for you, I will come again, and will receive you to myself; that where I am, you may be there also.

John 3: 16 (WEB)
16 For God so loved the world, that he gave his one and only Son, that whoever believes in him should not perish, but have eternal life.

John 8: 51 (MEV)
51 Truly, truly I say to you, if anyone keeps My word, he shall never see death.

2 Corinthians 5: 8 - 10 (NLT)
8 Yes, we are fully confident, and we would rather be away from these earthly bodies, for then we will be at home with the Lord. 9 So whether we are here in this body or away from this body, our goal is to please him. 10 For we must all stand before Christ to be judged. We will each receive whatever we deserve for the good or evil we have done in this earthly body.

1 Thessalonians 4: 13 - 14 (NIV)
13 Brothers and sisters, we do not want you to be uninformed about those who sleep in death, so that you do not grieve like the rest of mankind, who have no hope. 14 For we believe that Jesus died and rose again, and so we believe that God will bring with Jesus those who have fallen asleep in him.

1 Thessalonians 5: 10 - 11 (NIV)
10 He died for us so that, whether we are awake or asleep, we may live together with him. 11 There-fore encourage one another and build each other up, just as in fact you are doing.

Hebrews 9: 27 (NKJV)
27 And as it is appointed for men to die once, but after this the judgment,

1 John 5: 11 - 13 (WEB)
11 The testimony is this, that God gave to us eternal life, and this life is in his Son. 12 He who has the Son has the life. He who doesn't have God's Son doesn't have the life. 13 These things I have written to you who believe in the name of the Son of God, that you may know that you have eternal life, and that you may continue to believe in the name of the Son of God.

EXAMPLE

Matthew 5: 16 (WEB)
16 Even so, let your light shine before men; that they may see your good works, and glorify your Fa-ther who is in heaven.

Mark 10: 43 - 45 (NIVUK)
43 Not so with you. Instead, whoever wants to become great among you must be your servant, 44 and whoever wants to be first must be slave of all. 45 For even the Son of Man did not come to be served, but to serve, and to give his life as a ransom for many.'

John 13: 14 - 15 (CEV)
14 If I, your Lord and teacher, have washed your feet, you too must wash each other's feet. 15 I have given you an example: Just as I have done, you also must do.

John 13: 34 (NIV)
34 A new command I give you: Love one another. As I have loved you, so you must love one another.

John 14: 12 (NLT)
12 "I tell you the truth, anyone who believes in me will do the same works I have done, and even greater works, because I am going to be with the Father.

John 15: 10 (NCV)
10 I have obeyed my Father's commands, and I remain in his love. In the same way, if you obey my commands, you will remain in my love.

Romans 15: 5 - 7 (NIV)
5 May the God who gives endurance and encouragement give you the same attitude of mind toward each other that Christ Jesus had, 6 so that with one mind and one voice you may glorify the God and Father of our Lord Jesus Christ. 7 Accept one another, then, just as Christ accepted you, in order to bring praise to God.

Ephesians 5: 1 - 2 (ESV)
5 Therefore be imitators of God, as beloved children. 2 And walk in love, as Christ loved us and gave himself up for us, a fragrant offering and sacrifice to God.

Colossians 3: 12 - 13 (WEB)
12 Put on therefore, as God's chosen ones, holy and beloved, a heart of compassion, kindness, low-liness, humility, and perseverance; 13 bearing with one another, and forgiving each other, if any man has a complaint against any; even as Christ forgave you, so you also do.

Titus 2: 7 - 8 (NASB)
7 in all things show yourself to be an example of good deeds, with purity in doctrine, dignified, 8 sound in speech which is beyond reproach, so that the opponent will be put to shame, having noth-ing bad to say about us.

1 Peter 1: 15 - 16 (WEB)
15 but just as he who called you is holy, you yourselves also be holy in all of your behavior; 16 be-cause it is written, "You shall be holy; for I am holy."

1 Peter 2: 20 - 21 (RSV)
20 For what credit is it, if when you do wrong and are beaten for it you take it patiently? But if when you do right and suffer for it you take it patiently, you have God's approval. 21 For to this you have been called, because Christ also suffered for you, leaving you an example, that you should follow in his steps.

1 Peter 5: 2 - 3 (WEB)
2 Shepherd the flock of God which is among you, exercising the oversight, not under compulsion, but voluntarily, not for dishonest gain, but willingly; 3 neither as lording it over those entrusted to you, but making yourselves examples to the flock.

1 John 2: 6 (NASB)
6 the one who says he abides in Him ought himself to walk in the same manner as He walked.

1 John 4: 17 (ASV)
17 Herein is love made perfect with us, that we may have boldness in the day of judgment; because as he is, even so are we in this world.

FAITH

Matthew 8: 24 - 26 (NIV)
24 Suddenly a furious storm came up on the lake, so that the waves swept over the boat. But Jesus was sleeping. 25 The disciples went and woke him, saying, "Lord, save us! We're going to drown!" 26 He replied, "You of little faith, why are you so afraid?" Then he got up and rebuked the winds and the waves, and it was completely calm.

Matthew 9: 20 - 22 (LEB)
20 And behold, a woman who had been suffering with a hemorrhage twelve years approached from behind and touched the edge of his cloak, 21 for she said to herself, "If only I touch his cloak I will be healed." 22 But Jesus, turning around and seeing her, said, "Have courage, daughter! Your faith has healed you." And the woman was healed from that hour.

Matthew 9: 28 - 29 (WEB)
28 When he had come into the house, the blind men came to him. Jesus said to them, "Do you be-lieve that I am able to do this?" They told him, "Yes, Lord." 29 Then he touched their eyes, saying, "According to your faith be it done to you."

Matthew 14: 29 - 31 (GW)
29 Jesus said, "Come!" So Peter got out of the boat and walked on the water toward Jesus. 30 But when he noticed how strong the wind was, he became afraid and started to sink. He shouted, "Lord, save me!" 31 Immediately, Jesus reached out, caught hold of him, and said, "You have so little faith! Why did you doubt?"

Matthew 15: 27 - 28 (NCV)
27 The woman said, "Yes, Lord, but even the dogs eat the crumbs that fall from their masters' table." 28 Then Jesus answered, "Woman, you have great faith! I will do what you asked." And at that mo-ment the woman's daughter was healed.

Matthew 17: 20 (WEB)
20 He said to them, "Because of your unbelief. For most certainly I tell you, if you have faith as a grain of mustard seed, you will tell this mountain, 'Move from here to there,' and it will move; and nothing will be impossible for you.

Matthew 21: 18 - 19, 21, 22 (GW)
18 In the morning, as Jesus returned to the city, he became hungry. 19 When he saw a fig tree by the road, he went up to the tree and found nothing on it but leaves. He said to the tree, "May fruit never grow on you again!" At once the fig tree dried up. 21 Jesus answered them, "I can guarantee this truth: If you have faith and do not doubt, you will be able to do what I did to the fig tree. You could also say to this mountain, 'Be uprooted and thrown into the sea,' and it will happen. 22 Have faith that you will receive whatever you ask for in prayer."

Mark 11: 22 - 25 (NCV)
22 Jesus answered, "Have faith in God. 23 I tell you the truth, you can say to this mountain, 'Go, fall into the sea.' And if you have no doubts in your mind and believe that what you say will happen, God will do it for you. 24 So I tell you to believe that you have received the things you ask for in prayer, and God will give them to you. 25 When you are praying, if you

are angry with someone, forgive him so that your Father in heaven will also forgive your sins.

Mark 9: 23 - 24 (WEB)
23 Jesus said to him, "If you can believe, all things are possible to him who believes." 24 Immediately the father of the child cried out with tears, "I believe. Help my unbelief!"

Mark 16: 17 - 18 (HCSB)
17 And these signs will accompany those who believe: In My name they will drive out demons; they will speak in new languages; 18 they will pick up snakes; if they should drink anything deadly, it will never harm them; they will lay hands on the sick, and they will get well.

Romans 1: 17 (NCV)
17 The Good News shows how God makes people right with himself—that it begins and ends with faith. As the Scripture says, "But those who are right with God will live by faith."

Romans 8: 24 - 25 (NOG)
24 We were saved with this hope in mind. If we hope for something we already see, it's not really hope. Who hopes for what can be seen? 25 But if we hope for what we don't see, we eagerly wait for it with perseverance.

Romans 10: 17 (NKJV)
17 So then faith comes by hearing, and hearing by the word of God.

Romans 10: 6 - 8 (NCV)
6 But this is what the Scripture says about being made right through faith: "Don't say to yourself, 'Who will go up into heaven?'" (That means, "Who will go up to heaven and bring Christ down to earth?") 7 "And do not say, 'Who will go down into the world below?'" (That means, "Who will go down and bring Christ up from the dead?") 8 This is what the Scripture says: "The word is near you; it is in your mouth and in your heart." That is the teaching of faith that we are telling.

Romans 12: 3, 5 - 6 (AMP)
3 For by the grace (unmerited favor of God) given to me I warn everyone among you not to estimate and think of himself more highly than he ought [not to have an exaggerated opinion of his own impor-tance], but to rate his ability with sober judgment, each according to the degree of faith apportioned by God to him. 5 So we, numerous as we are, are one body in Christ (the Messiah) and individually we are parts one of another [mutually dependent on one another]. 6 Having gifts (faculties, talents, qualities) that differ according to the grace given us, let us use them: [He whose gift is] prophecy, [let him prophesy] according to the proportion of his faith;

2 Corinthians 5: 7 (NLT)
7 For we live by believing and not by seeing.

Hebrews 10: 35 - 38 (NCV)
35 So do not lose the courage you had in the past, which has a great reward. 36 You must hold on, so you can do what God wants and receive what he has promised. 37 For in a very short time, "The One who is coming will come and will not be delayed. 38 Those who are right with me will live by faith. But if they turn back with fear, I will not be pleased with them."

Hebrews 11: 1 - 3, 6 (NCV)
1 Faith means being sure of the things we hope for and knowing that something is real even if we do not see it. 2 Faith is the reason we remember great people who lived in the past. 3 It is by faith we un-derstand that the whole world was made by God's command so what we see was made by something that cannot be seen. 6 Without faith no one can please God. Anyone who comes to God must believe that he is real and that he rewards those who truly want to find him.

Hebrews 12: 2 (HCSB)
2 keeping our eyes on Jesus, the source and perfecter of our faith, who for the joy that lay before Him endured a cross and despised the shame and has sat down at the right hand of God's throne.

James 1: 5 - 6 (HCSB)
5 Now if any of you lacks wisdom, he should ask God, who gives to all generously and without criti - cizing, and it will be given to him. 6 But let him ask in faith without doubting. For the doubter is like the surging sea, driven and tossed by the wind.

James 2: 14 - 18 (NCV)
14 My brothers and sisters, if people say they have faith, but do nothing, their faith is worth nothing. Can faith like that save them? 15 A brother or sister in Christ might need clothes or food. 16 If you say to that person, "God be with you! I hope you stay warm and get plenty to eat," but you do not give what that person needs, your words are worth nothing. 17 In the same way, faith by itself—that does nothing—is dead. 18 Someone might say, "You have

faith, but I have deeds." Show me your faith without doing anything, and I will show you my faith by what I do.

James 5: 14 - 15 (NCV)
14 Anyone who is sick should call the church's elders. They should pray for and pour oil on the per-son in the name of the Lord. 15 And the prayer that is said with faith will make the sick person well; the Lord will heal that person. And if the person has sinned, the sins will be forgiven.

1 John 5: 4 - 5 (HCSB)
4 because whatever has been born of God conquers the world. This is the victory that has conquered the world: our faith. 5 And who is the one who conquers the world but the one who believes that Je-sus is the Son of God?

FALL SHORT

2 Chronicles 7: 14 - 15 (GNT)
14 if they pray to me and repent and turn away from the evil they have been doing, then I will hear them in heaven, forgive their sins, and make their land prosperous again. 15 I will watch over this Temple and be ready to hear all the prayers that are offered here,

Psalms 103: 10 - 13 (HCSB)
10 He has not dealt with us as our sins deserve or repaid us according to our offenses. 11 For as high as the heavens are above the earth, so great is His faithful love toward those who fear Him. 12 As far as the east is from the west, so far has He removed our transgressions from us. 13 As a father has compassion on his children, so the

Lord has compassion on those who fear Him.

Psalms 145: 14 (NKJV)
14 The Lord upholds all who fall, And raises up all who are bowed down.

Psalms 37: 23 - 24 (NLT)
23 The Lord directs the steps of the godly. He delights in every detail of their lives. 24 Though they stumble, they will never fall, for the Lord holds them by the hand.

Psalms 51: 1 - 2 (NKJV)
1 Have mercy upon me, O God, According to Your lovingkindness; According to the multitude of Your tender mercies, Blot out my transgressions. 2 Wash me thoroughly from my iniquity, And cleanse me from my sin.

Psalms 51: 10 - 11 (NKJV)
10 Create in me a clean heart, O God, And renew a steadfast spirit within me. 11 Do not cast me away from Your presence, And do not take Your Holy Spirit from me.

Psalms 56: 12 - 13 (NIV)
12 I am under vows to you, my God; I will present my thank offerings to you. 13 For you have deliv-ered me from death and my feet from stumbling, that I may walk before God in the light of life.

Psalms 94: 17 - 19 (ESV)
17 If the Lord had not been my help, my soul would soon have lived in the land of silence. 18 When I thought, "My foot slips," your steadfast love, O Lord, held me up. 19 When the cares of my heart are many, your consolations cheer my soul.

Proverbs 10: 9 (NLT)
9 People with integrity walk safely, but those who follow crooked paths will be exposed.

Proverbs 11: 28 (NIV)
28 Those who trust in their riches will fall, but the righteous will thrive like a green leaf.

Proverbs 16: 18 (HCSB)
18 Pride comes before destruction, and an arrogant spirit before a fall.

Proverbs 24: 16 (NLT)
16 The godly may trip seven times, but they will get up again. But one disaster is enough to overthrow the wicked.

Proverbs 28: 13 (NIV)
13 Whoever conceals their sins does not prosper, but the one who confesses and renounces them finds mercy.

Ecclesiastes 4: 9 - 10 (MEV)
9 Two are better than one,because there is a good reward for their labor together.10 For if they fall then one will help up his companion. But woe to him who is alone when he falls and has no one to help him up.

Ecclesiastes 7: 20 (AMP)
20 Surely there is not a righteous man upon earth who does good and never sins.

Isaiah 53: 6 (MEV)
6 All of us like sheep have gone astray; each of us has turned to his own way, but the Lord has laid on him the iniquity of us all.

Lamentations 3: 22 - 23 (MEV)
22 It is of the Lord's mercies that we are not consumed; His compassions do not fail. 23 They are new every morning; great is Your faithfulness.

Joel 2: 12 - 13 (GNT)
12 "But even now," says the Lord, "repent sincerely and return to me with fasting and weeping and mourning. 13 Let your broken heart show your sorrow; tearing your clothes is not enough." Come back to the Lord your God. He is kind and full of mercy; he is patient and keeps his promise; he is always ready to forgive and not punish.

Matthew 14: 29 - 31 (HCSB)
29 "Come!" He said. And climbing out of the boat, Peter started walking on the water and came to-ward Jesus. 30 But when he saw the strength of the wind, he was afraid. And beginning to sink he cried out, "Lord, save me!" 31 Immediately Jesus reached out His hand, caught hold of him, and said to him, "You of little faith, why did you doubt?"

Matthew 26: 41 (HCSB)
41 Stay awake and pray, so that you won't enter into temptation. The spirit is willing, but the flesh is weak."

Luke 15: 21 - 24 (NLT)
21 His son said to him, 'Father, I have sinned against both heaven and you, and I am no longer wor-thy of being called your son.' 22 "But his father said to the servants, 'Quick! Bring the finest robe in the house and put it on him. Get a ring for his finger and sandals for his feet. 23 And kill the calf we have been fattening. We must celebrate with a feast, 24 for this son of mine was dead and has now

returned to life. He was lost, but now he is found.' So the party began.

Romans 7: 15 - 22 (NIV)
15 I do not understand what I do. For what I want to do I do not do, but what I hate I do. 16 And if I do what I do not want to do, I agree that the law is good. 17 As it is, it is no longer I myself who do it, but it is sin living in me. 18 For I know that good itself does not dwell in me, that is, in my sinful nature. For I have the desire to do what is good, but I cannot carry it out. 19 For I do not do the good I want to do, but the evil I do not want to do—this I keep on doing. 20 Now if I do what I do not want to do, it is no longer I who do it, but it is sin living in me that does it. 21 So I find this law at work: Although I want to do good, evil is right there with me. 22 For in my inner being I delight in God's law;

Romans 7: 24 - 25 (NIV)
24 What a wretched man I am! Who will rescue me from this body that is subject to death? 25 Thanks be to God, who delivers me through Jesus Christ our Lord! So then, I myself in my mind am a slave to God's law, but in my sinful nature a slave to the law of sin.

1 Corinthians 10: 12 - 13 (NIVUK)
12 So, if you think you are standing firm, be careful that you don't fall! 13 No temptation has overtaken you except what is common to mankind. And God is faithful; he will not let you be tempted beyond what you can bear. But when you are tempted, he will also provide a way out so that you can endure it.

Galatians 5: 16 - 17 (NKJV)
16 I say then: Walk in the Spirit, and you shall not fulfill the lust of the flesh. 17

For the flesh lusts against the Spirit, and the Spirit against the flesh; and these are contrary to one another, so that you do not do the things that you wish.

Hebrews 7: 22, 25 (MEV)
22 Through this oath Jesus became the guarantor of a better covenant. 25 Therefore He is able to save to the uttermost those who come to God through Him, because He at all times lives to make intercession for them.

James 1: 5 (HCSB)
5 Now if any of you lacks wisdom, he should ask God, who gives to all generously and without criticiz-ing, and it will be given to him.

James 4: 10 (NCV)
10 Humble yourself in the Lord's presence, and he will honor you.

1 John 1: 8 - 9 (HCSB)
8 If we say, "We have no sin," we are deceiving ourselves, and the truth is not in us. 9 If we confess our sins, He is faithful and righteous to forgive us our sins and to cleanse us from all unrighteousness.

Jude 1: 24 (MEV)
24 Now to Him who is able to keep you from falling and to present you blameless before the presence of His glory with rejoicing,

FALSEHOOD

Exodus 23: 1 (GNT)
1 Do not spread false rumors, and do not help a guilty person by giving false testimony.

Deuteronomy 25: 15 - 16 (GW)
15 Use accurate and honest weights and measures. Then you will live for a long time in the land that the Lord your God is giving you. 16 Everyone who uses dishonest weights and measures is disgusting to the Lord.

Psalms 34: 13 - 15 (NIV)
13 keep your tongue from evil and your lips from telling lies. 14 Turn from evil and do good; seek peace and pursue it. 15 The eyes of the Lord are on the righteous, and his ears are attentive to their cry;

Psalms 58: 3 (NCV)
3 From birth, evil people turn away from God; they wander off and tell lies as soon as they are born.

Proverbs 6: 16 - 17, 19 (NKJV)
16 These six things the Lord hates, Yes, seven are an abomination to Him: 17 A proud look, A lying tongue, Hands that shed innocent blood, 19 A false witness who speaks lies, And one who sows dis-cord among brethren.

Proverbs 11: 1 (ESV)
1 A false balance is an abomination to the Lord, but a just weight is his delight.

Proverbs 14: 5 (MSG)
5 A true witness never lies; a false witness makes a business of it.

Proverbs 19: 5 (NKJV)
5 A false witness will not go unpunished, And he who speaks lies will not escape.

Proverbs 25: 18 (NLT)
18 Telling lies about others is as harmful as hitting them with an ax, wounding

them with a sword, or shooting them with a sharp arrow.

Matthew 12: 36 - 37 (TLB)
36 And I tell you this, that you must give account on Judgment Day for every idle word you speak. 37 Your words now reflect your fate then: either you will be justified by them or you will be con-demned.

John 8: 44 (GNT)
44 You are the children of your father, the Devil, and you want to follow your father's desires. From the very beginning he was a murderer and has never been on the side of truth, because there is no truth in him. When he tells a lie, he is only doing what is natural to him, because he is a liar and the father of all lies.

Ephesians 4: 25 - 27 (NET)
25 Therefore, having laid aside falsehood, each one of you speak the truth with his neighbor, for we are members of one another. 26 Be angry and do not sin; do not let the sun go down on the cause of your anger. 27 Do not give the devil an opportunity.

Colossians 3: 9 - 10 (NCV)
9 Do not lie to each other. You have left your old sinful life and the things you did before. 10 You have begun to live the new life, in which you are being made new and are becoming like the One who made you. This new life brings you the true knowledge of God.

1 Thessalonians 4: 6 - 7 (MEV)
6 and that no man take advantage of and defraud his brother in any matter, because the Lord is the avenger in all these things, as we also have

forewarned you and testified. 7 For God has not called us to uncleanness, but to holiness.

Titus 3: 2 (GNT)
2 Tell them not to speak evil of anyone, but to be peaceful and friendly, and always to show a gentle attitude toward everyone.

1 Peter 3: 10 - 12 (ESV)
10 For "Whoever desires to love life and see good days, let him keep his tongue from evil and his lips from speaking deceit; 11 let him turn away from evil and do good; let him seek peace and pursue it. 12 For the eyes of the Lord are on the righteous, and his ears are open to their prayer. But the face of the Lord is against those who do evil."

FAMILY

Exodus 20: 12 (NLT)
12 Honor your father and mother. Then you will live a long, full life in the land the Lord your God is giving you.

Deuteronomy 6: 5 - 7 (NLT)
5 And you must love the Lord your God with all your heart, all your soul, and all your strength. 6 And you must commit yourselves wholeheartedly to these commands that I am giving you today. 7 Repeat them again and again to your children. Talk about them when you are at home and when you are on the road, when you are going to bed and when you are getting up.

Nehemiah 4: 14 (NLT)
14 Then as I looked over the situation, I called together the nobles and the rest

of the people and said to them, "Don't be afraid of the enemy! Remember the Lord, who is great and glorious, and fight for your brothers, your sons, your daughters, your wives, and your homes!"

Psalms 68: 6 (NIV)
6 God sets the lonely in families, he leads out the prisoners with singing; but the rebellious live in a sun-scorched land.

Psalms 107: 41 (NIV)
41 But he lifted the needy out of their affliction and increased their families like flocks.

Psalms 127: 3 - 5 (NIV)
3 Children are a heritage from the Lord, offspring a reward from him. 4 Like arrows in the hands of a warrior are children born in one's youth. 5 Blessed is the man whose quiver is full of them. They will not be put to shame when they contend with their opponents in court.

Psalms 128: 1, 3, 4 (HCSB)
1 How happy is everyone who fears the Lord, who walks in His ways! 3 Your wife will be like a fruitful vine within your house, your sons, like young olive trees around your table. 4 In this very way the man who fears the Lord will be blessed.

Proverbs 17: 6 (NET)
6 Grandchildren are like a crown to the elderly, and the glory of children is their parents.

Proverbs 13: 22 (HCSB)
22 A good man leaves an inheritance to his grandchildren, but the sinner's wealth is stored up for the righteous.

Proverbs 17: 25 (HCSB)
25 A foolish son is grief to his father and bitterness to the one who bore him.

Proverbs 23: 24 - 25 (WEB)
24 The father of the righteous has great joy. Whoever fathers a wise child delights in him. 25 Let your father and your mother be glad! Let her who bore you rejoice!

Proverbs 29: 17 (NET)
17 Discipline your child, and he will give you rest; he will bring you happiness.

Malachi 4: 6 (HCSB)
6 And he will turn the hearts of fathers to their children and the hearts of children to their fathers. Otherwise, I will come and strike the land with a curse."

Acts 16: 31 (HCSB)
31 So they said, "Believe on the Lord Jesus, and you will be saved—you and your household."

Ephesians 5: 22, 25 (NET)
22 Wives, submit to your husbands as to the Lord, 25 Husbands, love your wives just as Christ loved the church and gave himself for her.

Ephesians 6: 1 - 4 (HCSB)
1 Children, obey your parents as you would the Lord, because this is right. 2 Honor your father and mother, which is the first commandment with a promise, 3 so that it may go well with you and that you may have a long life in the land. 4 Fathers, don't stir up anger in your children, but bring them up in the training and instruction of the Lord.

1 Timothy 3: 1, 4 - 5 (GNT)
1 This is a true saying: If a man is eager to be a church leader, he desires an excellent work. 4 he must be able to manage his own family well and make his children obey him with all respect. 5 For if a man does not know how to manage his own family, how can he take care of the church of God?

1 Timothy 5: 8 (GNT)
8 But if any do not take care of their relatives, especially the members of their own family, they have denied the faith and are worse than an unbeliever.

1 Peter 3: 1 (NIV)
1 Wives, in the same way submit yourselves to your own husbands so that, if any of them do not be-lieve the word, they may be won over without words by the behavior of their wives,

FAVOR

Nehemiah 1: 11 (NIV)
11 Lord, let your ear be attentive to the prayer of this your servant and to the prayer of your servants who delight in revering your name. Give your servant success today by granting him favor in the pres-ence of this man." I was cupbearer to the king.

Psalms 5: 12 (NIV)
12 Surely, Lord, you bless the righteous; you surround them with your favor as with a shield.

Psalms 84: 11 (NIV)
11 For the Lord God is a sun and shield; the Lord bestows favor and honor; no good thing does he withhold from those whose walk is blameless.

Psalms 90: 17 (NIV)
17 May the favor of the Lord our God rest on us; establish the work of our hands for us— yes, estab-lish the work of our hands.

Proverbs 3: 34 (GNT)
34 He has no use for conceited people, but shows favor to those who are humble.

Proverbs 8: 34 - 35 (NIV)
34 Blessed are those who listen to me, watching daily at my doors, waiting at my doorway. 35 For those who find me find life and receive favor from the Lord.

Proverbs 11: 27 (NIV)
27 Whoever seeks good finds favor, but evil comes to one who searches for it.

Proverbs 18: 22 (NIV)
22 He who finds a wife finds what is good and receives favor from the Lord.

Isaiah 61: 1 - 2 (MEV)
1 The Spirit of the Lord God is upon me because the Lord has anointed me to preach good news to the poor; He has sent me to heal the broken-hearted, to proclaim liberty to the captives, and the opening of the prison to those who are bound; 2 to proclaim the acceptable year of the Lord and the day of vengeance of our God; to comfort all who mourn,

Isaiah 66: 2 (AMP)
2 For all these things My hand has made, and so all these things have come into being [by and for Me], says

the Lord. But this is the man to whom I will look and have regard: he who is humble and of a broken or wounded spirit, and who trembles at My word and reveres My commands.

Daniel 1: 9 (NIV)
9 Now God had caused the official to show favor and compassion to Daniel,

Luke 2: 14 (NIVUK)
14 'Glory to God in the highest heaven, and on earth peace to those on whom his favour rests.'

2 Corinthians 1: 10 - 11 (NIV)
10 He has delivered us from such a deadly peril, and he will deliver us again. On him we have set our hope that he will continue to deliver us, 11 as you help us by your prayers. Then many will give thanks on our behalf for the gracious favor granted us in answer to the prayers of many.

2 Corinthians 6: 2 (NIV)
2 For he says, "In the time of my favor I heard you, and in the day of salvation I helped you." I tell you, now is the time of God's favor, now is the day of salvation.

James 4: 6 (NIV)
6 But he gives us more grace. That is why Scripture says: "God opposes the proud but shows favor to the humble."

FEAR

Deuteronomy 31: 6 (NKJV)
6 Be strong and of good courage, do not fear nor be afraid of them; for the Lord your God, He is the One who goes with

you. He will not leave you nor forsake you.

Joshua 1: 9 (HCSB)
9 Haven't I commanded you: be strong and courageous? Do not be afraid or discouraged, for the Lord your God is with you wherever you go.

Psalms 112: 1, 7 (WEB)
1 Praise Yah! Blessed is the man who fears Yahweh, who delights greatly in his commandments. 7 He will not be afraid of evil news. His heart is steadfast, trusting in Yahweh.

Psalms 23: 4 - 5 (MEV)
4 Even though I walk through the valley of the shadow of death, I will fear no evil; for You are with me; Your rod and Your staff, they comfort me. 5 You prepare a table before me in the presence of my enemies; You anoint my head with oil; my cup runs over.

Psalms 27: 1, 3, 5 (NLT)
1 The Lord is my light and my salvation— so why should I be afraid? The Lord is my fortress, pro-tecting me from danger, so why should I tremble? 3 Though a mighty army surrounds me, my heart will not be afraid. Even if I am attacked, I will remain confident. 5 For he will conceal me there when troubles come; he will hide me in his sanctuary. He will place me out of reach on a high rock.

Psalms 91: 1 - 16 (NKJV)
1 He who dwells in the secret place of the Most High Shall abide under the shadow of the Almighty. 2 I will say of the Lord, "He is my refuge and my fortress; My God, in Him I will trust." 3 Surely He shall deliver you from

the snare of the fowler And from the perilous pestilence. 4 He shall cover you with His feathers, And under His wings you shall take refuge; His truth shall be your shield and buckler. 5 You shall not be afraid of the terror by night, Nor of the arrow that flies by day, 6 Nor of the pestilence that walks in darkness, Nor of the destruction that lays waste at noonday. 7 A thousand may fall at your side, And ten thousand at your right hand; But it shall not come near you. 8 Only with your eyes shall you look, And see the reward of the wicked. 9 Because you have made the Lord, who is my ref-uge, Even the Most High, your dwelling place, 10 No evil shall befall you, Nor shall any plague come near your dwelling; 11 For He shall give His angels charge over you, To keep you in all your ways. 12 In their hands they shall bear you up, Lest you dash your foot against a stone. 13 You shall tread upon the lion and the cobra, The young lion and the serpent you shall trample underfoot. 14 "Because he has set his love upon Me, therefore I will deliver him; I will set him on high, because he has known My name. 15 He shall call upon Me, and I will answer him; I will be with him in trouble; I will deliver him and honor him. 16 With long life I will satisfy him, And show him My salvation."

Proverbs 1: 20, 33 (WEB)
20 Wisdom calls aloud in the street. She utters her voice in the public squares. 33 But whoever lis-tens to me will dwell securely, and will be at ease, without fear of harm.

Proverbs 3: 24 - 26 (NLT)
24 You can go to bed without fear; you will lie down and sleep soundly. 25 You

need not be afraid of sudden disaster or the destruction that comes upon the wicked, 26 for the Lord is your security. He will keep your foot from being caught in a trap.

Isaiah 41: 10 - 13 (NKJV)
10 Fear not, for I am with you; Be not dismayed, for I am your God. I will strengthen you, Yes, I will help you, I will uphold you with My righteous right hand.' 11 "Behold, all those who were incensed against you Shall be ashamed and disgraced; They shall be as nothing, And those who strive with you shall perish. 12 You shall seek them and not find them— Those who contended with you. Those who war against you Shall be as nothing, As a nonexistent thing. 13 For I, the Lord your God, will hold your right hand, Saying to you, 'Fear not, I will help you.'

Isaiah 43: 1 - 2 (NKJV)
1b Fear not, for I have redeemed you; I have called you by your name; You are Mine. 2 When you pass through the waters, I will be with you; And through the rivers, they shall not overflow you. When you walk through the fire, you shall not be burned, Nor shall the flame scorch you.

Isaiah 54: 14 - 17 (NKJV)
14 In righteousness you shall be established; You shall be far from oppression, for you shall not fear; And from terror, for it shall not come near you. 15 Indeed they shall surely assemble, but not because of Me. Whoever assembles against you shall fall for your sake. 16 "Behold, I have created the black-smith Who blows the coals in the fire, Who brings forth

an instrument for his work; And I have created the spoiler to destroy. 17 No weapon formed against you shall prosper, And every tongue which rises against you in judgment You shall condemn. This is the heritage of the servants of the Lord, And their righteousness is from Me," Says the Lord.

Mark 4: 38 - 40 (WEB)
38 He himself was in the stern, asleep on the cushion, and they woke him up, and told him, "Teacher, don't you care that we are dying?" 39 He awoke, and rebuked the wind, and said to the sea, "Peace! Be still!" The wind ceased, and there was a great calm. 40 He said to them, "Why are you so afraid? How is it that you have no faith?"

Luke 12: 32 (HCSB)
32 Don't be afraid, little flock, because your Father delights to give you the kingdom.

Romans 8: 15 (NCV)
15 The Spirit we received does not make us slaves again to fear; it makes us children of God. With that Spirit we cry out, "Father."

Romans 8: 30 - 31 (WEB)
30 Whom he predestined, those he also called. Whom he called, those he also justified. Whom he justified, those he also glorified. 31 What then shall we say about these things? If God is for us, who can be against us?

Romans 8: 37, 39 (MEV)
37 No, in all these things we are more than conquerors through Him who loved us. 39 neither height nor depth, nor any other created thing, shall

be able to separate us from the love of God, which is in Christ Jesus our Lord.

2 Timothy 1: 7 (NKJV)
7 For God has not given us a spirit of fear, but of power and of love and of a sound mind.

FORGIVENESS

Psalms 32: 1 - 2 (HCSB)
1 How joyful is the one whose transgression is forgiven, whose sin is covered! 2 How joyful is the man the Lord does not charge with sin and in whose spirit is no deceit!

Psalms 103: 10 - 12 (NKJV)
10 He has not dealt with us according to our sins, Nor punished us according to our iniquities. 11 For as the heavens are high above the earth, So great is His mercy toward those who fear Him; 12 As far as the east is from the west, So far has He removed our transgressions from us.

Psalms 103: 2 - 3 (NKJV)
2 Bless the Lord, O my soul, And forget not all His benefits: 3 Who forgives all your iniquities, Who heals all your diseases,

Isaiah 1: 18 - 19 (ESV)
18 Come now, let us reason together, says the Lord: though your sins are like scarlet, they shall be as white as snow; though they are red like crimson, they shall become like wool. 19 If you are willing and obedient, you shall eat the good of the land;

Joel 2:13 (NIV)
13 Rend your heart and not your garments. Return to the Lord your God, for he is gracious and com-passionate, slow to anger and abounding in love, and he relents from sending calamity.

Matthew 6: 14 - 15 (NKJV)
14 "For if you forgive men their trespasses, your heavenly Father will also forgive you. 15 But if you do not forgive men their trespasses, neither will your Father forgive your trespasses.

Mark 11: 25 (HCSB)
25 And whenever you stand praying, if you have anything against anyone, forgive him, so that your Father in heaven will also forgive you your wrongdoing.

Luke 17: 3 - 4 (NKJV)
3 Take heed to yourselves. If your brother sins against you, rebuke him; and if he repents, forgive him. 4 And if he sins against you seven times in a day, and seven times in a day returns to you, say-ing, 'I repent,' you shall forgive him."

Ephesians 4: 32 (GNT)
32 Instead, be kind and tender-hearted to one another, and forgive one another, as God has forgiven you through Christ.

1 John 1: 9 (HCSB)
9 If we confess our sins, He is faithful and righteous to forgive us our sins and to cleanse us from all unrighteousness.

FORNICATION

Leviticus 18: 20, 22, 23 (NASB)
20 You shall not have intercourse with your neighbor's wife, to be defiled with her. 22 You shall not lie with a male as one lies with a female; it is an abomination. 23 Also you shall not have intercourse with any animal to be defiled with it, nor shall any woman stand before an animal to mate with it; it is a perversion.

Proverbs 5: 15 - 21 (NIV)
15 Drink water from your own cistern, running water from your own well. 16 Should your springs over-flow in the streets, your streams of water in the public squares? 17 Let them be yours alone, never to be shared with strangers. 18 May your fountain be blessed, and may you rejoice in the wife of your youth. 19 A loving doe, a graceful deer— may her breasts satisfy you always, may you ever be in-toxicated with her love. 20 Why, my son, be intoxicated with another man's wife? Why embrace the bosom of a wayward woman? 21 For your ways are in full view of the Lord, and he examines all your paths.

Proverbs 6: 24 - 29 (NIV)
24 keeping you from your neighbor's wife, from the smooth talk of a wayward woman. 25 Do not lust in your heart after her beauty or let her captivate you with her eyes. 26 For a prostitute can be had for a loaf of bread, but another man's wife preys on your very life. 27 Can a man scoop fire into his lap without his clothes being burned? 28 Can a man walk on hot coals without his feet being scorched? 29 So is he who sleeps with another man's wife; no one who touches her will go unpunished.

Matthew 15: 19 (ESV)
19 For out of the heart come evil thoughts, murder, adultery, sexual immorality, theft, false witness, slander.

Matthew 5: 28 (ESV)
28 But I say to you that everyone who looks at a woman with lustful intent has already committed adultery with her in his heart.

Mark 10: 11 - 12 (HCSB)
11 And He said to them, "Whoever divorces his wife and marries another commits adultery against her. 12 Also, if she divorces her husband and marries another, she commits adultery."

1 Corinthians 6: 13, 15 (NET)
13 "Food is for the stomach and the stomach is for food, but God will do away with both." The body is not for sexual immorality, but for the Lord, and the Lord for the body. 15 Do you not know that your bodies are members of Christ? Should I take the members of Christ and make them members of a prostitute? Never!

1 Corinthians 6: 18 - 20 (NET)
18 Flee sexual immorality! "Every sin a person commits is outside of the body"—but the immoral per - son sins against his own body. 19 Or do you not know that your body is the temple of the Holy Spirit who is in you, whom you have from God, and you are not your own? 20 For you were bought at a price. Therefore glorify God with your body.

1 Corinthians 7: 1, 8 - 9 (MEV)
1 Now concerning the things about which you wrote to me: "It is good for a man not to touch a wom-an." 8 I say to the unmarried and widows that it is good for them if they live even as I am. 9 But if they cannot restrain themselves, let them marry. For it is better to marry than to burn with passion.

1 Corinthians 10: 13 (NLT)
13 The temptations in your life are no different from what others experience. And God is faithful. He will not allow the temptation to be more than you can stand. When you are tempted, he will show you a way out so that you can endure.

Galatians 5: 19 (NLT)
19 When you follow the desires of your sinful nature, the results are very clear: sexual immorality, impurity, lustful pleasures,

1 Thessalonians 4: 3 - 5 (HCSB)
3 For this is God's will, your sanctification: that you abstain from sexual immorality, 4 so that each of you knows how to control his own body in sanctification and honor, 5 not with lustful desires, like the Gentiles who don't know God.

Hebrews 13: 4 (NKJV)
4 Marriage is honorable among all, and the bed undefiled; but fornicators and adulterers God will judge.

FRETFUL

Joshua 1: 9 (NET)
9 I repeat, be strong and brave! Don't be afraid and don't panic, for I, the Lord your God, am with you in all you do.

2 Samuel 22: 7, 17 - 18 (NKJV)
7 In my distress I called upon the Lord, And cried out to my God; He heard my voice from His temple, And my cry entered His ears. 17 He sent from above, He took me, He drew me out of many waters. 18 He delivered me from

my strong enemy, From those who hated me; For they were too strong for me.

Psalms 4: 1 (NET)
1 When I call out, answer me, O God who vindicates me! Though I am hemmed in, you will lead me into a wide, open place. Have mercy on me and respond to my prayer!

Psalms 107: 9 (NKJV)
9 For He satisfies the longing soul, And fills the hungry soul with goodness.

Psalms 27: 13 - 14 (HCSB)
13 I am certain that I will see the Lord's goodness in the land of the living. 14 Wait for the Lord; be strong and courageous. Wait for the Lord.

Psalms 32: 7 (NET)
7 You are my hiding place; you protect me from distress. You surround me with shouts of joy from those celebrating deliverance.

Psalms 37: 1 - 2 (NET)
1 Do not fret when wicked men seem to succeed! Do not envy evildoers! 2 For they will quickly dry up like grass, and wither away like plants.

Psalms 37: 7 - 8 (NET)
7 Wait patiently for the Lord! Wait confidently for him! Do not fret over the apparent success of a sin-ner, a man who carries out wicked schemes! 8 Do not be angry and frustrated! Do not fret! That only leads to trouble!

Proverbs 24: 19 - 20 (MEV)
19 Do not fret because of evil men, nor be envious of the wicked; 20 for there

will be no reward to the evil man; the candle of the wicked will be put out.

Isaiah 26: 3 (ESV)
3 You keep him in perfect peace whose mind is stayed on you, because he trusts in you.

Isaiah 40: 29 - 31 (NET)
29 He gives strength to those who are tired; to the ones who lack power, he gives renewed energy. 30 Even youths get tired and weary; even strong young men clumsily stumble. 31 But those who wait for the Lord's help find renewed strength; they rise up as if they had eagles' wings, they run without growing weary, they walk without getting tired.

Isaiah 41: 10 - 11 (NET)
10 Don't be afraid, for I am with you! Don't be frightened, for I am your God! I strengthen you— yes, I help you— yes, I uphold you with my saving right hand! 11 Look, all who were angry at you will be ashamed and humiliated; your adversaries will be reduced to nothing and perish.

Matthew 11: 28 - 30 (NLT)
28 Then Jesus said, "Come to me, all of you who are weary and carry heavy burdens, and I will give you rest. 29 Take my yoke upon you. Let me teach you, because I am humble and gentle at heart, and you will find rest for your souls. 30 For my yoke is easy to bear, and the burden I give you is light."

Galatians 5: 22 - 23, 25 (HCSB)
22 But the fruit of the Spirit is love, joy, peace, patience, kindness, goodness, faith, 23 gentleness, self-control.

Against such things there is no law. 25 Since we live by the Spirit, we must also follow the Spirit.

Philippians 4: 6 - 8 (NKJV)

6 Be anxious for nothing, but in everything by prayer and supplication, with thanksgiving, let your requests be made known to God; 7 and the peace of God, which surpasses all understanding, will guard your hearts and minds through Christ Jesus. 8 Finally, brethren, whatever things are true, what - ever things are noble, whatever things are just, whatever things are pure, whatever things are lovely, whatever things are of good report, if there is any virtue and if there is anything praiseworthy—medi-tate on these things.

2 Timothy 1: 7 (NET)

7 For God did not give us a Spirit of fear but of power and love and self-control.

Hebrews 10: 35 - 36 (GNT)

35 Do not lose your courage, then, because it brings with it a great reward. 36 You need to be patient, in order to do the will of God and receive what he promises.

1 Peter 5: 6 - 9 (NIVUK)

6 Humble yourselves, therefore, under God's mighty hand, that he may lift you up in due time. 7 Cast all your anxiety on him because he cares for you. 8 Be alert and of sober mind. Your enemy the devil prowls around like a roaring lion looking for someone to devour. 9 Resist him, standing firm in the faith, because you know that the family of believers throughout the world is undergoing the same kind of sufferings.

1 John 4: 4 (HCSB)

4 You are from God, little children, and you have conquered them, because the One who is in you is greater than the one who is in the world.

FRIEND

Proverbs 12: 26 (NKJV)

26 The righteous should choose his friends carefully, For the way of the wicked leads them astray.

Proverbs 16: 28 (NKJV)

28 A perverse man sows strife, And a whisperer separates the best of friends.

Proverbs 17: 17 (NLT)

17 A friend is always loyal, and a brother is born to help in time of need.

Proverbs 18: 24 (NKJV)

A man who has friends must himself be friendly, But there is a friend who sticks closer than a brother.

Proverbs 19: 6 (NKJV)

6 Many entreat the favor of the nobility, And every man is a friend to one who gives gifts.

Proverbs 27: 6 (NKJV)

6 Faithful are the wounds of a friend, But the kisses of an enemy are deceitful.

Proverbs 27: 9 (NKJV)

9 Ointment and perfume delight the heart, And the sweetness of a man's friend gives delight by hearty counsel.

Proverbs 27: 14 (NKJV)
14 He who blesses his friend with a loud voice, rising early in the morning, It will be counted a curse to him.

Proverbs 27: 17 (NKJV)
17 As iron sharpens iron, So a man sharpens the countenance of his friend.

Ecclesiastes 4: 9 - 10 (NKJV)
9 Two are better than one, Because they have a good reward for their labor. 10 For if they fall, one will lift up his companion. But woe to him who is alone when he falls, For he has no one to help him up.

John 15: 13 - 14 (HCSB)
13 No one has greater love than this, that someone would lay down his life for his friends. 14 You are My friends if you do what I command you.

John 15: 15 - 16 (HCSB)
15 I do not call you slaves anymore, because a slave doesn't know what his master is doing. I have called you friends, because I have made known to you everything I have heard from My Father. 16 You did not choose Me, but I chose you. I appointed you that you should go out and produce fruit and that your fruit should remain, so that whatever you ask the Father in My name, He will give you.

2 Corinthians 6: 14 (CEB)
14 Don't be tied up as equal partners with people who don't believe. What does righteousness share with that which is outside the Law? What relationship does light have with darkness?

Galatians 6: 10 (HCSB)
10 Therefore, as we have opportunity, we must work for the good of all, especially for those who be-long to the household of faith.

Ephesians 4: 32 (NLT)
32 Instead, be kind to each other, tenderhearted, forgiving one another, just as God through Christ has forgiven you.

James 2: 23 (NIV)
23 And the scripture was fulfilled that says, "Abraham believed God, and it was credited to him as righteousness," and he was called God's friend.

James 4: 4 (GNT)
4 Unfaithful people! Don't you know that to be the world's friend means to be God's enemy? If you want to be the world's friend, you make yourself God's enemy.

GIVING

Leviticus 19: 9 - 10 (NKJV)
9 'When you reap the harvest of your land, you shall not wholly reap the corners of your field, nor shall you gather the gleanings of your harvest. 10 And you shall not glean your vineyard, nor shall you gather every grape of your vineyard; you shall leave them for the poor and the stranger: I am the Lord your God.

Psalms 112: 5, 9 (CEV)
5 Life will go well for those who freely lend and are honest in business. 9 They will always be remem-bered and

greatly praised, because they were kind and freely gave to the poor.

Psalms 41: 1 - 2 (NKJV)

1 Blessed is he who considers the poor; The Lord will deliver him in time of trouble. 2 The Lord will preserve him and keep him alive, And he will be blessed on the earth; You will not deliver him to the will of his enemies.

Proverbs 11: 24 - 25 (NIV)

24 One person gives freely, yet gains even more; another withholds unduly, but comes to poverty. 25 A generous person will prosper; whoever refreshes others will be refreshed.

Proverbs 22: 9 (CEV)

9 The Lord blesses everyone who freely gives food to the poor.

Proverbs 28: 27 (NIV)

27 Those who give to the poor will lack nothing, but those who close their eyes to them receive many curses.

Isaiah 58: 7 - 11 (NLT)

7 Share your food with the hungry, and give shelter to the homeless. Give clothes to those who need them, and do not hide from relatives who need your help. 8 "Then your salvation will come like the dawn, and your wounds will quickly heal. Your godliness will lead you forward, and the glory of the Lord will protect you from behind. 9 Then when you call, the Lord will answer. 'Yes, I am here,' he will quickly reply. "Remove the heavy yoke of oppression. Stop pointing your finger and spreading vicious rumors! 10 Feed the hungry, and help those in trouble. Then your light will shine out from the dark-ness, and the darkness around you will be as bright as noon. 11 The Lord will guide you continually, giving you water when you are dry and restoring your strength. You will be like a well-watered garden, like an ever-flowing spring.

Malachi 3: 10 - 11 (NASB)

10 Bring the whole tithe into the storehouse, so that there may be food in My house, and test Me now in this," says the Lord of hosts, "if I will not open for you the windows of heaven and pour out for you a blessing until it overflows. 11 Then I will rebuke the devourer for you, so that it will not destroy the fruits of the ground; nor will your vine in the field cast its grapes," says the Lord of hosts.

Matthew 25: 34 - 40 (ESV)

34 Then the King will say to those on his right, 'Come, you who are blessed by my Father, inherit the kingdom prepared for you from the foundation of the world. 35 For I was hungry and you gave me food, I was thirsty and you gave me drink, I was a stranger and you welcomed me, 36 I was naked and you clothed me, I was sick and you visited me, I was in prison and you came to me.' 37 Then the righteous will answer him, saying, 'Lord, when did we see you hungry and feed you, or thirsty and give you drink? 38 And when did we see you a stranger and welcome you, or naked and clothe you? 39 And when did we see you sick or in prison and visit you?' 40 And the King will answer them, 'Truly, I say to you, as you did it to one of the least of these my brothers, you did it to me.'

Matthew 6: 1 - 4 (WEB)

1 Be careful that you don't do your charitable giving before men, to be seen by them, or else you have no reward from your Father who is in heaven. 2 Therefore when you do merciful deeds, don't sound a trumpet before yourself, as the hypocrites do in the synagogues and in the streets, that they may get glory from men. Most certainly I tell you, they have received their reward. 3 But when you do merciful deeds, don't let your left hand know what your right hand does, 4 so that your merciful deeds may be in secret, then your Father who sees in secret will reward you openly.

Mark 9: 37 - 41 (NIV)

37 "Whoever welcomes one of these little children in my name welcomes me; and whoever welcomes me does not welcome me but the one who sent me." 38 "Teacher," said John, "we saw someone driving out demons in your name and we told him to stop, because he was not one of us." 39 "Do not stop him," Jesus said. "For no one who does a miracle in my name can in the next moment say any - thing bad about me, 40 for whoever is not against us is for us. 41 Truly I tell you, anyone who gives you a cup of water in my name because you belong to the Messiah will certainly not lose their reward.

Luke 6: 38 (NCV)

38 Give, and you will receive. You will be given much. Pressed down, shaken together, and running over, it will spill into your lap. The way you give to others is the way God will give to you.

Acts 20: 35 (ESV)

35 In all things I have shown you that by working hard in this way we must help the weak and remem-ber the words of the Lord Jesus, how he himself said, 'It is more blessed to give than to receive.'

Romans 12: 9, 13 (NKJV)

9 Let love be without hypocrisy. Abhor what is evil. Cling to what is good. 13 distributing to the needs of the saints, given to hospitality.

2 Corinthians 8: 9, 12 - 14 (MEV)

9 For you know the grace of our Lord Jesus Christ, that though He was rich, yet for your sakes He became poor, that through His poverty you might be rich. 12 For if there is a willing mind first, the gift is accepted according to what a man possesses and not according to what he does not possess. 13 I do not mean that other men have relief, and you be burdened, 14 but for equality, that your abun - dance now at this time may supply their need, and their abundance may supply your need—that there may be equality.

2 Corinthians 9: 6 - 8 (GNT)

6 Remember that the person who plants few seeds will have a small crop; the one who plants many seeds will have a large crop. 7 You should each give, then, as you have decided, not with regret or out of a sense of duty; for God loves the one who gives gladly. 8 And God is able to give you more than you need, so that you will always have all you need for yourselves and more than enough for every good cause.

Ephesians 4: 28 (WEB)
28 Let him who stole steal no more; but rather let him labor, producing with his hands something that is good, that he may have something to give to him who has need.

James 1: 27 (NIV)
27 Religion that God our Father accepts as pure and faultless is this: to look after orphans and wid-ows in their distress and to keep oneself from being polluted by the world.

James 2: 14 - 16 (ISV)
14 What good does it do, my brothers, if someone claims to have faith but does not prove it with actions? This kind of faith cannot save him, can it? 15 Suppose a brother or sister does not have any clothes or daily food 16 and one of you tells them, "Go in peace! Stay warm and eat heartily." If you do not provide for their bodily needs, what good does it do?

GOD HEARING

2 Chronicles 33: 12 - 13 (AMP)
12 When he was in affliction, he besought the Lord his God and humbled himself greatly before the God of his fathers. 13 He prayed to Him, and God, entreated by him, heard his supplication and brought him again to Jerusalem to his kingdom. Then Manasseh knew that the Lord is God.

Psalms 4: 3 (GW)
3 Know that the Lord singles out godly people for himself. The Lord hears me when I call to him.

Psalms 5: 3 (NET)
3 Lord, in the morning you will hear me; in the morning I will present my case to you and then wait expectantly for an answer.

Psalms 10: 17 (NKJV)
17 Lord, You have heard the desire of the humble; You will prepare their heart; You will cause Your ear to hear,

Psalms 18: 6 (NKJV)
6 In my distress I called upon the Lord, And cried out to my God; He heard my voice from His temple, And my cry came before Him, even to His ears.

Psalms 22: 24 (NLV)
24 For He has not turned away from the suffering of the one in pain or trouble. He has not hidden His face from him. But He has heard his cry for help.

Psalms 34: 15, 17 (NKJV)
15 The eyes of the Lord are on the righteous, And His ears are open to their cry. 17 The righteous cry out, and the Lord hears, And delivers them out of all their troubles.

Psalms 55: 17 (NKJV)
17 Evening and morning and at noon I will pray, and cry aloud, And He shall hear my voice.

Psalms 69: 33 (NKJV)
33 For the Lord hears the poor, And does not despise His prisoners.

Psalms 102: 17, 19 - 20 (NKJV)
17 He shall regard the prayer of the destitute, And shall not despise their prayer. 19 For He looked down from the height of His sanctuary; From heaven the Lord viewed the earth, 20

To hear the groan-ing of the prisoner,
To release those appointed to death,

Psalms 145: 19 (NKJV)
19 He will fulfill the desire of those
who fear Him; He also will hear their
cry and save them.

Proverbs 15: 29 (NLV)
29 The Lord is far from the sinful, but
He hears the prayer of those who are
right with Him.

Isaiah 59: 1 (NET)
1 Look, the Lord's hand is not too weak
to deliver you; his ear is not too deaf to
hear you.

Isaiah 65: 24 (NKJV)
24 It shall come to pass That before
they call, I will answer; And while they
are still speaking, I will hear.

John 9: 31 (NKJV)
31 Now we know that God does not hear
sinners; but if anyone is a worshiper of
God and does His will, He hears him.

1 Peter 3: 12 (NKJV)
12 For the eyes of the Lord are on the
righteous, And His ears are open to
their prayers; But the face of the Lord
is against those who do evil.

1 John 5: 14 - 15 (ESV)
14 And this is the confidence that
we have toward him, that if we ask
anything according to his will he hears
us. 15 And if we know that he hears us
in whatever we ask, we know that we
have the requests that we have asked
of him.

GOD NOT HEARING

2 Chronicles 7: 14 (NIV)
14 if my people, who are called by my
name, will humble themselves and pray
and seek my face and turn from their
wicked ways, then I will hear from
heaven, and I will forgive their sin and
will heal their land.

Psalms 66: 18 (ASV)
18 If I regard iniquity in my heart, The
Lord will not hear:

Proverbs 15: 29 (NCV)
29 The Lord does not listen to the
wicked, but he hears the prayers of
those who do right.

Isaiah 59: 2 (ASV)
2 but your iniquities have separated
between you and your God, and your
sins have hid his face from you, so that
he will not hear.

Zechariah 7: 11 - 13 (ESV)
11 But they refused to pay attention
and turned a stubborn shoulder and
stopped their ears that they might
not hear. 12 They made their hearts
diamond-hard lest they should hear
the law and the words that the Lord of
hosts had sent by his Spirit through the
former prophets. Therefore great anger
came from the Lord of hosts. 13 "As I
called, and they would not hear, so they
called, and I would not hear," says the
Lord of hosts,

John 9: 31 (ASV)
31 We know that God heareth not
sinners: but if any man be a worshipper
of God, and do his will, him he heareth.

1 Peter 3: 12 (NKJV)
12 For the eyes of the Lord are on the righteous and his ears are attentive to their prayer, but the face of the Lord is against those who do evil.

1 Peter 3: 7 (GNT)
7 In the same way you husbands must live with your wives with the proper understanding that they are more delicate than you. Treat them with respect, because they also will receive, together with you, God's gift of life. Do this so that nothing will interfere with your prayers.

GOD WITH US

Deuteronomy 31: 6 (AMP)
6 Be strong, courageous, and firm; fear not nor be in terror before them, for it is the Lord your God Who goes with you; He will not fail you or forsake you.

Psalms 46: 1 (NIRV)
1 God is our place of safety. He gives us strength. He is always there to help us in times of trouble.

Jeremiah 23: 23 (ESV)
23 "Am I a God at hand, declares the Lord, and not a God far away?

Matthew 18: 20 (MEV)
20 For where two or three are assembled in My name, there I am in their midst."

Luke 17: 21 (MEV)
21 Nor will they say, 'Here it is!' or 'There it is!' For remember, the kingdom of God is within you.

John 14: 21, 23 (GNT)
21 "Those who accept my commandments and obey them are the ones who love me. My Father will love those who love me; I too will love them and reveal myself to them." 23 Jesus answered him, "Those who love me will obey my teaching. My Father will love them, and my Father and I will come to them and live with them.

John 15: 4 - 5, 7 (NIV)
4 Remain in me, as I also remain in you. No branch can bear fruit by itself; it must remain in the vine. Neither can you bear fruit unless you remain in me. 5 "I am the vine; you are the branches. If you remain in me and I in you, you will bear much fruit; apart from me you can do nothing. 7 If you remain in me and my words remain in you, ask whatever you wish, and it will be done for you.

Romans 8: 11 (NIV)
11 And if the Spirit of him who raised Jesus from the dead is living in you, he who raised Christ from the dead will also give life to your mortal bodies because of his Spirit who lives in you.

Romans 8: 35 - 39 (NIV)
35 Who shall separate us from the love of Christ? Shall trouble or hardship or persecution or famine or nakedness or danger or sword? 36 As it is written: "For your sake we face death all day long; we are considered as sheep to be slaughtered." 37 No, in all these things we are more than conquerors through him who loved us. 38 For I am convinced that neither death nor life, neither angels nor

de-mons, neither the present nor the future, nor any powers, 39 neither height nor depth, nor anything else in all creation, will be able to separate us from the love of God that is in Christ Jesus our Lord.

1 Corinthians 1: 9 (CEV)
9 God can be trusted, and he chose you to be partners with his Son, our Lord Jesus Christ.

Ephesians 3: 20 (DRA)
20 Now to him who is able to do all things more abundantly than we desire or understand, according to the power that worketh in us;

Ephesians 4: 6 (NLV)
6 There is one God. He is the Father of us all. He is over us all. He is the One working through us all. He is the One living in us all.

James 4: 8, 10 (NCV)
8 Come near to God, and God will come near to you. You sinners, clean sin out of your lives. You who are trying to follow God and the world at the same time, make your thinking pure. 10 Humble yourself in the Lord's presence, and he will honor you.

1 John 4: 4 (WEB)
4 You are of God, little children, and have overcome them; because greater is he who is in you than he who is in the world.

Revelation 3: 20 (NKJV)
20 Behold, I stand at the door and knock. If anyone hears My voice and opens the door, I will come in to him and dine with him, and he with Me.

GOD'S FAITHFULNESS

Numbers 23: 19 - 20 (NKJV)
19 God is not a man, that He should lie, Nor a son of man, that He should repent. Has He said, and will He not do? Or has He spoken, and will He not make it good? 20 Behold, I have received a com-mand to bless; He has blessed, and I cannot reverse it.

Psalms 9: 10 (GNT)
10 Those who know you, Lord, will trust you; you do not abandon anyone who comes to you.

Psalms 25: 10 (NET)
10 The Lord always proves faithful and reliable to those who follow the demands of his covenant.

Psalms 36: 5 (NIV)
5 Your love, Lord, reaches to the heavens, your faithfulness to the skies.

Psalms 89: 34 (NLT)
34 No, I will not break my covenant; I will not take back a single word I said.

Psalms 91: 4 (NET)
4 He will shelter you with his wings; you will find safety under his wings. His faithfulness is like a shield or a protective wall.

Isaiah 46: 9 - 11 (ESV)
9 remember the former things of old; for I am God, and there is no other; I am God, and there is none like me, 10 declaring the end from the beginning and from ancient times things not yet done, saying, 'My counsel shall stand, and I will accomplish all my purpose,'

11 calling a bird of prey from the east, the man of my counsel from a far country. I have spoken, and I will bring it to pass; I have purposed, and I will do it.

Isaiah 54: 9 - 10 (NIV)
9 To me this is like the days of Noah, when I swore that the waters of Noah would never again cover the earth. So now I have sworn not to be angry with you, never to rebuke you again. 10 Though the mountains be shaken and the hills be removed, yet my unfailing love for you will not be shaken nor my covenant of peace be removed," says the Lord, who has compassion on you.

1 Corinthians 10: 13 (NIV)
13 No temptation has overtaken you except what is common to mankind. And God is faithful; he will not let you be tempted beyond what you can bear. But when you are tempted, he will also provide a way out so that you can endure it.

2 Corinthians 1: 18 - 20 (NLT)
18 As surely as God is faithful, our word to you does not waver between "Yes" and "No." 19 For Jesus Christ, the Son of God, does not waver between "Yes" and "No." He is the one whom Silas, Timothy, and I preached to you, and as God's ultimate "Yes," he always does what he says. 20 For all of God's promises have been fulfilled in Christ with a resounding "Yes!" And through Christ, our "Amen" (which means "Yes") ascends to God for his glory.

1 Thessalonians 5: 23 - 24 (NKJV)
23 Now may the God of peace Himself sanctify you completely; and may your whole spirit, soul, and body be preserved blameless at the coming of our Lord Jesus Christ. 24 He who calls you is faithful, who also will do it.

2 Timothy 2: 13 (AMP)
13 If we are faithless [do not believe and are untrue to Him], He remains true (faithful to His Word and His righteous character), for He cannot deny Himself.

Hebrews 10: 23 (AMP)
23 So let us seize and hold fast and retain without wavering the hope we cherish and confess and our acknowledgement of it, for He Who promised is reliable (sure) and faithful to His word.

GOD'S LOVE

Psalms 17: 7 (NIV)
7 Show me the wonders of your great love, you who save by your right hand those who take refuge in you from their foes.

Psalms 23: 6 (NIV)
6 Surely your goodness and love will follow me all the days of my life, and I will dwell in the house of the Lord forever.

Psalms 31: 7 - 8 (NLT)
7 I will be glad and rejoice in your unfailing love, for you have seen my troubles, and you care about the anguish of my soul. 8 You have not handed me over to my enemies but have set me in a safe place.

Psalms 36: 5 - 8 (NIV)
5 Your love, Lord, reaches to the heavens, your faithfulness to the

skies. 6 Your righteousness is like the highest mountains, your justice like the great deep. You, Lord, preserve both people and animals. 7 How priceless is your unfailing love, O God! People take refuge in the shadow of your wings. 8 They feast on the abundance of your house; you give them drink from your river of delights.

Psalms 42: 8 (NIV)
8 By day the Lord directs his love, at night his song is with me — a prayer to the God of my life.

Psalms 44: 3 (NIV)
3 It was not by their sword that they won the land, nor did their arm bring them victory; it was your right hand, your arm, and the light of your face, for you loved them.

Psalms 51: 1 (NCV)
1 God, be merciful to me because you are loving. Because you are always ready to be merciful, wipe out all my wrongs.

Psalms 52: 8 (NIV)
8 But I am like an olive tree flourishing in the house of God; I trust in God's unfailing love for ever and ever.

Psalms 57: 3 (NIV)
3 He sends from heaven and saves me, rebuking those who hotly pursue me — God sends forth his love and his faithfulness.

Psalms 66: 20 (NIV)
20 Praise be to God, who has not rejected my prayer or withheld his love from me!

Psalms 86: 5, 15 (NIV)
5 You, Lord, are forgiving and good, abounding in love to all who call to you. 15 But you, Lord, are a compassionate and gracious God, slow to anger, abounding in love and faithfulness.

Psalms 91: 14 (NIV)
14 "Because he loves me," says the Lord, "I will rescue him; I will protect him, for he acknowledges my name.

Psalms 103: 11 (HCSB)
11 For as high as the heavens are above the earth,so great is His faithful love toward those who fear Him.

Joel 2: 13 (HCSB)
13 Tear your hearts, not just your clothes, and return to the Lord your God. For He is gracious and compassionate, slow to anger, rich in faithful love, and He relents from sending disaster.

Zephaniah 3: 17 (GNT)
17 The Lord your God is with you; his power gives you victory. The Lord will take delight in you, and in his love he will give you new life. He will sing and be joyful over you,

John 3: 16 (WEB)
16 For God so loved the world, that he gave his one and only Son, that whoever believes in him should not perish, but have eternal life.

John 16: 27 (NIV)
27 No, the Father himself loves you because you have loved me and have believed that I came from God.

Romans 5: 5 (NKJV)
5 Now hope does not disappoint, because the love of God has been

poured out in our hearts by the Holy Spirit who was given to us.

Romans 8: 38 - 39 (CEV)

38 I am sure that nothing can separate us from God's love—not life or death, not angels or spirits, not the present or the future, 39 and not powers above or powers below. Nothing in all creation can sepa-rate us from God's love for us in Christ Jesus our Lord!

Ephesians 2: 4 - 5 (ESV)

4 But God, being rich in mercy, because of the great love with which he loved us, 5 even when we were dead in our trespasses, made us alive together with Christ—by grace you have been saved—

Ephesians 3: 16 - 19 (ESV)

16 that according to the riches of his glory he may grant you to be strengthened with power through his Spirit in your inner being, 17 so that Christ may dwell in your hearts through faith—that you, be-ing rooted and grounded in love, 18 may have strength to comprehend with all the saints what is the breadth and length and height and depth, 19 and to know the love of Christ that surpasses knowl-edge, that you may be filled with all the fullness of God.

Ephesians 5: 1 - 2 (CEV)

1 Do as God does. After all, you are his dear children. 2 Let love be your guide. Christ loved us and offered his life for us as a sacrifice that pleases God.

Ephesians 6: 23 (ESV)

23 Peace be to the brothers, and love with faith, from God the Father and the Lord Jesus Christ.

2 Thessalonians 2: 16 - 17 (NLT)

16 Now may our Lord Jesus Christ himself and God our Father, who loved us and by his grace gave us eternal comfort and a wonderful hope, 17 comfort you and strengthen you in every good thing you do and say.

2 Timothy 1: 7 (NKJV)

7 For God has not given us a spirit of fear, but of power and of love and of a sound mind.

Titus 3: 3 - 5 (NLT)

3 Once we, too, were foolish and disobedient. We were misled and became slaves to many lusts and pleasures. Our lives were full of evil and envy, and we hated each other. 4 But— When God our Sav-ior revealed his kindness and love, 5 he saved us, not because of the righteous things we had done, but because of his mercy. He washed away our sins, giving us a new birth and new life through the Holy Spirit.

1 John 3: 1 (NIVUK)

3 See what great love the Father has lavished on us, that we should be called children of God! And that is what we are! The reason the world does not know us is that it did not know him.

1 John 3: 17 (HCSB)

17 If anyone has this world's goods and sees his brother in need but closes his eyes to his need— how can God's love reside in him?

1 John 4: 7 - 8, 10, 16 (HCSB)

7 Dear friends, let us love one another, because love is from God, and everyone who loves has been born of God and knows God. 8 The one who does not

love does not know God, because God is love. 10 Love consists in this: not that we loved God, but that He loved us and sent His Son to be the propi-tiation for our sins. 16 And we have come to know and to believe the love that God has for us. God is love, and the one who remains in love remains in God, and God remains in him.

GOD'S TRUTH

Numbers 23: 19 (NLT)
19 God is not a man, so he does not lie. He is not human, so he does not change his mind. Has he ever spoken and failed to act? Has he ever promised and not carried it through?

Deuteronomy 32: 4 (GNT)
4 The Lord is your mighty defender, perfect and just in all his ways; Your God is faithful and true; he does what is right and fair.

Psalms 25: 5 (NLT)
5 Lead me by your truth and teach me, for you are the God who saves me. All day long I put my hope in you.

Psalms 119: 160 (MEV)
160 Your word is true from the beginning, and every one of Your righteous judgments endures forev-er.

Proverbs 30: 5 (NIV)
5 Every word of God is flawless; he is a shield to those who take refuge in him.

Mark 11: 22 - 24 (NIVUK)
22 'Have faith in God,' Jesus answered. 23 'Truly I tell you, if anyone says to this mountain, "Go, throw yourself

into the sea," and does not doubt in their heart but believes that what they say will happen, it will be done for them. 24 Therefore I tell you, whatever you ask for in prayer, believe that you have received it, and it will be yours.

John 1: 14 (GW)
14 The Word became human and lived among us. We saw his glory. It was the glory that the Father shares with his only Son, a glory full of kindness and truth.

John 15: 26 (NOG)
26 "The helper whom I will send to you from the Father will come. This helper, the Spirit of Truth who comes from the Father, will declare the truth about me.

John 16: 13 (NASB)
13 But when He, the Spirit of truth, comes, He will guide you into all the truth; for He will not speak on His own initiative, but whatever He hears, He will speak; and He will disclose to you what is to come.

John 17: 17 (NET)
17 Set them apart in the truth; your word is truth.

Acts 17: 11 (NCV)
11 These people were more willing to listen than the people in Thessalonica. The Bereans were eager to hear what Paul and Silas said and studied the Scriptures every day to find out if these things were true.

Ephesians 6: 13 - 14 (WEB)
13 Therefore put on the whole armor of God, that you may be able to withstand in the evil day, and having done all, to stand. 14 Stand therefore, having the

utility belt of truth buckled around your waist, and having put on the breastplate of righteousness,

Hebrews 6: 16 - 18 (NIV)
16 People swear by someone greater than themselves, and the oath confirms what is said and puts an end to all argument. 17 Because God wanted to make the unchanging nature of his purpose very clear to the heirs of what was promised, he confirmed it with an oath. 18 God did this so that, by two unchangeable things in which it is impossible for God to lie, we who have fled to take hold of the hope set before us may be greatly encouraged.

GOD'S WILL

Matthew 8: 2 - 3 (HCSB)
2 Right away a man with a serious skin disease came up and knelt before Him, saying, "Lord, if You are willing, You can make me clean." 3 Reaching out His hand He touched him, saying, "I am willing; be made clean." Immediately his disease was healed.

John 14: 13 - 14 (WEB)
13 Whatever you will ask in my name, that will I do, that the Father may be glorified in the Son. 14 If you will ask anything in my name, I will do it.

John 9: 31 (WEB)
31 We know that God doesn't listen to sinners, but if anyone is a worshiper of God, and does his will, he listens to him.

Romans 12: 2 (NLT)
2 Don't copy the behavior and customs of this world, but let God transform you into a new person by changing the way you think. Then you will learn to know God's will for you, which is good and pleas-ing and perfect.

Ephesians 1: 5 - 7 (MEV)
5 He predestined us to adoption as sons to Himself through Jesus Christ according to the good plea-sure of His will, 6 to the praise of the glory of His grace which He graciously bestowed on us in the Beloved. 7 In Him we have redemption through His blood and the forgiveness of sins according to the riches of His grace,

Ephesians 5: 17 (WEB)
17 Therefore don't be foolish, but understand what the will of the Lord is.

1 Thessalonians 4: 3 - 5 (NET)
3 For this is God's will: that you become holy, that you keep away from sexual immorality, 4 that each of you know how to possess his own body in holiness and honor, 5 not in lustful passion like the Gen-tiles who do not know God.

1 Thessalonians 5: 18 (NET)
18 in everything give thanks. For this is God's will for you in Christ Jesus.

James 1: 27 (NASB)
27 Pure and undefiled religion in the sight of our God and Father is this: to visit orphans and widows in their distress, and to keep oneself unstained by the world.

1 Peter 2: 15 (NKJV)
15 For this is the will of God, that by doing good you may put to silence the ignorance of foolish men

1 Peter 3: 17 (NKJV)
17 For it is better, if it is the will of God, to suffer for doing good than for doing evil.

GOD'S WORD

Joshua 1: 8 (NIV)
8 Keep this Book of the Law always on your lips; meditate on it day and night, so that you may be careful to do everything written in it. Then you will be prosperous and successful.

Psalms 119: 89 (NKJV)
89 Forever, O Lord, Your word is settled in heaven.

Psalms 119: 105 (NOG)
105 Your word is a lamp for my feet and a light for my path.

Psalms 119: 130 (NASB)
130 The unfolding of Your words gives light; It gives understanding to the simple.

Psalms 147: 15 (NIV)
15 He sends his command to the earth; his word runs swiftly.

Proverbs 4: 20 - 23 (NKJV)
20 My son, give attention to my words; Incline your ear to my sayings. 21 Do not let them depart from your eyes; Keep them in the midst of your heart; 22 For they are life to those who find them, And health to all their flesh. 23 Keep your heart with all diligence, For out of it spring the issues of life.

Isaiah 30: 21 (MEV)
21 Your ears shall hear a word behind you, saying, "This is the way, walk in it," whenever you turn to the right hand and when you turn to the left.

Isaiah 46: 9 - 11 (NCV)
9 Remember what happened long ago. Remember that I am God, and there is no other God. I am God, and there is no one like me. 10 From the beginning I told you what would happen in the end. A long time ago I told you things that have not yet happened. When I plan something, it happens. What I want to do, I will do. 11 I am calling a man from the east to carry out my plan; he will come like a hawk from a country far away. I will make what I have said come true; I will do what I have planned.

Isaiah 55: 10 - 11 (CEV)
10 Rain and snow fall from the sky. But they don't return without watering the earth that produces seeds to plant and grain to eat. 11 That's how it is with my words. They don't return to me without doing everything I send them to do.

Jeremiah 1: 12 (MEV)
12 Then the Lord said to me, "You have seen well. For I will hasten My word to perform it."

Jeremiah 23: 29 (NLT)
29 Does not my word burn like fire?" says the Lord. "Is it not like a mighty hammer that smashes a rock to pieces?

John 10: 27 (NKJV)
27 My sheep hear My voice, and I know them, and they follow Me.

John 6: 63 (NKJV)
63 It is the Spirit who gives life; the flesh profits nothing. The words that I speak to you are spirit, and they are life.

Romans 10: 17 (NKJV)
17 So then faith comes by hearing, and hearing by the word of God.

Ephesians 6: 13, 17 - 18 (WEB)
13 Therefore put on the whole armor of God, that you may be able to withstand in the evil day, and having done all, to stand. 17 And take the helmet of salvation, and the sword of the Spirit, which is the word of God; 18 with all prayer and requests, praying at all times in the Spirit, and being watchful to this end in all perseverance and requests for all the saints:

2 Timothy 3: 16 - 17 (GNT)
16 All Scripture is inspired by God and is useful for teaching the truth, rebuking error, correcting faults, and giving instruction for right living, 17 so that the person who serves God may be fully qualified and equipped to do every kind of good deed.

Hebrews 4: 12 (NCV)
12 God's word is alive and working and is sharper than a double-edged sword. It cuts all the way into us, where the soul and the spirit are joined, to the center of our joints and bones. And it judges the thoughts and feelings in our hearts.

James 1: 21 - 25 (NIV)
21 Therefore, get rid of all moral filth and the evil that is so prevalent and humbly accept the word planted in you, which can save you. 22 Do not merely listen to the word, and so deceive yourselves. Do what it says. 23 Anyone who listens to the word but does not do what it says is like someone who looks at his face in a mirror 24 and, after looking at himself, goes away and immediately forgets what he looks like. 25 But whoever looks intently into the perfect law that gives freedom, and continues in it—not forgetting what they have heard, but doing it—they will be blessed in what they do.

1 Peter 2: 2 (NIV)
2 Like newborn babies, crave pure spiritual milk, so that by it you may grow up in your salvation,

Revelation 1: 3 (NKJV)
3 Blessed is he who reads and those who hear the words of this prophecy, and keep those things which are written in it; for the time is near.

GOODNESS

Psalms 31: 19 (HCSB)
19 How great is Your goodness that You have stored up for those who fear You and accomplished in the sight of everyone for those who take refuge in You.

Psalms 34: 8, 10 (NET)
8 Taste and see that the Lord is good! How blessed is the one who takes shelter in him! 10 Even young lions sometimes lack food and are hungry, but those who seek the Lord lack no good thing.

Psalms 84: 11 (NET)
11 For the Lord God is our sovereign protector. The Lord bestows favor and honor; he withholds no good thing from those who have integrity.

Psalms 103: 5 (NIV)

5 who satisfies your desires with good things so that your youth is renewed like the eagle's.

Psalms 107: 9 (NKJV)
9 For He satisfies the longing soul, And fills the hungry soul with goodness.

Proverbs 18: 22 (ESV)
22 He who finds a wife finds a good thing and obtains favor from the Lord.

Isaiah 58: 11 (TLB)
11 And the Lord will guide you continually, and satisfy you with all good things, and keep you healthy too; and you will be like a well-watered garden, like an ever-flowing spring.

Luke 6: 45 (RSV)
45 The good man out of the good treasure of his heart produces good, and the evil man out of his evil treasure produces evil; for out of the abundance of the heart his mouth speaks.

Acts 10: 38 (NLT)
38 And you know that God anointed Jesus of Nazareth with the Holy Spirit and with power. Then Je-sus went around doing good and healing all who were oppressed by the devil, for God was with him.

1 Corinthians 10: 24 (NIVUK)
24 No one should seek their own good, but the good of others.

Galatians 5: 22 - 23 (NIV)
22 But the fruit of the Spirit is love, joy, peace, forbearance, kindness, goodness, faithfulness, 23 gen-tleness and self-control. Against such things there is no law.

Galatians 6: 9 - 10 (HCSB)
9 So we must not get tired of doing good, for we will reap at the proper time if we don't give up. 10 Therefore, as we have opportunity, we must work for the good of all, especially for those who belong to the household of faith.

Ephesians 2: 10 (NIVUK)
10 For we are God's handiwork, created in Christ Jesus to do good works, which God prepared in advance for us to do.

Ephesians 4: 29 (ESV)
29 Let no corrupting talk come out of your mouths, but only such as is good for building up, as fits the occasion, that it may give grace to those who hear.

Ephesians 6: 8 (ESV)
8 knowing that whatever good anyone does, this he will receive back from the Lord, whether he is a bondservant or is free.

Hebrews 13: 20 - 21 (NIV)
20 Now may the God of peace, who through the blood of the eternal covenant brought back from the dead our Lord Jesus, that great Shepherd of the sheep, 21 equip you with everything good for doing his will, and may he work in us what is pleasing to him, through Jesus Christ, to whom be glory for ever and ever. Amen.

James 1: 17 (TLB)
17 But whatever is good and perfect comes to us from God, the Creator of all light, and he shines forever without change or shadow.

James 3: 17 (TLB)
17 But the wisdom that comes from heaven is first of all pure and full of

quiet gentleness. Then it is peace-loving and courteous. It allows discussion and is willing to yield to others; it is full of mercy and good deeds. It is wholehearted and straightforward and sincere.

1 Peter 2: 15 (NKJV)
15 For this is the will of God, that by doing good you may put to silence the ignorance of foolish men—

GOSSIP

Psalms 34: 13 - 15 (NKJV)
13 Keep your tongue from evil, And your lips from speaking deceit. 14 Depart from evil and do good; Seek peace and pursue it. 15 The eyes of the Lord are on the righteous, And His ears are open to their cry.

Psalms 101: 5 (NIV)
5 Whoever slanders their neighbor in secret, I will put to silence; whoever has haughty eyes and a proud heart, I will not tolerate.

Proverbs 12: 18 (NIV)
18 The words of the reckless pierce like swords, but the tongue of the wise brings healing.

Proverbs 17: 9 (NKJV)
9 He who covers a transgression seeks love, But he who repeats a matter separates friends.

Proverbs 18: 8 (NET)
8 The words of a gossip are like choice morsels; they go down into the person's innermost being.

Proverbs 20: 3 (DRA)
3 It is an honour for a man to separate himself from quarrels: but all fools are meddling with reproach-es.

Proverbs 26: 20 - 22 (NET)
20 Where there is no wood, a fire goes out, and where there is no gossip, contention ceases. 21 Like charcoal is to burning coals, and wood to fire, so is a contentious person to kindle strife. 22 The words of a gossip are like delicious morsels; they go down into a person's innermost being.

Matthew 12: 36 - 37 (NET)
36 I tell you that on the day of judgment, people will give an account for every worthless word they speak. 37 For by your words you will be justified, and by your words you will be condemned.

Matthew 15: 19 (TLB)
19 For from the heart come evil thoughts, murder, adultery, fornication, theft, lying, and slander.

Luke 6: 31 (NIVUK)
31 Do to others as you would have them do to you.

Luke 6: 45 (RSV)
45 The good man out of the good treasure of his heart produces good, and the evil man out of his evil treasure produces evil; for out of the abundance of the heart his mouth speaks.

Ephesians 4: 29, 31 (NET)
29 You must let no unwholesome word come out of your mouth, but only what is beneficial for the building up of the one in need, that it may give grace to those who hear. 31 You must put away

all bitterness, anger, wrath, quarreling, and slanderous talk—indeed all malice.

Titus 2: 3 (NET)
3 Older women likewise are to exhibit behavior fitting for those who are holy, not slandering, not slaves to excessive drinking, but teaching what is good.

Titus 3: 2 (MEV)
2 to speak evil of no one, not to be contentious, but gentle, showing all humility toward everyone.

1 Peter 3: 10 - 11 (NCV)
10 The Scripture says, "A person must do these things to enjoy life and have many happy days. He must not say evil things, and he must not tell lies. 11 He must stop doing evil and do good. He must look for peace and work for it.

GRACE

1 Samuel 1: 17 - 18 (MEV)
17 Then Eli answered and said, "Go in peace, and the God of Israel grant you your request that you have asked of Him." 18 And she said, "Let your handmaid find grace in your sight." So the woman went her way and ate, and her face was not sad as before.

Psalms 84: 11 (AMP)
11 For the Lord God is a Sun and Shield; the Lord bestows [present] grace and favor and [future] glo-ry (honor, splendor, and heavenly bliss)! No good thing will He withhold from those who walk uprightly.

Proverbs 4: 7 - 9 (NKJV)
7 Wisdom is the principal thing; Therefore get wisdom. And in all your getting, get understanding. 8 Exalt her, and she will promote you; She will bring you honor, when you embrace her. 9 She will place on your head an ornament of grace; A crown of glory she will deliver to you.

John 1: 16 - 17 (NIV)
16 Out of his fullness we have all received grace in place of grace already given. 17 For the law was given through Moses; grace and truth came through Jesus Christ.

2 Corinthians 9: 7 - 9 (NKJV)
7 So let each one give as he purposes in his heart, not grudgingly or of necessity; for God loves a cheerful giver. 8 And God is able to make all grace abound toward you, that you, always having all sufficiency in all things, may have an abundance for every good work. 9 As it is written: "He has dis-persed abroad, He has given to the poor; His righteousness endures forever."

2 Corinthians 12: 9 - 10 (NKJV)
9 And He said to me, "My grace is sufficient for you, for My strength is made perfect in weakness." Therefore most gladly I will rather boast in my infirmities, that the power of Christ may rest upon me. 10 Therefore I take pleasure in infirmities, in reproaches, in needs, in persecutions, in distresses, for Christ's sake. For when I am weak, then I am strong.

Ephesians 2: 8 (GNT)
8 For it is by God's grace that you have been saved through faith. It is not the

result of your own ef-forts, but God's gift, so that no one can boast about it.

Ephesians 4: 29 (ESV)
29 Let no corrupting talk come out of your mouths, but only such as is good for building up, as fits the occasion, that it may give grace to those who hear.

Ephesians 4: 7 (AMP)
7 Yet grace (God's unmerited favor) was given to each of us individually [not indiscriminately, but in different ways] in proportion to the measure of Christ's [rich and bounteous] gift.

Ephesians 6: 24 (ESV)
24 Grace be with all who love our Lord Jesus Christ with love incorruptible.

Colossians 4: 6 (NIV)
6 Let your conversation be always full of grace, seasoned with salt, so that you may know how to answer everyone.

2 Thessalonians 2: 16 - 17 (NLT)
16 Now may our Lord Jesus Christ himself and God our Father, who loved us and by his grace gave us eternal comfort and a wonderful hope, 17 comfort you and strengthen you in every good thing you do and say.

Titus 2: 11 - 12 (NKJV)
11 For the grace of God that brings salvation has appeared to all men, 12 teaching us that, denying ungodliness and worldly lusts, we should live soberly, righteously, and godly in the present age,

Titus 3: 4 - 7 (HCSB)
4 But when the kindness of God our Savior and His love for mankind appeared, 5 He saved us— not by works of righteousness that we had done, but according to His mercy, through the washing of regeneration and renewal by the Holy Spirit. 6 He poured out this Spirit on us abundantly through Jesus Christ our Savior, 7 so that having been justified by His grace, we may become heirs with the hope of eternal life.

Hebrews 4: 16 (TLB)
16 So let us come boldly to the very throne of God and stay there to receive his mercy and to find grace to help us in our times of need.

Hebrews 12: 14 - 15 (MEV)
14 Pursue peace with all people, and holiness, without which no one will see the Lord: 15 looking carefully lest anyone fall short of the grace of God; lest any root of bitterness springing up cause trou-ble, and by this many become defiled;

James 4: 6 - 7 (HCSB)
6 But He gives greater grace. Therefore He says: God resists the proud, but gives grace to the hum-ble. 7 Therefore, submit to God. But resist the Devil, and he will flee from you.

1 Peter 4: 10 - 11 (NIVUK)
10 Each of you should use whatever gift you have received to serve others, as faithful stewards of God's grace in its various forms. 11 If anyone speaks, they should do so as one who speaks the very words of God. If anyone serves, they should do so with the strength God provides, so that in all things God may be praised through Jesus Christ. To him be the glory and the power for ever and ever. Amen.

GRIEF

2 Samuel 12: 22 - 23 (RSV)
22 He said, "While the child was still alive, I fasted and wept; for I said, 'Who knows whether the Lord will be gracious to me, that the child may live?' 23 But now he is dead; why should I fast? Can I bring him back again? I shall go to him, but he will not return to me."

Psalms 6: 7 - 9 (AMP)
7 My eye grows dim because of grief; it grows old because of all my enemies. 8 Depart from me, all you workers of iniquity, for the Lord has heard the voice of my weeping. 9 The Lord has heard my supplication; the Lord receives my prayer.

Psalms 116: 15 (AMP)
15 Precious (important and no light matter) in the sight of the Lord is the death of His saints (His lov-ing ones).

Psalms 119: 28 (NASB)
28 My soul weeps because of grief; Strengthen me according to Your word.

Psalms 42: 11 (MEV)
11 Why, my soul, are you cast down? Why do you groan within me? Wait for God; I will yet thank Him, For He is my deliverance and my God.

Isaiah 26: 3 (AMP)
3 You will guard him and keep him in perfect and constant peace whose mind [both its inclination and its character] is stayed on You, because he commits himself to You, leans on You, and hopes confi-dently in You.

Isaiah 61: 1 - 2 (MEV)
1 The Spirit of the Lord God is upon me because the Lord has anointed me to preach good news to the poor; He has sent me to heal the broken-hearted, to proclaim liberty to the captives, and the opening of the prison to those who are bound; 2 to proclaim the acceptable year of the Lord and the day of vengeance of our God; to comfort all who mourn,

Jeremiah 31: 25 (ESV)
25 For I will satisfy the weary soul, and every languishing soul I will replenish."

Matthew 5: 4 (MEV)
4 Blessed are those who mourn, for they shall be comforted.

Matthew 11: 28 - 29 (RSV)
28 Come to me, all who labor and are heavy laden, and I will give you rest. 29 Take my yoke upon you, and learn from me; for I am gentle and lowly in heart, and you will find rest for your souls.

John 11: 33 (ASV)
33 When Jesus therefore saw her weeping, and the Jews also weeping who came with her, he groaned in the spirit, and was troubled,

John 14: 1 - 2, 18 (NOG)
1 "Don't be troubled. Believe in God, and believe in me. 2 My Father's house has many rooms. If that were not true, would I have told you that I'm going to prepare a place for you? 18 "I will not leave you all alone. I will come back to you.

Acts 2: 39 (NKJV)
39 For the promise is to you and to your children, and to all who are afar off, as many as the Lord our God will call.

1 Thessalonians 4: 13 - 14 (NIV)
13 Brothers and sisters, we do not want you to be uninformed about those who sleep in death, so that you do not grieve like the rest of mankind, who have no hope. 14 For we believe that Jesus died and rose again, and so we believe that God will bring with Jesus those who have fallen asleep in him.

GROWING

Psalms 92: 12 - 13 (NKJV)
12 The righteous shall flourish like a palm tree, He shall grow like a cedar in Lebanon. 13 Those who are planted in the house of the Lord Shall flourish in the courts of our God.

Psalms 138: 8 (NKJV)
8 The Lord will perfect that which concerns me; Your mercy, O Lord, endures forever; Do not forsake the works of Your hands.

Proverbs 4: 18 (GNT)
18 The road the righteous travel is like the sunrise, getting brighter and brighter until daylight has come.

Malachi 4: 2 - 3 (NLT)
2 "But for you who fear my name, the Sun of Righteousness will rise with healing in his wings. And you will go free, leaping with joy like calves let out to pasture. 3 On the day when I act, you will tread upon the wicked as if they were dust under your feet," says the Lord of Heaven's Armies.

Mark 4: 30 - 32 (NIVUK)
30 Again he said, 'What shall we say the kingdom of God is like, or what parable shall we use to describe it? 31 It is like a mustard seed, which is the smallest of all seeds on earth. 32 Yet when planted, it grows and becomes the largest of all garden plants, with such big branches that the birds can perch in its shade.'

Ephesians 3: 17 - 19 (NIV)
17 so that Christ may dwell in your hearts through faith. And I pray that you, being rooted and estab-lished in love, 18 may have power, together with all the Lord's holy people, to grasp how wide and long and high and deep is the love of Christ, 19 and to know this love that surpasses knowledge— that you may be filled to the measure of all the fullness of God.

Philippians 1: 9 - 10 (NKJV)
9 And this I pray, that your love may abound still more and more in knowledge and all discernment, 10 that you may approve the things that are excellent, that you may be sincere and without offense till the day of Christ,

Colossians 3: 16 - 17 (NIVUK)
16 Let the message of Christ dwell among you richly as you teach and admonish one another with all wisdom through psalms, hymns, and songs from the Spirit, singing to God with gratitude in your hearts. 17 And whatever you do, whether in word or deed, do it all in the name of the Lord Jesus, giving thanks to God the Father through him.

1 Timothy 4: 14 - 16 (NIV)
14 Do not neglect your gift, which was given you through prophecy when the body of elders laid their hands on you. 15 Be diligent in these matters; give yourself

wholly to them, so that everyone may see your progress. 16 Watch your life and doctrine closely. Persevere in them, because if you do, you will save both yourself and your hearers.

1 Peter 2: 2 - 3 (NIV)
2 Like newborn babies, crave pure spiritual milk, so that by it you may grow up in your salvation, 3 now that you have tasted that the Lord is good.

2 Peter 3: 18 (NIV)
18 But grow in the grace and knowledge of our Lord and Savior Jesus Christ. To him be glory both now and forever! Amen.

GUIDANCE

Deuteronomy 8: 5 - 6 (NCV)
5 Know in your heart that the Lord your God corrects you as a parent corrects a child. 6 Obey the commands of the Lord your God, living as he has commanded you and respecting him.

Psalms 119: 105 (GNT)
105 Your word is a lamp to guide me and a light for my path.

Psalms 143: 8, 10 (MEV)
8 Cause me to hear Your lovingkindness in the morning; for in You I have my trust; cause me to know the way I should walk, for I lift up my soul unto You. 10 Teach me to do Your will, for You are my God; may Your good spirit lead me onto level ground.

Psalms 16: 7, 11 (NLT)
7 I will bless the Lord who guides me; even at night my heart instructs me.

11 You will show me the way of life, granting me the joy of your presence and the pleasures of living with you forever.

Psalms 23: 3 (NIV)
3 he refreshes my soul. He guides me along the right paths for his name's sake.

Psalms 32: 8 (NLT)
8 The Lord says, "I will guide you along the best pathway for your life. I will advise you and watch over you.

Psalms 37: 23 - 24 (NIV)
23 The Lord makes firm the steps of the one who delights in him; 24 though he may stumble, he will not fall, for the Lord upholds him with his hand.

Psalms 48: 14 (NIV)
14 For this God is our God for ever and ever; he will be our guide even to the end.

Proverbs 3: 1, 5 - 6 (MEV)
1 My son, do not forget my teaching, but let your heart keep my commandments; 3 Trust in the Lord with all your heart, and lean not on your own understanding; 6 in all your ways acknowledge Him, and He will direct your paths.

Proverbs 16: 3, 9 (NET)
3 Commit your works to the Lord, and your plans will be established. 9 A person plans his course, but the Lord directs his steps.

Isaiah 30: 21 (MEV)
21 Your ears shall hear a word behind you, saying, "This is the way, walk in

it," whenever you turn to the right hand and when you turn to the left.

Isaiah 42: 16 (NET)
16 I will lead the blind along an unfamiliar way; I will guide them down paths they have never traveled. I will turn the darkness in front of them into light, and level out the rough ground. This is what I will do for them. I will not abandon them.

Isaiah 48: 17 (NIV)
17 This is what the Lord says—your Redeemer, the Holy One of Israel: "I am the Lord your God, who teaches you what is best for you, who directs you in the way you should go.

Isaiah 58: 11 (AMP)
11 And the Lord shall guide you continually and satisfy you in drought and in dry places and make strong your bones. And you shall be like a watered garden and like a spring of water whose waters fail not.

Romans 8: 14 (WEB)
14 For as many as are led by the Spirit of God, these are children of God.

James 1: 5 (MEV)
5 If any of you lacks wisdom, let him ask of God, who gives to all men liberally and without criticism, and it will be given to him.

HEALING

Exodus 15: 26 (NKJV)
26 and said, "If you diligently heed the voice of the Lord your God and do what is right in His sight, give ear to His commandments and keep all His statutes, I will put none of the diseases on you which I have brought on the Egyptians. For I am the Lord who heals you."

Exodus 23: 25 (NKJV)
25 "So you shall serve the Lord your God, and He will bless your bread and your water. And I will take sickness away from the midst of you.

Deuteronomy 7: 14 - 15 (NLT)
14 You will be blessed above all the nations of the earth. None of your men or women will be child-less, and all your livestock will bear young. 15 And the Lord will protect you from all sickness. He will not let you suffer from the terrible diseases you knew in Egypt, but he will inflict them on all your enemies!

Psalms 30: 2 (NIV)
2 Lord my God, I called to you for help, and you healed me.

Deuteronomy 30: 19 - 20 (ESV)
19 I call heaven and earth to witness against you today, that I have set before you life and death, blessing and curse. Therefore choose life, that you and your offspring may live, 20 loving the Lord your God, obeying his voice and holding fast to him, for he is your life and length of days, that you may dwell in the land that the Lord swore to your fathers, to Abraham, to Isaac, and to Jacob, to give them.

Psalms 34: 19 (NKJV)
19 Many are the afflictions of the righteous, But the Lord delivers him out of them all.

Psalms 91: 3, 9 - 10, 16 (NIV)
3 Surely he will save you from the fowler's snare and from the deadly pestilence. 9 If you say, "The Lord is my refuge," and you make the Most High your dwelling, 10 no harm will overtake you, no disaster will come near your tent. 16 With long life I will satisfy him and show him my salvation."

Psalms 103: 2 - 5 (NIV)
2 Praise the Lord, my soul, and forget not all his benefits— 3 who forgives all your sins and heals all your diseases, 4 who redeems your life from the pit and crowns you with love and compassion, 5 who satisfies your desires with good things so that your youth is renewed like the eagle's.

Psalms 107: 17, 19 - 21 (ESV)
17 Some were fools through their sinful ways, and because of their iniquities suffered affliction; 19 Then they cried to the Lord in their trouble, and he delivered them from their distress. 20 He sent out his word and healed them, and delivered them from their destruction. 21 Let them thank the Lord for his steadfast love, for his wondrous works to the children of man!

Psalms 118: 17 (GW)
17 I will not die, but I will live and tell what the Lord has done.

Proverbs 4: 4 (NIV)
4 Then he taught me, and he said to me, "Take hold of my words with all your heart; keep my com-mands, and you will live.

Proverbs 4: 20 - 24 (HCSB)
20 listen closely to my sayings. 21 Don't lose sight of them; keep them

within your heart. 22 For they are life to those who find them, and health to one's whole body. 23 Guard your heart above all else, for it is the source of life. 24 Don't let your mouth speak dishonestly, and don't let your lips talk devi-ously.

Isaiah 40: 31 (HCSB)
31 but those who trust in the Lord will renew their strength; they will soar on wings like eagles; they will run and not grow weary; they will walk and not faint.

Isaiah 41: 10 (HCSB)
10 Do not fear, for I am with you; do not be afraid, for I am your God. I will strengthen you; I will help you; I will hold on to you with My righteous right hand.

Isaiah 53: 5 (NKJV)
5 But He was wounded for our transgressions, He was bruised for our iniquities; The chastisement for our peace was upon Him, And by His stripes we are healed.

Isaiah 58: 7 - 8 (NCV)
7 Share your food with the hungry and bring poor, homeless people into your own homes. When you see someone who has no clothes, give him yours, and don't refuse to help your own relatives. 8 Then your light will shine like the dawn, and your wounds will quickly heal. Your God will walk before you, and the glory of the Lord will protect you from behind.

Jeremiah 17: 14 (NKJV)
14 Heal me, O Lord, and I shall be healed; Save me, and I shall be saved, For You are my praise.

Malachi 4: 2 (NLT)
2 "But for you who fear my name, the Sun of Righteousness will rise with healing in his wings. And you will go free, leaping with joy like calves let out to pasture.

Matthew 14: 14 (HCSB)
14 As He stepped ashore, He saw a huge crowd, felt compassion for them, and healed their sick.

Matthew 4: 23 - 24 (NIV)
23 Jesus went throughout Galilee, teaching in their synagogues, proclaiming the good news of the kingdom, and healing every disease and sickness among the people. 24 News about him spread all over Syria, and people brought to him all who were ill with various diseases, those suffering severe pain, the demon-possessed, those having seizures, and the paralyzed; and he healed them.

Matthew 8: 2 - 3 (NET)
2 And a leper approached, and bowed low before him, saying, "Lord, if you are willing, you can make me clean." 3 He stretched out his hand and touched him saying, "I am willing. Be clean!" Immediately his leprosy was cleansed.

Matthew 8: 7 - 8 (RSV)
7 And he said to him, "I will come and heal him." 8 But the centurion answered him, "Lord, I am not worthy to have you come under my roof; but only say the word, and my servant will be healed.

Matthew 8: 16 - 17 (WEB)
16 When evening came, they brought to him many possessed with demons. He cast out the spirits with a word,

and healed all who were sick; 17 that it might be fulfilled which was spoken through Isa-iah the prophet, saying: "He took our infirmities, and bore our diseases."

Matthew 9: 22 (WE)
22 Jesus turned around. He saw her and said, 'Daughter, be glad. You were healed because you believed.' And right away the woman was healed.

Matthew 9: 28 - 30 (NKJV)
28 And when He had come into the house, the blind men came to Him. And Jesus said to them, "Do you believe that I am able to do this?" They said to Him, "Yes, Lord." 29 Then He touched their eyes, saying, "According to your faith let it be to you." 30 And their eyes were opened. And Jesus sternly warned them, saying, "See that no one knows it."

Matthew 15: 30 - 31 (GNT)
30 Large crowds came to him, bringing with them the lame, the blind, the crippled, the dumb, and many other sick people, whom they placed at Jesus' feet; and he healed them. 31 The people were amazed as they saw the dumb speaking, the crippled made whole, the lame walking, and the blind seeing; and they praised the God of Israel.

Matthew 18: 18 - 19 (NCV)
18 "I tell you the truth, the things you don't allow on earth will be the things God does not allow. And the things you allow on earth will be the things that God allows. 19 "Also, I tell you that if two of you on earth agree about something and pray for it, it will be done for you by my Father in heaven.

Matthew 21: 14 (MEV)

14 The blind and the lame came to Him in the temple, and He healed them.

Mark 5: 27 - 29, 34 (RSV)

27 She had heard the reports about Jesus, and came up behind him in the crowd and touched his garment. 28 For she said, "If I touch even his garments, I shall be made well." 29 And immediately the hemorrhage ceased; and she felt in her body that she was healed of her disease. 34 And he said to her, "Daughter, your faith has made you well; go in peace, and be healed of your disease."

Mark 9: 23 - 24, 29 (NLT)

23 "What do you mean, 'If I can'?" Jesus asked. "Anything is possible if a person believes." 24 The father instantly cried out, "I do believe, but help me overcome my unbelief!" 29 Jesus replied, "This kind can be cast out only by prayer."

Mark 10: 51 - 52 (NCV)

51 Jesus asked him, "What do you want me to do for you?" The blind man answered, "Teacher, I want to see." 52 Jesus said, "Go, you are healed because you believed." At once the man could see, and he followed Jesus on the road.

Mark 16: 17 - 18 (RSV)

17 And these signs will accompany those who believe: in my name they will cast out demons; they will speak in new tongues; 18 they will pick up serpents, and if they drink any deadly thing, it will not hurt them; they will lay their hands on the sick, and they will recover.

Luke 6: 19 (WEB)

19 All the multitude sought to touch him, for power came out of him and healed them all.

Luke 9: 2 (NET)

2 and he sent them out to proclaim the kingdom of God and to heal the sick.

Luke 13: 16 (NCV)

16 This woman that I healed, a daughter of Abraham, has been held by Satan for eighteen years. Surely it is not wrong for her to be freed from her sickness on a Sabbath day!

Acts 5: 16 (HCSB)

16 In addition, a large group came together from the towns surrounding Jerusalem, bringing sick peo-ple and those who were tormented by unclean spirits, and they were all healed.

Acts 10: 38 (LEB)

38 Jesus of Nazareth—how God anointed him with the Holy Spirit and with power, who went about doing good and healing all who were oppressed by the devil, because God was with him.

Romans 8: 2, 11 (MEV)

2 For the law of the Spirit of life in Christ Jesus has set me free from the law of sin and death. 11 But if the Spirit of Him who raised Jesus from the dead lives in you, He who raised Christ from the dead will also give life to your mortal bodies through His Spirit that lives in you.

2 Corinthians 4: 18 (DRA)

18 While we look not at the things which are seen, but at the things which are not seen. For the things which are

seen, are temporal; but the things which are not seen, are eternal.

2 Corinthians 10: 3 - 5 (ASV)

3 For though we walk in the flesh, we do not war according to the flesh 4 (for the weapons of our war-fare are not of the flesh, but mighty before God to the casting down of strongholds), 5 casting down imaginations, and every high thing that is exalted against the knowledge of God, and bringing every thought into captivity to the obedience of Christ;

2 Timothy 1: 7 (NCV)

7 God did not give us a spirit that makes us afraid but a spirit of power and love and self-control.

James 4: 7 (HCSB)

7 Therefore, submit to God. But resist the Devil, and he will flee from you.

James 5: 14 - 16 (NKJV)

14 Is anyone among you sick? Let him call for the elders of the church, and let them pray over him, anointing him with oil in the name of the Lord. 15 And the prayer of faith will save the sick, and the Lord will raise him up. And if he has committed sins, he will be forgiven. 16 Confess your trespasses to one another, and pray for one another, that you may be healed. The effective, fervent prayer of a righteous man avails much.

1 Peter 2: 24 (NKJV)

24 who Himself bore our sins in His own body on the tree, that we, having died to sins, might live for righteousness—by whose stripes you were healed.

3 John 1: 2 (NASB)

2 Beloved, I pray that in all respects you may prosper and be in good health, just as your soul prospers.

HEALTH

Exodus 15: 26 (NKJV)

26 and said, "If you diligently heed the voice of the Lord your God and do what is right in His sight, give ear to His commandments and keep all His statutes, I will put none of the diseases on you which I have brought on the Egyptians. For I am the Lord who heals you."

Exodus 23: 25 (NKJV)

25 "So you shall serve the Lord your God, and He will bless your bread and your water. And I will take sickness away from the midst of you.

Deuteronomy 30: 19 - 20 (NLT)

19 "Today I have given you the choice between life and death, between blessings and curses. Now I call on heaven and earth to witness the choice you make. Oh, that you would choose life, so that you and your descendants might live! 20 You can make this choice by loving the Lord your God, obeying him, and committing yourself firmly to him. This is the key to your life. And if you love and obey the Lord, you will live long in the land the Lord swore to give your ancestors Abraham, Isaac, and Jacob."

Psalms 121: 7 - 8 (NKJV)

7 The Lord shall preserve you from all evil; He shall preserve your soul. 8 The Lord shall preserve your going out and

your coming in From this time forth, and even forevermore.

Psalms 91: 3, 9 - 10, 16 (NIV)
3 Surely he will save you from the fowler's snare and from the deadly pestilence. 9 If you say, "The Lord is my refuge," and you make the Most High your dwelling, 10 no harm will overtake you, no di-saster will come near your tent. 16 With long life I will satisfy him and show him my salvation."

Proverbs 3: 7 - 8 (MEV)
7 Do not be wise in your own eyes; fear the Lord and depart from evil. 8 It will be health to your body, and strength to your bones.

Proverbs 4: 20 - 23 (NKJV)
20 My son, give attention to my words; Incline your ear to my sayings. 21 Do not let them depart from your eyes; Keep them in the midst of your heart; 22 For they are life to those who find them, And health to all their flesh. 23 Keep your heart with all diligence, For out of it spring the issues of life.

Proverbs 16: 24 (WEB)
24 Pleasant words are a honeycomb, sweet to the soul, and health to the bones.

Proverbs 18: 21 (HCSB)
21 Life and death are in the power of the tongue, and those who love it will eat its fruit.

Lamentations 3: 33 (NIV)
33 For he does not willingly bring affliction or grief toone.

Malachi 4: 2 - 3 (NLT)
2 "But for you who fear my name, the Sun of Righteousness will rise with healing in his wings. And you will go free, leaping with joy like calves let out to pasture. 3 On the day when I act, you will tread upon the wicked as if they were dust under your feet," says the Lord of Heaven's Armies.

Matthew 4: 23 (NIV)
23 Jesus went throughout Galilee, teaching in their synagogues, proclaiming the good news of the kingdom, and healing every disease and sickness among the people.

Matthew 15: 30 - 31 (NLT)
30 A vast crowd brought to him people who were lame, blind, crippled, those who couldn't speak, and many others. They laid them before Jesus, and he healed them all. 31 The crowd was amazed! Those who hadn't been able to speak were talking, the crippled were made well, the lame were walk-ing, and the blind could see again! And they praised the God of Israel.

Matthew 21: 14 (MEV)
14 The blind and the lame came to Him in the temple, and He healed them.

Mark 5: 27 - 29, 34 (WEB)
27 having heard the things concerning Jesus, came up behind him in the crowd, and touched his clothes. 28 For she said, "If I just touch his clothes, I will be made well." 29 Immediately the flow of her blood was dried up, and she felt in her body that she was healed of her affliction. 34 He said to her, "Daughter, your faith has made you well. Go in peace, and be cured of your disease."

Mark 10: 51 - 52 (NCV)
51 Jesus asked him, "What do you want me to do for you?" The blind man

answered, "Teacher, I want to see." 52 Jesus said, "Go, you are healed because you believed." At once the man could see, and he followed Jesus on the road.

Mark 16: 17 - 18 (HCSB)
17 And these signs will accompany those who believe: In My name they will drive out demons; they will speak in new languages; 18 they will pick up snakes; if they should drink anything deadly, it will never harm them; they will lay hands on the sick, and they will get well."

Acts 5: 16 (NIV)
16 Crowds gathered also from the towns around Jerusalem, bringing their sick and those tormented by impure spirits, and all of them were healed.

Romans 8: 2, 11 (WEB)
2 For the law of the Spirit of life in Christ Jesus made me free from the law of sin and of death. 11 But if the Spirit of him who raised up Jesus from the dead dwells in you, he who raised up Christ Jesus from the dead will also give life to your mortal bodies through his Spirit who dwells in you.

1 Thessalonians 5: 23 - 24 (RSV)
23 May the God of peace himself sanctify you wholly; and may your spirit and soul and body be kept sound and blameless at the coming of our Lord Jesus Christ. 24 He who calls you is faithful, and he will do it.

James 5: 14 - 16 (NKJV)
14 Is anyone among you sick? Let him call for the elders of the church, and let them pray over him, anointing him with oil in the name of the Lord. 15 And the prayer of faith will save the sick, and the Lord will raise him up. And if he has committed sins, he will be forgiven. 16 Confess your trespasses to one another, and pray for one another, that you may be healed. The effective, fervent prayer of a righteous man avails much.

1 Peter 2: 24 (NIV)
24 "He himself bore our sins" in his body on the cross, so that we might die to sins and live for righ-teousness; "by his wounds you have been healed."

3 John 1: 2 (NASB)
2 Beloved, I pray that in all respects you may prosper and be in good health, just as your soul pros-pers.

HEARING GOD

Exodus 15: 26 (AMP)
26 Saying, If you will diligently hearken to the voice of the Lord your God and will do what is right in His sight, and will listen to and obey His commandments and keep all His statutes, I will put none of the diseases upon you which I brought upon the Egyptians, for I am the Lord Who heals you.

Exodus 19: 5 (LEB)
5 And now if you will carefully listen to my voice and keep my covenant, you will be a treasured pos-session for me out of all the peoples, for all the earth is mine,

Deuteronomy 30: 19 - 20 (MEV)
19 I call heaven and earth to witnesses against you this day, that I have set before you life and death, blessing and

curse. Therefore choose life, that both you and your descendants may live; 20 that you may love the Lord your God, that you may obey His voice, and that you may cling to Him, for He is your life and the length of your days; and that you may dwell in the land that the Lord swore to your fathers, to Abraham, Isaac, and Jacob, to give them.

Psalms 19: 1 - 4 (ESV)

1 The heavens declare the glory of God, and the sky above proclaims his handiwork. 2 Day to day pours out speech, and night to night reveals knowledge. 3 There is no speech, nor are there words, whose voice is not heard. 4 Their voice goes out through all the earth, and their words to the end of the world. In them he has set a tent for the sun,

Psalms 29: 4 - 5, 7 - 8 (NIV)

4 The voice of the Lord is powerful; the voice of the Lord is majestic. 5 The voice of the Lord breaks the cedars; the Lord breaks in pieces the cedars of Lebanon. 7 The voice of the Lord strikes with flashes of lightning. 8 The voice of the Lord shakes the desert; the Lord shakes the Desert of Kadesh.

Psalms 32: 8 - 9 (NKJV)

8 I will instruct you and teach you in the way you should go; I will guide you with My eye. 9 Do not be like the horse or like the mule, Which have no understanding, Which must be harnessed with bit and bridle, Else they will not come near you.

Psalms 39: 4 (NET)

4 O Lord, help me understand my mortality and the brevity of life! Let me realize how quickly my life will pass!

Proverbs 4: 4 (NIV)

4 Then he taught me, and he said to me, "Take hold of my words with all your heart; keep my com-mands, and you will live.

Proverbs 8: 33 - 35 (AMP)

33 Hear instruction and be wise, and do not refuse or neglect it. 34 Blessed (happy, fortunate, to be envied) is the man who listens to me, watching daily at my gates, waiting at the posts of my doors. 35 For whoever finds me [Wisdom] finds life and draws forth and obtains favor from the Lord.

Isaiah 30: 21 (MEV)

21 Your ears shall hear a word behind you, saying, "This is the way, walk in it," whenever you turn to the right hand and when you turn to the left.

Isaiah 55: 3 (TLB)

3 Come to me with your ears wide open. Listen, for the life of your soul is at stake. I am ready to make an everlasting covenant with you, to give you all the unfailing mercies and love that I had for King David.

Matthew 10: 19 - 20 (WEB)

19 But when they deliver you up, don't be anxious how or what you will say, for it will be given you in that hour what you will say. 20 For it is not you who speak, but the Spirit of your Father who speaks in you.

John 10: 3, 27 (NIV)

3 The gatekeeper opens the gate for him, and the sheep listen to his voice. He calls his own sheep by name and leads them out. 27 My sheep listen to my voice; I know them, and they follow me.

John 8: 47 (NIV)
47 Whoever belongs to God hears what God says.

John 16: 15 (NLT)
15 All that belongs to the Father is mine; this is why I said, 'The Spirit will tell you whatever he re-ceives from me.'

Romans 10: 17 (ESV)
17 So faith comes from hearing, and hearing through the word of Christ.

Hebrews 3: 7 - 9, 12 (NLT)
7 That is why the Holy Spirit says, "Today when you hear his voice, 8 don't harden your hearts as Israel did when they rebelled, when they tested me in the wilderness. 9 There your ancestors tested and tried my patience, even though they saw my miracles for forty years. 12 Be careful then, dear brothers and sisters. Make sure that your own hearts are not evil and unbelieving, turning you away from the living God.

Revelation 3: 20 (ESV)
20 Behold, I stand at the door and knock. If anyone hears my voice and opens the door, I will come in to him and eat with him, and he with me.

HEARING VOICES

Leviticus 19: 31 (NIV)
31 Do not turn to mediums or seek out spiritists, for you will be defiled by them. I am the Lord your God.

Psalms 32: 7 (NKJV)
7 You are my hiding place; You shall preserve me from trouble; You shall surround me with songs of deliverance. Selah

Isaiah 30: 21 (NLT)
21 Your own ears will hear him. Right behind you a voice will say, "This is the way you should go," whether to the right or to the left.

John 10: 27 (NLT)
27 My sheep listen to my voice; I know them, and they follow me.

John 16: 13 (NASB)
13 But when He, the Spirit of truth, comes, He will guide you into all the truth; for He will not speak on His own initiative, but whatever He hears, He will speak; and He will disclose to you what is to come.

1 Corinthians 14: 33 (NCV)
33 God is not a God of confusion but a God of peace. As is true in all the churches of God's people,

Philippians 4: 8 - 9 (NKJV)
8 Finally, brethren, whatever things are true, whatever things are noble, whatever things are just, whatever things are pure, whatever things are lovely, whatever things are of good report, if there is any virtue and if there is anything praiseworthy—meditate on these things. 9 The things which you learned and received and heard and saw in me, these do, and the God of peace will be with you.

1 Thessalonians 5: 19 - 22 (NIV)
19 Do not quench the Spirit. 20 Do not treat prophecies with contempt 21 but test them all; hold on to what is good, 22 reject every kind of evil

2 Timothy 1: 7 (NKJV)
7 For God has not given us a spirit of fear, but of power and of love and of a sound mind.

James 3: 16 (NKJV)
16 For where envy and self-seeking exist, confusion and every evil thing are there.

1 John 4: 3 (WEB)
3 and every spirit who doesn't confess that Jesus Christ has come in the flesh is not of God, and this is the spirit of the Antichrist, of whom you have heard that it comes. Now it is in the world already.

Revelation 3: 20 (NIV)
20 Here I am! I stand at the door and knock. If anyone hears my voice and opens the door, I will come in and eat with that person, and they with me.

HEAVEN

2 Chronicles 18: 18 (GNT)
18 Micaiah went on: "Now listen to what the Lord says! I saw the Lord sitting on his throne in heaven, with all his angels standing beside him.

Psalms 11: 4 (NLT)
4 But the Lord is in his holy Temple; the Lord still rules from heaven. He watches everyone closely, examining every person on earth.

Psalms 19: 1 - 2 (NET)
1 The heavens declare the glory of God; the sky displays his handiwork. 2 Day after day it speaks out; night after night it reveals his greatness.

Psalms 33: 6 (NKJV)
6 By the word of the Lord the heavens were made, And all the host of them by the breath of His mouth.

Psalms 57: 3 (HCSB)
3 He reaches down from heaven and saves me, challenging the one who tramples me.Selah God sends His faithful love and truth.

Psalms 119: 89 (HCSB)
89 Lord, Your word is forever; it is firmly fixed in heaven.

Matthew 5: 11 - 12 (NET)
11 "Blessed are you when people insult you and persecute you and say all kinds of evil things about you falsely on account of me. 12 Rejoice and be glad because your reward is great in heaven, for they persecuted the prophets before you in the same way.

Matthew 7: 21 (AMP)
21 Not everyone who says to Me, Lord, Lord, will enter the kingdom of heaven, but he who does the will of My Father Who is in heaven.

Matthew 10: 7 - 8 (NASB)
7 And as you go, preach, saying, 'The kingdom of heaven is at hand.' 8 Heal the sick, raise the dead, cleanse the lepers, cast out demons. Freely you received, freely give.

Matthew 16: 19 (NET)
19 I will give you the keys of the kingdom of heaven. Whatever you bind on earth will have been bound in heaven, and whatever you release on earth will have been released in heaven."

Matthew 18: 19 (CEV)
19 Again I assure you that if two of you agree on earth about anything you ask, then my Father who is in heaven will do it for you.

Luke 10: 18 - 19 (RSV)
18 And he said to them, "I saw Satan fall like lightning from heaven. 19 Behold, I have given you au-thority to tread upon serpents and scorpions, and over all the power of the enemy; and nothing shall hurt you.

Luke 11: 2 (MEV)
2 He said to them, "When you pray, say: Our Father, who is in heaven, hallowed be Your name. Your kingdom come; Your will be done on earth, as it is in heaven.

John 14: 2 - 3 (ASV)
2 In my Father's house are many mansions; if it were not so, I would have told you; for I go to prepare a place for you. 3 And if I go and prepare a place for you, I come again, and will receive you unto my-self; that where I am, there ye may be also.

John 3: 27 (WEB)
27 John answered, "A man can receive nothing, unless it has been given him from heaven.

Ephesians 1: 3 (NKJV)
3 Blessed be the God and Father of our Lord Jesus Christ, who has blessed us with every spiritual blessing in the heavenly places in Christ,

Ephesians 2: 6 (NCV)
6 And he raised us up with Christ and gave us a seat with him in the heavens. He did this for those in Christ Jesus.

Romans 8: 26 (NKJV)
26 Likewise the Spirit also helps in our weaknesses. For we do not know what we should pray for as we ought, but the Spirit Himself makes intercession for us with groanings which cannot be uttered.

HEAVY LADEN

Genesis 28: 15 (ESV)
15 Behold, I am with you and will keep you wherever you go, and will bring you back to this land. For I will not leave you until I have done what I have promised you.

2 Chronicles 33: 12 (ESV)
12 And when he was in distress, he entreated the favor of the Lord his God and humbled himself greatly before the God of his fathers.

Psalms 6: 7 - 9 (GW)
7 My eyes blur from grief. They fail because of my enemies. 8 Get away from me, all you troublemak-ers, because the Lord has heard the sound of my crying. 9 The Lord has heard my plea for mercy. The Lord accepts my prayer.

Psalms 12: 5 (NKJV)
5 "For the oppression of the poor, for the sighing of the needy, Now I will arise," says the Lord; "I will set him in the safety for which he yearns."
Psalms 30: 11 - 12 (NLT)
11 You have turned my mourning into joyful dancing. You have taken away my clothes of mourning and clothed me with joy, 12 that I might sing praises

to you and not be silent. O Lord my God, I will give you thanks forever!

Psalms 34: 18 (NIV)

18 The Lord is close to the brokenhearted and saves those who are crushed in spirit.

Psalms 37: 24 (NIV)

24 though he may stumble, he will not fall, for the Lord upholds him with his hand.

Psalms 42: 11 (NIV)

11 Why, my soul, are you downcast? Why so disturbed within me? Put your hope in God, for I will yet praise him, my Savior and my God.

Psalms 55: 22 (NLT)

22 Give your burdens to the Lord, and he will take care of you. He will not permit the godly to slip and fall.

Psalms 68: 9 (NIV)

9 You gave abundant showers, O God; you refreshed your weary inheritance.

Psalms 119: 28 (NKJV)

28 My soul melts from heaviness; Strengthen me according to Your word.

Psalms 121: 1 - 3 (HCSB)

1 I lift my eyes toward the mountains. Where will my help come from? 2 My help comes from the Lord, the Maker of heaven and earth. 3 He will not allow your foot to slip; your Protector will not slum-ber.

Psalms 126: 5 - 6 (HCSB)

5 Those who sow in tears will reap with shouts of joy. 6 Though one goes along weeping, carrying the bag of seed, he will surely come back with shouts of joy, carrying his sheaves.

Psalms 138: 7 - 8 (NASB)

7 Though I walk in the midst of trouble, You will revive me; You will stretch forth Your hand against the wrath of my enemies, And Your right hand will save me. 8 The Lord will accomplish what concerns me; Your lovingkindness, O Lord, is everlasting; Do not forsake the works of Your hands.

Proverbs 4: 11 - 13 (NASB)

11 I have directed you in the way of wisdom; I have led you in upright paths. 12 When you walk, your steps will not be impeded; And if you run, you will not stumble. 13 Take hold of instruction; do not let go. Guard her, for she is your life.

Isaiah 40: 29, 31 (NIV)

29 He gives strength to the weary and increases the power of the weak. 31 but those who hope in the Lord will renew their strength. They will soar on wings like eagles; they will run and not grow weary, they will walk and not be faint.

Isaiah 42: 16 (ESV)

16 And I will lead the blind in a way that they do not know, in paths that they have not known I will guide them. I will turn the darkness before them into light, the rough places into level ground. These are the things I do, and I do not forsake them.

Jeremiah 12: 5 (NASB)

5 If you have run with footmen and they have tired you out, Then how can you compete with horses? If you fall down in a land of peace, How will you do in the thicket of the Jordan?

Jeremiah 31: 25 (NASB)
25 For I satisfy the weary ones and refresh everyone who languishes.

Matthew 11: 28 - 29 (ESV)
28 Come to me, all who labor and are heavy laden, and I will give you rest. 29 Take my yoke upon you, and learn from me, for I am gentle and lowly in heart, and you will find rest for your souls.

2 Corinthians 1: 3 - 4 (NKJV)
3 Blessed be the God and Father of our Lord Jesus Christ, the Father of mercies and God of all comfort, 4 who comforts us in all our tribulation, that we may be able to comfort those who are in any trouble, with the comfort with which we ourselves are comforted by God.

Romans 8: 26 (NKJV)
26 Likewise the Spirit also helps in our weaknesses. For we do not know what we should pray for as we ought, but the Spirit Himself makes intercession for us with groanings which cannot be uttered.

HELPER

Exodus 23: 20 - 23 (NET)
20 "I am going to send an angel before you to protect you as you journey and to bring you into the place that I have prepared. 21 Take heed because of him, and obey his voice; do not rebel against him, for he will not pardon your transgressions, for my name is in him. 22 But if you diligently obey him and do all that I command, then I will be an enemy to your enemies, and I will be an adversary to your adversaries. 23 For

my angel will go before you and bring you to the Amorites, the Hittites, the Perizzites, the Canaanites, the Hivites, and the Jebusites, and I will destroy them completely.

1 Samuel 2: 8 - 9 (ESV)
8 He raises up the poor from the dust; he lifts the needy from the ash heap to make them sit with princes and inherit a seat of honor. For the pillars of the earth are the Lord's, and on them he has set the world. 9 "He will guard the feet of his faithful ones, but the wicked shall be cut off in darkness, for not by might shall a man prevail.

Psalms 27: 5 (AMP)
5 For in the day of trouble He will hide me in His shelter; in the secret place of His tent will He hide me; He will set me high upon a rock.

Psalms 28: 7 (NLT)
7 The Lord is my strength and shield. I trust him with all my heart. He helps me, and my heart is filled with joy. I burst out in songs of thanksgiving.

Psalms 34: 7 (NIV)
7 The angel of the Lord encamps around those who fear him, and he delivers them.

Psalms 34: 19 (MEV)
19 Many are the afflictions of the righteous, but the Lord delivers him out of them all.

Psalms 37: 23 - 24 (GNT)
23 The Lord guides us in the way we should go and protects those who please him. 24 If they fall, they will not stay down, because the Lord will help them up.

Psalms 40: 1 - 2 (GNT)

1 I waited patiently for the Lord's help; then he listened to me and heard my cry. 2 He pulled me out of a dangerous pit, out of the deadly quicksand. He set me safely on a rock and made me secure.

Psalms 63: 5 - 7 (NLT)

5 You satisfy me more than the richest feast. I will praise you with songs of joy. 6 I lie awake thinking of you, meditating on you through the night. 7 Because you are my helper, I sing for joy in the shadow of your wings.

Psalms 91: 14 - 15 (NKJV)

14 Because he has set his love upon Me, therefore I will deliver him; I will set him on high, because he has known My name. 15 He shall call upon Me, and I will answer him; I will be with him in trouble; I will deliver him and honor him.

Psalms 105: 12, 14 (NCV)

12 Then God's people were few in number. They were strangers in the land. 14 But the Lord did not let anyone hurt them; he warned kings not to harm them.

Psalms 116: 6 (GNT)

6 The Lord protects the helpless; when I was in danger, he saved me.

Psalms 118: 13 - 16 (GNT)

13 I was fiercely attacked and was being defeated, but the Lord helped me. 14 The Lord makes me powerful and strong; he has saved me. 15 Listen to the glad shouts of victory in the tents of God's people: "The Lord's mighty power has done it! 16 His power has brought us victory— his mighty pow-er in battle!"

Psalms 118: 5 - 10 (GNT)

5 In my distress I called to the Lord; he answered me and set me free. 6 The Lord is with me, I will not be afraid; what can anyone do to me? 7 It is the Lord who helps me, and I will see my enemies de-feated. 8 It is better to trust in the Lord than to depend on people. 9 It is better to trust in the Lord than to depend on human leaders. 10 Many enemies were around me; but I destroyed them by the power of the Lord!

Psalms 121: 1 - 3 (MEV)

1 I will lift up my eyes to the hills, from where does my help come? 2 My help comes from the Lord, who made heaven and earth. 3 He will not let your foot slip; He who keeps you will not slumber.

Psalms 145: 14 (NIV)

14 The Lord upholds all who fall and lifts up all who are bowed down.

Isaiah 30: 21 (MEV)

21 Your ears shall hear a word behind you, saying, "This is the way, walk in it," whenever you turn to the right hand and when you turn to the left.

Isaiah 40: 29 - 31 (NET)

29 He gives strength to those who are tired; to the ones who lack power, he gives renewed energy 30 Even youths get tired and weary; even strong young men clumsily stumble. 31 But those who wait for the Lord's help find renewed strength; they rise up as if they had eagles' wings, they run without

growing weary, they walk without getting tired.

Isaiah 41: 10 (NIV)
10 So do not fear, for I am with you do not be dismayed, for I am your God. I will strengthen you and help you; I will uphold you with my righteous right hand.

Isaiah 41: 17 (NLT)
17 When the poor and needy search for water and there is none, and their tongues are parched from thirst, then I, the Lord, will answer them. I, the God of Israel, will never abandon them.

Isaiah 54: 14 - 15, 17 (NKJV)
14 In righteousness you shall be established; You shall be far from oppression, for you shall not fear; And from terror, for it shall not come near you. 15 Indeed they shall surely assemble, but not because of Me. Whoever assembles against you shall fall for your sake. 17 No weapon formed against you shall prosper, And every tongue which rises against you in judgment You shall condemn. This is the heritage of the servants of the Lord, And their righteousness is from Me," Says the Lord.

Zephaniah 3: 17 (NCV)
17 The Lord your God is with you; the mighty One will save you. He will rejoice over you. You will rest in his love; he will sing and be joyful about you.

John 14: 16 - 17 (NKJV)
16 And I will pray the Father, and He will give you another Helper, that He may abide with you for-ever— 17 the Spirit of truth, whom the world cannot

receive, because it neither sees Him nor knows Him; but you know Him, for He dwells with you and will be in you.

1 Corinthians 15: 57 - 58 (HCSB)
57 But thanks be to God, who gives us the victory through our Lord Jesus Christ! 58 Therefore, my dear brothers, be steadfast, immovable, always excelling in the Lord's work, knowing that your labor in the Lord is not in vain.

2 Corinthians 2: 14 (WEB)
14 Now thanks be to God, who always leads us in triumph in Christ, and reveals through us the sweet aroma of his knowledge in every place.

Philippians 4: 11 - 13 (NLT)
11 Not that I was ever in need, for I have learned how to be content with whatever I have. 12 I know how to live on almost nothing or with everything. I have learned the secret of living in every situa-tion, whether it is with a full stomach or empty, with plenty or little. 13 For I can do everything through Christ,[a] who gives me strength.

Hebrews 4: 16 (TLB)
16 So let us come boldly to the very throne of God and stay there to receive his mercy and to find grace to help us in our times of need.

Hebrews 13: 6 (NKJV)
6 So we may boldly say: "The Lord is my helper; I will not fear. What can man do to me?"

James 1: 5 (HCSB)
5 Now if any of you lacks wisdom, he should ask God, who gives to all

generously and without criticiz-ing, and it will be given to him.

Jude 1: 24 (GNT)
24 To him who is able to keep you from falling and to bring you faultless and joyful before his glorious presence

HIGH MINDEDNESS

Psalms 12: 3 (NKJV)
3 May the Lord cut off all flattering lips, And the tongue that speaks proud things,

Psalms 18: 27 (NIV)
27 You save the humble but bring low those whose eyes are haughty.

Psalms 101: 5 (AMP)
5 Whoso privily slanders his neighbor, him will I cut off [from me]; he who has a haughty look and a proud and arrogant heart I cannot and I will not tolerate.

Proverbs 3: 7 - 8 (NKJV)
7 Do not be wise in your own eyes; Fear the Lord and depart from evil. 8 It will be health to your flesh, And strength to your bones.

Proverbs 6: 16 - 17 (NASB)
16 There are six things which the Lord hates, Yes, seven which are an abomination to Him: 17 Haughty eyes, a lying tongue, And hands that shed innocent blood,

Proverbs 16: 5, 18 (NIV)
5 The Lord detests all the proud of heart. Be sure of this: They will not go unpunished. 18 Pride goes before destruction, a haughty spirit before a fall.

Proverbs 18: 11 - 12 (AMP)
11 The rich man's wealth is his strong city, and as a high protecting wall in his own imagination and conceit. 12 Haughtiness comes before disaster, but humility before honor.

Proverbs 21: 4 (NLV)
4 Eyes lifted high and a proud heart is sin and is the lamp of the sinful.

Proverbs 26: 12 (NKJV)
12 Do you see a man wise in his own eyes? There is more hope for a fool than for him.

Proverbs 28: 25 (NLV)
25 A proud man starts fights, but all will go well for the man who trusts in the Lord.

Ecclesiastes 7: 8 (DARBY)
8 Better is the end of a thing than its beginning; better is a patient spirit than a proud spirit.

Isaiah 64: 6 (TLB)
6 We are all infected and impure with sin. When we put on our prized robes of righteousness, we find they are but filthy rags. Like autumn leaves we fade, wither, and fall. And our sins, like the wind, sweep us away.

Isaiah 65: 5 (ESV)
5 who say, "Keep to yourself, do not come near me, for I am too holy for you." These are a smoke in my nostrils, a fire that burns all the day.

Matthew 7: 1 - 5 (NIV)
1 "Don't judge others, or you will be judged. 2 You will be judged in the same way that you judge others, and the amount you give to others will be

given to you. 3 "Why do you notice the little piece of dust in your friend's eye, but you don't notice the big piece of wood in your own eye? 4 How can you say to your friend, 'Let me take that little piece of dust out of your eye'? Look at yourself! You still have that big piece of wood in your own eye. 5 You hypocrite! First, take the wood out of your own eye. Then you will see clearly to take the dust out of your friend's eye.

Luke 18: 9, 11 - 14 (NIV)
9 To some who were confident of their own righteousness and looked down on everyone else, Jesus told this parable: 11 The Pharisee stood by himself and prayed: 'God, I thank you that I am not like other people—robbers, evildoers, adulterers—or even like this tax collector. 12 I fast twice a week and give a tenth of all I get.' 13 "But the tax collector stood at a distance. He would not even look up to heaven, but beat his breast and said, 'God, have mercy on me, a sinner.' 14 "I tell you that this man, rather than the other, went home justified before God. For all those who exalt themselves will be humbled, and those who humble themselves will be exalted."

Romans 12: 16 - 18 (NIV)
16 Live in harmony with one another. Do not be proud, but be willing to associate with people of low position. Do not be conceited. 17 Do not repay anyone evil for evil. Be careful to do what is right in the eyes of everyone. 18 If it is possible, as far as it depends on you, live at peace with everyone.

1 Corinthians 13: 4 - 7 (NIVUK)
4 Love is patient, love is kind. It does not envy, it does not boast, it is not proud. 5 It does not dishon-our others, it is not self-seeking, it is not easily angered, it keeps no record of wrongs. 6 Love does not delight in evil but rejoices with the truth. 7 It always protects, always trusts, always hopes, always perseveres.

2 Corinthians 10: 17 - 18 (NIV)
17 But, "Let the one who boasts boast in the Lord." 18 For it is not the one who commends himself who is approved, but the one whom the Lord commends.

HOLY SPIRIT IN YOU

Proverbs 1: 23 (ESV)
23 If you turn at my reproof, behold, I will pour out my spirit to you; I will make my words known to you.

Isaiah 30: 21 (NIV)
21 Whether you turn to the right or to the left, your ears will hear a voice behind you, saying, "This is the way; walk in it."

Isaiah 59: 21 (GNT)
21 And I make a covenant with you: I have given you my power and my teachings to be yours forever, and from now on you are to obey me and teach your children and your descendants to obey me for all time to come.

Jeremiah 23: 23 - 24 (AMP)
23 Am I a God at hand, says the Lord, and not a God afar off? 24 Can anyone hide himself in secret places so that I cannot see him? says the Lord. Do not I fill heaven and earth? says the Lord.

Luke 11: 13 (NLT)
13 So if you sinful people know how to give good gifts to your children, how

much more will your heavenly Father give the Holy Spirit to those who ask him.

John 14: 16 - 17, 20 (NKJV)
16 And I will pray the Father, and He will give you another Helper, that He may abide with you for-ever— 17 the Spirit of truth, whom the world cannot receive, because it neither sees Him nor knows Him; but you know Him, for He dwells with you and will be in you. 20 At that day you will know that I am in My Father, and you in Me, and I in you.

Acts 1: 4 - 5, 8 (NIV)
4 On one occasion, while he was eating with them, he gave them this command: "Do not leave Jeru-salem, but wait for the gift my Father promised, which you have heard me speak about. 5 For John baptized with water, but in a few days you will be baptized with the Holy Spirit." 8 But you will receive power when the Holy Spirit comes on you; and you will be my witnesses in Jerusalem, and in all Ju-dea and Samaria, and to the ends of the earth."

Acts 2: 4 (NIV)
4 All of them were filled with the Holy Spirit and began to speak in other tongues as the Spirit enabled them.

Acts 4: 31 (NIV)
31 After they prayed, the place where they were meeting was shaken. And they were all filled with the Holy Spirit and spoke the word of God boldly.

Acts 10: 44 - 47 (GNT)
44 While Peter was still speaking, the Holy Spirit came down on all those who were listening to his message. 45 The Jewish believers who had come from Joppa with Peter were amazed that God had poured out his gift of the Holy Spirit on the Gentiles also. 46 For they heard them speaking in strange tongues and praising God's greatness. Peter spoke up: 47 "These people have received the Holy Spirit, just as we also did. Can anyone, then, stop them from being baptized with water?"

Romans 5: 5 (MEV)
5 And hope does not disappoint, because the love of God is shed abroad in our hearts by the Holy Spirit who has been given to us.

Romans 8: 26 - 27 (MEV)
26 Likewise, the Spirit helps us in our weaknesses, for we do not know what to pray for as we ought, but the Spirit Himself intercedes for us with groanings too deep for words. 27 He who searches the hearts knows what the mind of the Spirit is, because He intercedes for the saints according to the will of God.

1 Corinthians 6: 19 - 20 (NIVUK)
19 Do you not know that your bodies are temples of the Holy Spirit, who is in you, whom you have received from God? You are not your own; 20 you were bought at a price. Therefore honour God with your bodies.

Galatians 3: 14 (HCSB)
14 The purpose was that the blessing of Abraham would come to the Gentiles by Christ Jesus, so that we could receive the promised Spirit through faith.

Galatians 5: 16 - 17 (HCSB)
16 I say then, walk by the Spirit and you will not carry out the desire of the flesh. 17 For the flesh de-sires what is against the Spirit, and the Spirit desires what is

against the flesh; these are opposed to each other, so that you don't do what you want.

1 John 2: 27 (NIVUK)

27 As for you, the anointing you received from him remains in you, and you do not need anyone to teach you. But as his anointing teaches you about all things and as that anointing is real, not counter-feit – just as it has taught you, remain in him.

HOPE

Psalms 33: 18, 22 (NKJV)

18 Behold, the eye of the Lord is on those who fear Him, On those who hope in His mercy, 22 Let Your mercy, O Lord, be upon us, Just as we hope in You.

Psalms 42: 11 (NKJV)

11 Why are you cast down, O my soul? And why are you disquieted within me? Hope in God; For I shall yet praise Him, The help of my countenance and my God.

Psalms 119: 49 - 50 (NIV)

49 Remember your word to your servant, for you have given me hope. 50 My comfort in my suffering is this: Your promise preserves my life.

Psalms 147: 11 (MEV)

11 but the Lord takes pleasure in those who fear Him, in those who hope in His mercy.

Proverbs 10:28 (NLV)

28 The hope of those who are right with God is joy, but the hope of the sinful comes to nothing.

Jeremiah 29: 11 (GNT)

11 I alone know the plans I have for you, plans to bring you prosperity and not disaster, plans to bring about the future you hope for.

Lamentations 3: 22 - 26 (NKJV)

22 Through the Lord's mercies we are not consumed, Because His compassions fail not. 23 They are new every morning; Great is Your faithfulness. 24 "The Lord is my portion," says my soul, "There-fore I hope in Him!" 25 The Lord is good to those who wait for Him, To the soul who seeks Him. 26 It is good that one should hope and wait quietly For the salvation of the Lord.

Habakkuk 3: 17 - 28 (GNT)

17 Even though the fig trees have no fruit and no grapes grow on the vines, even though the olive crop fails and the fields produce no grain, even though the sheep all die and the cattle stalls are emp - ty, 18 I will still be joyful and glad, because the Lord God is my savior. 19 The Sovereign Lord gives me strength. He makes me sure-footed as a deer and keeps me safe on the mountains.

Zechariah 9: 12 (NIV)

12 Return to your fortress, you prisoners of hope; even now I announce that I will restore twice as much to you.

Romans 5: 3 - 5 (MEV)

3 Not only so, but we also boast in tribulation, knowing that tribulation produces patience, 4 patience produces character, and character produces hope. 5 And hope does not disappoint, because the love of God is shed abroad in our hearts by the Holy Spirit who has been given to us.

Romans 8: 24 - 25 (MEV)
24 For we are saved through hope, but hope that is seen is not hope, for why does a man still hope for what he sees? 25 But if we hope for what we do not see, we wait for it with patience.

Romans 15: 13 (NKJV)
13 Now may the God of hope fill you with all joy and peace in believing, that you may abound in hope by the power of the Holy Spirit.

Ephesians 1: 18 - 23 (GNT)
18 I ask that your minds may be opened to see his light, so that you will know what is the hope to which he has called you, how rich are the wonderful blessings he promises his people, 19 and how very great is his power at work in us who believe. This power working in us is the same as the mighty strength 20 which he used when he raised Christ from death and seated him at his right side in the heavenly world. 21 Christ rules there above all heavenly rulers, authorities, powers, and lords; he has a title superior to all titles of authority in this world and in the next. 22 God put all things under Christ's feet and gave him to the church as supreme Lord over all things. 23 The church is Christ's body, the completion of him who himself completes all things everywhere.

Hebrews 11: 1 - 3, 6 (HCSB)
1 Now faith is the reality of what is hoped for, the proof of what is not seen. 2 For our ancestors won God's approval by it. 3 By faith we understand that the universe was created by God's command, so that what is seen has been made from things that are not visible. 6 Now without faith it is impossible to please God, for the one who draws near

to Him must believe that He exists and rewards those who seek Him.

1 Peter 1: 21 (MEV)
21 Through Him you believe in God who raised Him up from the dead and gave Him glory, so that your faith and hope might be in God.

HOUSING

Psalms 112: 1, 3 (ESV)
1 Praise the Lord! Blessed is the man who fears the Lord, who greatly delights in his commandments! 3 Wealth and riches are in his house, and his righteousness endures forever.

Psalms 113: 9 (ESV)
9 He gives the barren woman a home, making her the joyous mother of children. Praise the Lord!

Proverbs 1: 33 (MEV)
33 But whoever listens to me will dwell safely, and will be secure from fear of evil.

Proverbs 2: 20 - 21 (AMP)
20 So may you walk in the way of good men, and keep to the paths of the [consistently] righteous (the upright, in right standing with God). 21 For the upright shall dwell in the land, and the men of integrity, blameless and complete [in God's sight], shall remain in it;

Proverbs 24: 3 - 4 (NKJV)
3 Through wisdom a house is built, And by understanding it is established; 4 By knowledge the rooms are filled With all precious and pleasant riches.

Isaiah 32: 18 (NIV)
18 My people will live in peaceful dwelling places, in secure homes, in undisturbed places of rest.

Matthew 6: 33 (NCV)
33 Seek first God's kingdom and what God wants. Then all your other needs will be met as well.

Matthew 7: 11 (WEB)
11 If you then, being evil, know how to give good gifts to your children, how much more will your Fa-ther who is in heaven give good things to those who ask him!

Acts 17: 26 (AMP)
26 And He made from one [common origin, one source, one blood] all nations of men to settle on the face of the earth, having definitely determined [their] allotted periods of time and the fixed boundaries of their habitation (their settlements, lands, and abodes),

Ephesians 3: 20 (WEB)
20 Now to him who is able to do exceedingly abundantly above all that we ask or think, according to the power that works in us,

Philippians 4: 19 (NCV)
19 My God will use his wonderful riches in Christ Jesus to give you everything you need.

HOW LONG

Joshua 18: 3 (NLT)
3 Then Joshua asked them, "How long are you going to wait before taking possession of the remain-ing land the Lord, the God of your ancestors, has given to you?"

Psalms 12: 5 (HCSB)
5 "Because of the oppression of the afflicted and the groaning of the poor, I will now rise up," says the Lord. "I will put the one who longs for it in a safe place."

Psalms 13: 1 - 6 (NLT)
1 O Lord, how long will you forget me? Forever? How long will you look the other way? 2 How long must I struggle with anguish in my soul, with sorrow in my heart every day? How long will my enemy have the upper hand? 3 Turn and answer me, O Lord my God! Restore the sparkle to my eyes, or I will die. 4 Don't let my enemies gloat, saying, "We have defeated him!" Don't let them rejoice at my downfall. 5 But I trust in your unfailing love. I will rejoice because you have rescued me. 6 I will sing to the Lord because he is good to me.

Psalms 31: 2 - 4 (NIV)
2 Turn your ear to me, come quickly to my rescue; be my rock of refuge, a strong fortress to save me. 3 Since you are my rock and my fortress, for the sake of your name lead and guide me. 4 Keep me free from the trap that is set for me, for you are my refuge.

Psalms 35: 17 - 18, 22 (MEV)
17 Lord, how long will You look on? Rescue my soul from their destructions, my life from the lions. 18 I will give You thanks in the great congregation; I will praise You among a mighty people. 22 This You have seen, O Lord; do not be silent; O Lord, be not far from me.

Psalms 118: 21 - 24 (NIV)

21 I will give you thanks, for you answered me; you have become my salvation. 22 The stone the builders rejected has become the cornerstone; 23 the Lord has done this, and it is marvelous in our eyes. 24 The Lord has done it this very day; let us rejoice today and be glad.

Psalms 143: 7 - 8 (GW)

7 Answer me quickly, O Lord. My spirit is worn out. Do not hide your face from me, or I will be like those who go into the pit. 8 Let me hear about your mercy in the morning, because I trust you. Let me know the way that I should go, because I long for you.

Jeremiah 1: 12 (NKJV)

12 Then the Lord said to me, "You have seen well, for I am ready to perform My word."

Luke 18: 7 - 8 (RSV)

7 And will not God vindicate his elect, who cry to him day and night? Will he delay long over them? 8 I tell you, he will vindicate them speedily. Nevertheless, when the Son of man comes, will he find faith on earth?

2 Corinthians 6: 1 - 2 (ESV)

1 Working together with him, then, we appeal to you not to receive the grace of God in vain. 2 For he says, "In a favorable time I listened to you, and in a day of salvation I have helped you." Behold, now is the favorable time; behold, now is the day of salvation.

HUMBLE

2 Chronicles 7: 14 (GW)

14 However, if my people, who are called by my name, will humble themselves, pray, search for me, and turn from their evil ways, then I will hear their prayer from heaven, forgive their sins, and heal their country.

Psalms 9: 12 (NKJV)

12 When He avenges blood, He remembers them; He does not forget the cry of the humble.

Psalms 10: 17 (AMP)

17 O Lord, You have heard the desire and the longing of the humble and oppressed; You will prepare and strengthen and direct their hearts, You will cause Your ear to hear,

Psalms 22: 26 (HCSB)

26 The humble will eat and be satisfied; those who seek the Lord will praise Him. May your hearts live forever!

Psalms 25: 9 (NIV)

9 He guides the humble in what is right and teaches them his way.

Psalms 147: 6 (NIV)

6 The Lord sustains the humble but casts the wicked to the ground.

Proverbs 3: 34 (GNT)

34 He has no use for conceited people, but shows favor to those who are humble.

Proverbs 11: 2 (NIV)

2 When pride comes, then comes disgrace, but with humility comes wisdom.

Proverbs 15: 1, 33 (NIV)
1 A gentle answer turns away wrath, but a harsh word stirs up anger. 33 Wisdom's instruction is to fear the Lord, and humility comes before honor.

Proverbs 16: 19 (NKJV)
19 Better to be of a humble spirit with the lowly, Than to divide the spoil with the proud.

Proverbs 22: 4 (NKJV)
4 By humility and the fear of the Lord Are riches and honor and life.

Isaiah 29: 19 (NIV)
19 Once more the humble will rejoice in the Lord; the needy will rejoice in the Holy One of Israel.

Isaiah 57: 15 (NIV)
15 For this is what the high and exalted One says— he who lives forever, whose name is holy: "I live in a high and holy place, but also with the one who is contrite and lowly in spirit, to revive the spirit of the lowly and to revive the heart of the contrite.

Micah 6: 8 (NKJV)
8 He has shown you, O man, what is good; And what does the Lord require of you But to do justly, To love mercy, And to walk humbly with your God?

Matthew 18: 3 - 4 (NLT)
3 Then he said, "I tell you the truth, unless you turn from your sins and become like little children, you will never get into the Kingdom of Heaven. 4 So anyone who becomes as humble as this little child is the greatest in the Kingdom of Heaven.

Matthew 23: 12 (NET)
12 And whoever exalts himself will be humbled, and whoever humbles himself will be exalted.

1 Corinthians 13: 4 - 7 (NIVUK)
4 Love is patient, love is kind. It does not envy, it does not boast, it is not proud. 5 It does not dishon-our others, it is not self-seeking, it is not easily angered, it keeps no record of wrongs. 6 Love does not delight in evil but rejoices with the truth. 7 It always protects, always trusts, always hopes, always perseveres.

Colossians 3: 12 (NET)
12 Therefore, as the elect of God, holy and dearly loved, clothe yourselves with a heart of mercy, kindness, humility, gentleness, and patience,

James 4: 6 (NIV)
6 But he gives us more grace. That is why Scripture says: "God opposes the proud but shows favor to the humble."

1 Peter 3: 3 - 4 (NIV)
3 Your beauty should not come from outward adornment, such as elaborate hairstyles and the wear-ing of gold jewelry or fine clothes. 4 Rather, it should be that of your inner self, the unfading beauty of a gentle and quiet spirit, which is of great worth in God's sight.

1 Peter 5: 6 (NKJV)
6 Therefore humble yourselves under the mighty hand of God, that He may exalt you in due time,

IMPOSSIBLE

Genesis 18: 14 (NASB)
14 Is anything too difficult for the Lord? At the appointed time I will return to you, at this time next year, and Sarah will have a son."

Isaiah 59: 1 (NET)
1 Look, the Lord's hand is not too weak to deliver you; his ear is not too deaf to hear you.

Jeremiah 32: 27 (AMP)
27 Behold, I am the Lord, the God of all flesh; is there anything too hard for Me?

Matthew 10: 1 (HCSB)
Summoning His 12 disciples, He gave them authority over unclean spirits, to drive them out and to heal every disease and sickness.

Matthew 17: 20 (WEB)
20 He said to them, "Because of your unbelief. For most certainly I tell you, if you have faith as a grain of mustard seed, you will tell this mountain, 'Move from here to there,' and it will move; and nothing will be impossible for you.

Matthew 18: 19 - 20 (MEV)
19 "Again I say to you, that if two of you agree on earth about anything they ask, it will be done for them by My Father who is in heaven. 20 For where two or three are assembled in My name, there I am in their midst."

Matthew 21: 20 - 22 (GW)
20 The disciples were surprised to see this. They asked, "How did the fig tree dry up so quickly?" 21 Jesus answered them, "I can guarantee this truth: If you have faith and do not doubt, you will be able to do what I did to the fig tree. You could also say to this mountain, 'Be uprooted and thrown into the sea,' and it will happen. 22 Have faith that you will receive whatever you ask for in prayer.

Mark 9: 23 (CEV)
23 Jesus replied, "Why do you say 'if you can'? Anything is possible for someone who has faith!"

Luke 1: 37 (GW)
37 But nothing is impossible for God.
Luke 18: 25 - 27 (NKJV)
25 Indeed, it is easier for a camel to go through the eye of a needle than for a rich person to enter God's kingdom." 26 Those who heard him asked, "Who, then, can be saved?" 27 Jesus said, "The things that are impossible for people to do are possible for God to do."

John 14: 12 - 14 (RSV)
12 I assure you that whoever believes in me will do the works that I do. They will do even greater works than these because I am going to the Father. 13 I will do whatever you ask for in my name, so that the Father can be glorified in the Son. 14 When you ask me for anything in my name, I will do it.

INSIGHT

Psalms 16: 7, 11 (NKJV)
7 I will bless the Lord who has given me counsel; My heart also instructs me in the night seasons. 11 You will show me the path of life; In Your presence is

fullness of joy; At Your right hand are pleasures forevermore.

Psalms 19: 8 - 11 (NIV)
8 The precepts of the Lord are right, giving joy to the heart. The commands of the Lord are radiant, giving light to the eyes. 9 The fear of the Lord is pure, enduring forever. The decrees of the Lord are firm, and all of them are righteous. 10 They are more precious than gold, than much pure gold; they are sweeter than honey, than honey from the honeycomb. 11 By them your servant is warned; in keeping them there is great reward.

Psalms 51: 6 (AMP)
6 Behold, You desire truth in the inner being; make me therefore to know wisdom in my inmost heart.

Proverbs 1: 23 (GW)
23 Turn to me when I warn you. I will generously pour out my spirit for you. I will make my words known to you.

Proverbs 1: 7 (NASB)
7 The fear of the Lord is the beginning of knowledge; Fools despise wisdom and instruction.

Proverbs 2: 3, 7 (GNT)
3 Yes, beg for knowledge; plead for insight. 7 He provides help and protection for those who are righ-teous and honest.

Proverbs 4: 5 - 7, 11 - 12 (NKJV)
5 Get wisdom! Get understanding! Do not forget, nor turn away from the words of my mouth. 6 Do not forsake her, and she will preserve you; Love her, and she will keep you. 7 Wisdom is the principal thing; Therefore get wisdom. And in all your getting, get understanding. 11 I have taught you in the way of wisdom; I have led you in right paths. 12 When you walk, your steps will not be hindered, And when you run, you will not stumble.

Proverbs 28: 5 (NLV)
5 Sinful men do not understand what is right and fair, but those who look to the Lord understand all things.

Ecclesiastes 2: 26 (NKJV)
26 For God gives wisdom and knowledge and joy to a man who is good in His sight; but to the sinner He gives the work of gathering and collecting, that he may give to him who is good before God. This also is vanity and grasping for the wind.

Isaiah 30: 21 (NLT)
21 Your own ears will hear him. Right behind you a voice will say, "This is the way you should go," whether to the right or to the left.

Isaiah 50: 4 (NLT)
4 The Sovereign Lord has given me his words of wisdom, so that I know how to comfort the weary. Morning by morning he wakens me and opens my understanding to his will.

Matthew 10: 19 - 20 (WEB)
19 But when they deliver you up, don't be anxious how or what you will say, for it will be given you in that hour what you will say. 20 For it is not you who speak, but the Spirit of your Father who speaks in you.

Romans 8: 14 (WEB)
14 For as many as are led by the Spirit of God, these are children of God.t:

1 Corinthians 2: 14 - 16 (WEB)
14 Now the natural man doesn't receive the things of God's Spirit, for they are foolishness to him, and he can't know them, because they are spiritually discerned. 15 But he who is spiritual discerns all things, and he himself is judged by no one. 16 "For who has known the mind of the Lord, that he should instruct him?" But we have Christ's mind.

1 Corinthians 12: 8 (ASV)
8 For to one is given through the Spirit the word of wisdom; and to another the word of knowledge, according to the same Spirit.

2 Corinthians 4: 6 (NET)
6 For God, who said "Let light shine out of darkness," is the one who shined in our hearts to give us the light of the glorious knowledge of God in the face of Christ.

Colossians 1: 9 - 10 (RSV)
9 And so, from the day we heard of it, we have not ceased to pray for you, asking that you may be filled with the knowledge of his will in all spiritual wisdom and understanding, 10 to lead a life worthy of the Lord, fully pleasing to him, bearing fruit in every good work and increasing in the knowledge of God.

2 Timothy 3: 16 - 17 (GNT)
16 All Scripture is inspired by God and is useful for teaching the truth, rebuking error, correcting faults, and giving instruction for right living, 17 so that the person who serves God may be fully qualified and equipped to do every kind of good deed.

Hebrews 4: 12 (NLV)
12 God's Word is living and powerful. It is sharper than a sword that cuts both ways. It cuts straight into where the soul and spirit meet and it divides them. It cuts into the joints and bones. It tells what the heart is thinking about and what it wants to do.

1 John 4: 1 (WEB)
1 Beloved, do not believe every spirit, but test the spirits, whether they are of God; because many false prophets have gone out into the world.

INSTRUCT CHILDREN

Deuteronomy 11: 18 - 19 (GW)
18 Take these words of mine to heart and keep them in mind. Write them down, tie them around your wrist, and wear them as headbands as a reminder. 19 Teach them to your children, and talk about them when you're at home or away, when you lie down or get up.

Proverbs 6: 20 - 22 (HCSB)
20 My son, keep your father's command, and don't reject your mother's teaching. 21 Always bind them to your heart; tie them around your neck. 22 When you walk here and there, they will guide you; when you lie down, they will watch over you; when you wake up, they will talk to you.

Proverbs 13: 24 (NCV)
24 If you do not punish your children, you don't love them, but if you love your children, you will cor-rect them.

Proverbs 19: 18 (NIV)
18 Discipline your children, for in that there is hope; do not be a willing party to their death.

Proverbs 22: 6 (NET)
6 Train a child in the way that he should go, and when he is old he will not turn from it.

Proverbs 23: 22 (NIV)
22 Listen to your father, who gave you life, and do not despise your mother when she is old.

Proverbs 29: 17 (HCSB)
17 Discipline your son, and it will bring you peace of mind and give you delight.

Isaiah 59: 21 (GNT)
21 And I make a covenant with you: I have given you my power and my teachings to be yours forever, and from now on you are to obey me and teach your children and your descendants to obey me for all time to come.

Jeremiah 10: 24 (ESV)
24 Correct me, O Lord, but in justice; not in your anger, lest you bring me to nothing.

Ephesians 6: 1 - 4 (WEB)
1 Children, obey your parents in the Lord, for this is right. 2 "Honor your father and mother," which is the first commandment with a promise: 3 "that it may be well with you, and you may live long on the earth." 4 You fathers, don't provoke your children to wrath, but nurture them in the discipline and instruction of the Lord.

Colossians 3: 21 (HCSB)
21 Fathers, do not exasperate your children, so they won't become discouraged.

INSTRUCTION

Psalms 16: 7, 11 (NKJV)
7 I will bless the Lord who has given me counsel; My heart also instructs me in the night seasons. 11 You will show me the path of life; In Your presence is fullness of joy; At Your right hand are pleasures forevermore.

Psalms 25: 12 - 13 (NLT)
12 Who are those who fear the Lord? He will show them the path they should choose. 13 They will live in prosperity, and their children will inherit the land.

Psalms 27: 11 (NIV)
11 Teach me your way, Lord; lead me in a straight path because of my oppressors.

Psalms 32: 8 (HCSB)
8 I will instruct you and show you the way to go; with My eye on you, I will give counsel.

Psalms 94: 12 (NET)
12 How blessed is the one whom you instruct, O Lord, the one whom you teach from your law,

Psalms 143: 8, 10 (NKJV)
8 Cause me to hear Your lovingkindness in the morning, For in You do I trust; Cause me to know the way in which I should walk, For I lift up my soul to You. 10 Teach me to do Your will, For

You are my God; Your Spirit is good. Lead me in the land of uprightness.

Proverbs 3: 1, 5 - 6 (NET)
1 My child, do not forget my teaching, but let your heart keep my commandments, 5 Trust in the Lord with all your heart, and do not rely on your own understanding. 6 Acknowledge him in all your ways, and he will make your paths straight.

Proverbs 6: 20, 23 (HCSB)
20 My son, keep your father's command, and don't reject your mother's teaching. 23 For a command is a lamp, teaching is a light, and corrective discipline is the way to life.

Isaiah 30: 21 (NET)
21 You will hear a word spoken behind you, saying, "This is the correct way, walk in it," whether you are heading to the right or the left.

Isaiah 48: 17 (NET)
17 This is what the Lord, your protector, says, the Holy One of Israel: "I am the Lord your God, who teaches you how to succeed, who leads you in the way you should go.

Matthew 10: 19 - 20 (WEB)
19 But when they deliver you up, don't be anxious how or what you will say, for it will be given you in that hour what you will say. 20 For it is not you who speak, but the Spirit of your Father who speaks in you.

2 Timothy 3: 16 - 17 (GNT)
16 All Scripture is inspired by God and is useful for teaching the truth, rebuking error, correcting faults, and giving instruction for right living, 17 so that the person who serves God may be fully qualified and equipped to do every kind of good deed.

INTERACTION

Leviticus 19: 18 (NIV)
18 Do not seek revenge or bear a grudge against anyone among your people, but love your neighbor as yourself. I am the Lord.

Deuteronomy 15: 7 - 8, 11 (NKJV)
7 "If there is among you a poor man of your brethren, within any of the gates in your land which the Lord your God is giving you, you shall not harden your heart nor shut your hand from your poor broth-er, 8 but you shall open your hand wide to him and willingly lend him sufficient for his need, whatever he needs. 11 For the poor will never cease from the land; therefore I command you, saying, 'You shall open your hand wide to your brother, to your poor and your needy, in your land.'

Psalms 37: 8 - 9 (HCSB)
8 Refrain from anger and give up your rage; do not be agitated—it can only bring harm. 9 For evildo-ers will be destroyed, but those who put their hope in the Lord will inherit the land.

Psalms 41: 1 (NKJV)
1 Blessed is he who considers the poor; The Lord will deliver him in time of trouble.

Psalms 133: 1 (NIV)
1 How good and pleasant it is when God's people live together in unity!

Proverbs 16: 28 (CEV)

28 Gossip is no good! It causes hard feelings and comes between friends.

Proverbs 17: 14 (GNT)

14 The start of an argument is like the first break in a dam; stop it before it goes any further.

Proverbs 19: 17 (NIV)

17 Whoever is kind to the poor lends to the Lord, and he will reward them for what they have done.

Proverbs 25: 17 (GNT)

17 Don't visit your neighbors too often; they may get tired of you and come to hate you.

Matthew 5: 43 - 48 (NOG)

43 "You have heard that it was said, 'Love your neighbor, and hate your enemy.' 44 But I tell you this: Love your enemies, and pray for those who persecute you. 45 In this way you show that you are chil-dren of your Father in heaven. He makes his sun rise on people whether they are good or evil. He lets rain fall on them whether they are just or unjust. 46 If you love those who love you, do you deserve a reward? Even the tax collectors do that! 47 Are you doing anything remarkable if you welcome only your friends? Everyone does that! 48 That is why you must be perfect as your Father in heaven is perfect.

Matthew 6: 14 - 15 (NIV)

14 For if you forgive other people when they sin against you, your heavenly Father will also forgive you. 15 But if you do not forgive others their sins, your Father will not forgive your sins.

Matthew 7: 1 - 4 (NCV)

1 Don't judge others, or you will be judged. 2 You will be judged in the same way that you judge others, and the amount you give to others will be given to you. 3 "Why do you notice the little piece of dust in your friend's eye, but you don't notice the big piece of wood in your own eye? 4 How can you say to your friend, 'Let me take that little piece of dust out of your eye'? Look at yourself! You still have that big piece of wood in your own eye.

Matthew 18: 21 - 22 (NCV)

21 Then Peter came to Jesus and asked, "Lord, when my fellow believer sins against me, how many times must I forgive him? Should I forgive him as many as seven times?" 22 Jesus answered, "I tell you, you must forgive him more than seven times. You must forgive him even if he wrongs you seven-ty times seven.

Luke 6: 27 - 31, 35, 37 (NIVUK)

27 'But to you who are listening I say: love your enemies, do good to those who hate you, 28 bless those who curse you, pray for those who ill-treat you. 29 If someone slaps you on one cheek, turn to them the other also. If someone takes your coat, do not withhold your shirt from them. 30 Give to everyone who asks you, and if anyone takes what belongs to you, do not demand it back. 31 Do to others as you would have them do to you. 35 But love your enemies, do good to them, and lend to them without expecting to get anything back. Then your reward will be great, and you will be children of the Most High, because he is kind to the ungrateful and wicked. 37 'Do not judge, and you will not be judged.

Do not condemn, and you will not be condemned. Forgive, and you will be forgiven.

John 13: 14 - 15 (CEV)
14 And if your Lord and teacher has washed your feet, you should do the same for each other. 15 I have set the example, and you should do for each other exactly what I have done for you.

Romans 12: 9 - 13 (ESV)
9 Let love be genuine. Abhor what is evil; hold fast to what is good. 10 Love one another with broth-erly affection. Outdo one another in showing honor. 11 Do not be slothful in zeal, be fervent in spirit, serve the Lord. 12 Rejoice in hope, be patient in tribulation, be constant in prayer. 13 Contribute to the needs of the saints and seek to show hospitality.

Romans 14: 1 (NIV)
1 Accept the one whose faith is weak, without quarreling over disputable matters.

1 Corinthians 1: 10 (NIV)
10 I appeal to you, brothers and sisters, in the name of our Lord Jesus Christ, that all of you agree with one another in what you say and that there be no divisions among you, but that you be perfectly united in mind and thought.

1 Corinthians 6: 1 - 5 (HCSB)
1 If any of you has a legal dispute against another, do you dare go to court before the unrighteous, and not before the saints? 2 Or don't you know that the saints will judge the world? And if the world is judged by you, are you unworthy to judge the smallest cases? 3 Don't you know that we will judge angels—not to mention ordinary matters? 4 So if you have cases pertaining to this life, do you select those who have no standing in the church to judge? 5 I say this to your shame! Can it be that there is not one wise person among you who is able to arbitrate between his brothers?

Galatians 5: 13 (NLT)
13 For you have been called to live in freedom, my brothers and sisters. But don't use your freedom to satisfy your sinful nature. Instead, use your freedom to serve one another in love.

Ephesians 4: 25, 29 - 32 (ESV)
25 Therefore, having put away falsehood, let each one of you speak the truth with his neighbor, for we are members one of another. 29 Let no corrupting talk come out of your mouths, but only such as is good for building up, as fits the occasion, that it may give grace to those who hear. 30 And do not grieve the Holy Spirit of God, by whom you were sealed for the day of redemption. 31 Let all bitterness and wrath and anger and clamor and slander be put away from you, along with all malice. 32 Be kind to one another, tenderhearted, forgiving one another, as God in Christ forgave you.

Philippians 2: 3 - 4 (NIV)
3 Do nothing out of selfish ambition or vain conceit. Rather, in humility value others above yourselves, 4 not looking to your own interests but each of you to the interests of the others.

Philippians 4: 5 - 6 (NIV)
5 Let your gentleness be evident to all. The Lord is near. 6 Do not be

anxious about anything, but in every situation, by prayer and petition, with thanksgiving, present your requests to God.

Colossians 3: 23 - 25 (NIVUK)
23 Whatever you do, work at it with all your heart, as working for the Lord, not for human masters, 24 since you know that you will receive an inheritance from the Lord as a reward. It is the Lord Christ you are serving. 25 Anyone who does wrong will be repaid for their wrongs, and there is no favouritism.

1 Peter 3: 8 - 9 (NLT)
8 Finally, all of you should be of one mind. Sympathize with each other. Love each other as brothers and sisters. Be tenderhearted, and keep a humble attitude. 9 Don't repay evil for evil. Don't retaliate with insults when people insult you. Instead, pay them back with a blessing. That is what God has called you to do, and he will grant you his blessing.

JEALOUSY

Psalms 37: 1 - 4 (NIV)
1 Do not fret because of those who are evil or be envious of those who do wrong; 2 for like the grass they will soon wither, like green plants they will soon die away. 3 Trust in the Lord and do good; dwell in the land and enjoy safe pasture. 4 Take delight in the Lord, and he will give you the desires of your heart.

Proverbs 3: 31 - 32 (NKJV)
31 Do not envy the oppressor, And choose none of his ways; 32 For the perverse person is an abomi-nation to the Lord, But His secret counsel is with the upright.

Proverbs 14: 30 (NKJV)
30 A sound heart is life to the body, But envy is rottenness to the bones.

Proverbs 23: 17 - 18 (CEV)
17 Don't be jealous of sinners, but always honor the Lord. 18 Then you will truly have hope for the future.

Proverbs 24: 1 - 2 (NIV)
1 Do not envy the wicked, do not desire their company; 2 for their hearts plot violence, and their lips talk about making trouble.

Proverbs 27: 4 (NIV)
4 Anger is cruel and fury overwhelming, but who can stand before jealousy?

Ecclesiastes 4: 4 (TLB)
4 Then I observed that the basic motive for success is the driving force of envy and jealousy! But this, too, is foolishness, chasing the wind.

Ezekiel 35: 11 (NLT)
11 Therefore, as surely as I live, says the Sovereign Lord, I will pay back your angry deeds with my own. I will punish you for all your acts of anger, envy, and hatred. And I will make myself known to Israel by what I do to you.

Mark 7: 20 - 23 (NIVUK)
20 He went on: 'What comes out of a person is what defiles them. 21 For it is from within, out of a person's heart, that evil thoughts come – sexual immorality, theft, murder, 22 adultery, greed, malice, deceit, lewdness, envy, slander, arrogance and folly. 23 All

these evils come from inside and defile a person.'

1 Corinthians 3: 3 (NLT)
3 for you are still controlled by your sinful nature. You are jealous of one another and quarrel with each other. Doesn't that prove you are controlled by your sinful nature? Aren't you living like people of the world?

1 Corinthians 13: 4 - 5 (NIVUK)
4 Love is patient, love is kind. It does not envy, it does not boast, it is not proud. 5 It does not dishon-our others, it is not self-seeking, it is not easily angered, it keeps no record of wrongs.

Galatians 5: 21 - 22, 25 - 26 (NIV)
21 and envy; drunkenness, orgies, and the like. I warn you, as I did before, that those who live like this will not inherit the kingdom of God. 22 But the fruit of the Spirit is love, joy, peace, forbearance, kindness, goodness, faithfulness, 25 Since we live by the Spirit, let us keep in step with the Spirit. 26 Let us not become conceited, provoking and envying each other.

James 3: 14 - 16 (NLT)
14 But if you harbor bitter envy and selfish ambition in your hearts, do not boast about it or deny the truth. 15 Such "wisdom" does not come down from heaven but is earthly, unspiritual, demonic. 16 For where you have envy and selfish ambition, there you find disorder and every evil practice.

1 Peter 2: 1 - 3 (NIV)
1 Therefore, rid yourselves of all malice and all deceit, hypocrisy, envy, and slander of every kind. 2 Like newborn babies, crave pure spiritual milk, so that by it you may grow up in your salvation, 3 now that you have tasted that the Lord is good.

JOY

Nehemiah 8: 10 (GNT)
10 Now go home and have a feast. Share your food and wine with those who don't have enough. Today is holy to our Lord, so don't be sad. The joy that the Lord gives you will make you strong.

Psalms 16: 11 (NIV)
11 You make known to me the path of life; you will fill me with joy in your presence, with eternal plea-sures at your right hand.

Psalms 30: 5 (NCV)
5 His anger lasts only a moment, but his kindness lasts for a lifetime. Crying may last for a night, but joy comes in the morning.

Psalms 97: 11 - 12 (ESV)
11 Light is sown for the righteous, and joy for the upright in heart. 12 Rejoice in the Lord, O you righ-teous, and give thanks to his holy name!

Psalms 126: 5 - 6 (GNT)
5 Let those who wept as they planted their crops, gather the harvest with joy! 6 Those who wept as they went out carrying the seed will come back singing for joy, as they bring in the harvest.

Proverbs 12: 20 (NIV)
20 Deceit is in the hearts of those who plot evil, but those who promote peace have joy.

Proverbs 15: 23, 30 (NIV)
23 A person finds joy in giving an apt reply— and how good is a timely word! 30 Light in a messen-ger's eyes brings joy to the heart, and good news gives health to the bones.

Isaiah 55: 12 (NCV)
12 So you will go out with joy and be led out in peace. The mountains and hills will burst into song before you, and all the trees in the fields will clap their hands.

Jeremiah 15: 16 (NKJV)
16 Your words were found, and I ate them, And Your word was to me the joy and rejoicing of my heart; For I am called by Your name, O Lord God of hosts.

Jeremiah 31:13 (NKJV)
13 Then shall the virgin rejoice in the dance, And the young men and the old, together; For I will turn their mourning to joy, Will comfort them, And make them rejoice rather than sorrow.

Habakkuk 3: 17 - 18 (GNT)
17 Even though the fig trees have no fruit and no grapes grow on the vines, even though the olive crop fails and the fields produce no grain, even though the sheep all die and the cattle stalls are emp-ty, 18 I will still be joyful and glad, because the Lord God is my savior.

Zephaniah 3:17 (GNT)
17 The Lord your God is with you; his power gives you victory. The Lord will take delight in you, and in his love he will give you new life. He will sing and be joyful over you,

Matthew 13: 44 (NIVUK)
44 'The kingdom of heaven is like treasure hidden in a field. When a man found it, he hid it again, and then in his joy went and sold all he had and bought that field.

Matthew 25: 21 (WEB)
21 His lord said to him, 'Well done, good and faithful servant. You have been faithful over a few things, I will set you over many things. Enter into the joy of your lord.'

John 16: 23 - 24 (NET)
23 At that time you will ask me nothing. I tell you the solemn truth, whatever you ask the Father in my name he will give you. 24 Until now you have not asked for anything in my name. Ask and you will receive it, so that your joy may be complete.

Romans 14: 17 - 18 (NLT)
17 For the Kingdom of God is not a matter of what we eat or drink, but of living a life of goodness and peace and joy in the Holy Spirit. 18 If you serve Christ with this attitude, you will please God, and oth-ers will approve of you, too.

Romans 15: 13 (GNT)
13 May God, the source of hope, fill you with all joy and peace by means of your faith in him, so that your hope will continue to grow by the power of the Holy Spirit.

Galatians 5: 22 - 23 (NCV)
22 But the Spirit produces the fruit of love, joy, peace, patience, kindness, goodness, faithfulness, 23 gentleness, self-control. There is no law that says these things are wrong.

KNOWLEDGE

Psalms 16: 7, 11 (NKJV)
7 I will bless the Lord who has given me counsel; My heart also instructs me in the night seasons. 11 You will show me the path of life; In Your presence is fullness of joy; At Your right hand are pleasures forevermore.

Psalms 19: 8 - 11 (NIV)
8 The precepts of the Lord are right, giving joy to the heart. The commands of the Lord are radiant, giving light to the eyes. 9 The fear of the Lord is pure, enduring forever. The decrees of the Lord are firm, and all of them are righteous. 10 They are more precious than gold, than much pure gold; they are sweeter than honey, than honey from the honeycomb. 11 By them your servant is warned; in keeping them there is great reward.

Psalms 51: 6 (AMP)
6 Behold, You desire truth in the inner being; make me therefore to know wisdom in my inmost heart.

Proverbs 1: 2 - 3 (NLT)
2 Their purpose is to teach people wisdom and discipline, to help them understand the insights of the wise. 3 Their purpose is to teach people to live disciplined and successful lives, to help them do what is right, just, and fair.

Proverbs 16: 3, 9 (HCSB)
3 Commit your activities to the Lord, and your plans will be achieved. 9 A man's heart plans his way, but the Lord determines his steps.

Proverbs 2: 3, 7 (GNT)
3 Yes, beg for knowledge; plead for insight. 7 He provides help and protection for those who are righ-teous and honest.

Proverbs 4: 5 - 7, 11 - 12 (NKJV)
5 Get wisdom! Get understanding! Do not forget, nor turn away from the words of my mouth. 6 Do not forsake her, and she will preserve you; Love her, and she will keep you. 7 Wisdom is the principal thing; Therefore get wisdom. And in all your getting, get understanding. 11 I have taught you in the way of wisdom; I have led you in right paths. 12 When you walk, your steps will not be hindered, And when you run, you will not stumble.

Proverbs 28: 5 (NLV)
5 Sinful men do not understand what is right and fair, but those who look to the Lord understand all things.

Ecclesiastes 2: 26 (NKJV)
26 To the person who pleases him, God gives wisdom, knowledge and happiness, but to the sinner he gives the task of gathering and storing up wealth to hand it over to the one who pleases God. This too is meaningless, a chasing after the wind.

Isaiah 30: 21 (NLT)
21 Your own ears will hear him. Right behind you a voice will say, "This is the way you should go," whether to the right or to the left.

Isaiah 50: 4 (NLT)
4 The Sovereign Lord has given me his words of wisdom, so that I know how to comfort the weary. Morning by

morning he wakens me and opens my understanding to his will.

Matthew 10: 19 - 20 (WEB)

19 But when they deliver you up, don't be anxious how or what you will say, for it will be given you in that hour what you will say. 20 For it is not you who speak, but the Spirit of your Father who speaks in you.

Romans 8: 14 (WEB)

14 For as many as are led by the Spirit of God, these are children of God.

1 Corinthians 2: 14 - 16 (WEB)

14 Now the natural man doesn't receive the things of God's Spirit, for they are foolishness to him, and he can't know them, because they are spiritually discerned. 15 But he who is spiritual discerns all things, and he himself is judged by no one. 16 "For who has known the mind of the Lord, that he should instruct him?" But we have Christ's mind.

1 Corinthians 12: 8 (ASV)

8 For to one is given through the Spirit the word of wisdom; and to another the word of knowledge, according to the same Spirit:

2 Corinthians 4: 6 (NET)

6 For God, who said "Let light shine out of darkness," is the one who shined in our hearts to give us the light of the glorious knowledge of God in the face of Christ.

Colossians 1: 9 - 10 (RSV)

9 And so, from the day we heard of it, we have not ceased to pray for you, asking that you may be filled with the knowledge of his will in all spiritual wisdom and understanding, 10 to lead

a life worthy of the Lord, fully pleasing to him, bearing fruit in every good work and increasing in the knowledge of God.

2 Timothy 3: 16 - 17 (GNT)

16 All Scripture is inspired by God and is useful for teaching the truth, rebuking error, correcting faults, and giving instruction for right living, 17 so that the person who serves God may be fully qualified and equipped to do every kind of good deed.

Hebrews 4: 12 (NLV)

12 God's Word is living and powerful. It is sharper than a sword that cuts both ways. It cuts straight into where the soul and spirit meet and it divides them. It cuts into the joints and bones. It tells what the heart is thinking about and what it wants to do.

1 John 4: 1 (WEB)

1 Beloved, do not believe every spirit, but test the spirits, whether they are of God; because many false prophets have gone out into the world.

LATER YEARS

Deuteronomy 5: 33 (HCSB)

33 Follow the whole instruction the Lord your God has commanded you, so that you may live, pros-per, and have a long life in the land you will possess.

Psalms 91: 16 (NET)

16 I will satisfy him with long life, and will let him see my salvation.

Psalms 92: 12 - 14 (NKJV)

12 The righteous shall flourish like a palm tree, He shall grow like a cedar

in Lebanon. 13 Those who are planted in the house of the Lord Shall flourish in the courts of our God. 14 They shall still bear fruit in old age; They shall be fresh and flourishing,

Proverbs 3: 1 - 2 (NET)
1 My child, do not forget my teaching, but let your heart keep my commandments, 2 for they will provide a long and full life, and they will add well-being to you.

Proverbs 9: 10 - 11 (NKJV)
10 The fear of the Lord is the beginning of wisdom, And the knowledge of the Holy One is under-standing. 11 For by me your days will be multiplied, And years of life will be added to you.

Proverbs 10: 27 (NCV)
27 Whoever respects the Lord will have a long life, but the life of an evil person will be cut short.

Proverbs 16: 31 (ESV)
31 Gray hair is a crown of glory; it is gained in a righteous life.

Proverbs 17: 6 (NET)
6 Grandchildren are like a crown to the elderly, and the glory of children is their parents.

Proverbs 20: 29 (ESV)
29 The glory of young men is their strength, but the splendor of old men is their gray hair.

Isaiah 46: 4 (NIV)
4 Even to your old age and gray hairs I am he, I am he who will sustain you. I have made you and I will carry you; I will sustain you and I will rescue you.

Joel 2: 28 (WEB)

28 It will happen afterward, that I will pour out my Spirit on all flesh; and your sons and your daugh-ters will prophesy. Your old men will dream dreams. Your young men will see visions.

Luke 1: 36 - 37 (AMP)
36 And listen! Your relative Elizabeth in her old age has also conceived a son, and this is now the sixth month with her who was called barren. 37 For with God nothing is ever impossible and no word from God shall be without power or impossible of fulfillment.

Titus 2: 1 - 5 (NET)
1 But as for you, communicate the behavior that goes with sound teaching. 2 Older men are to be temperate, dignified, self-controlled, sound in faith, in love, and in endurance. 3 Older women likewise are to exhibit behavior fitting for those who are holy, not slandering, not slaves to excessive drinking, but teaching what is good. 4 In this way they will train the younger women to love their husbands, to love their children, 5 to be self-controlled, pure, fulfilling their duties at home, kind, being subject to their own husbands, so that the message of God may not be discredited.

LONELY

Genesis 2: 18 (NLT)
18 Then the Lord God said, "It is not good for the man to be alone. I will make a helper who is just right for him."

Psalms 25: 16 - 17 (NIV)

16 Turn to me and be gracious to me, for I am lonely and afflicted. 17 Relieve the troubles of my heart and free me from my anguish.

Genesis 28: 15 (NIV)

15 I am with you and will watch over you wherever you go, and I will bring you back to this land. I will not leave you until I have done what I have promised you."

Psalms 68: 6 (WEB)

6 God sets the lonely in families. He brings out the prisoners with singing, but the rebellious dwell in a sun-scorched land.

Psalms 102: 1 - 2, 7, 17 (NCV)

1 Lord, listen to my prayer; let my cry for help come to you. 2 Do not hide from me in my time of trou-ble. Pay attention to me. When I cry for help, answer me quickly. 7 I lie awake. I am like a lonely bird on a housetop. 17 He will answer the prayers of the needy; he will not reject their prayers.

Psalms 147: 3 (WEB)

3 He heals the broken in heart, and binds up their wounds.

Ecclesiastes 4: 9 - 12 (NCV)

9 Two people are better than one, because they get more done by working together. 10 If one falls down, the other can help him up. But it is bad for the person who is alone and falls, because no one is there to help. 11 If two lie down together, they will be warm, but a person alone will not be warm. 12 An enemy might defeat one person, but two people together can defend themselves; a rope that is woven of three strings is hard to break.

Isaiah 41: 10 (NCV)

10 So don't worry, because I am with you. Don't be afraid, because I am your God. I will make you strong and will help you; I will support you with my right hand that saves you.

Luke 5: 16 (GW)

16 But he would go away to places where he could be alone for prayer.

John 14: 18 - 19 (NCV)

18 "I will not leave you all alone like orphans; I will come back to you. 19 In a little while the world will not see me anymore, but you will see me. Because I live, you will live, too.

1 Timothy 5: 5 (NIV)

5 The widow who is really in need and left all alone puts her hope in God and continues night and day to pray and to ask God for help.

LORD

Psalms 23: 1 (NIV)

1 The Lord is my shepherd, I lack nothing.

Psalms 24: 1, 8 (NIV)

1 The earth is the Lord's, and everything in it, the world, and all who live in it; 8 Who is this King of glory? The Lord strong and mighty, the Lord mighty in battle.

Psalms 68: 19 (GNT)

19 Praise the Lord, who carries our burdens day after day; he is the God who saves us.

Psalms 86: 5 - 7 (NKJV)
5 For You, Lord, are good, and ready to forgive, And abundant in mercy to all those who call upon You. 6 Give ear, O Lord, to my prayer; And attend to the voice of my supplications. 7 In the day of my trouble I will call upon You, For You will answer me.

Psalms 97: 9 (NCV)
9 You are the Lord Most High over all the earth; you are supreme over all gods.

Isaiah 33: 22 (NIV)
22 For the Lord is our judge, the Lord is our lawgiver, the Lord is our king; it is he who will save us.

Isaiah 40: 10 - 11 (NLT)
10 Yes, the Sovereign Lord is coming in power. He will rule with a powerful arm. See, he brings his reward with him as he comes. 11 He will feed his flock like a shepherd. He will carry the lambs in his arms, holding them close to his heart. He will gently lead the mother sheep with their young.

Isaiah 44: 6 (NIV)
6 This is what the Lord says— Israel's King and Redeemer, the Lord Almighty: I am the first and I am the last; apart from me there is no God.

Isaiah 44: 24 (NLT)
24 This is what the Lord says— your Redeemer and Creator: "I am the Lord, who made all things. I alone stretched out the heavens. Who was with me when I made the earth?

Isaiah 49: 13, 25 (NLT)
13 Sing for joy, O heavens! Rejoice, O earth! Burst into song, O mountains!

For the Lord has comfort-ed his people and will have compassion on them in their suffering. 25 But the Lord says, "The cap-tives of warriors will be released, and the plunder of tyrants will be retrieved. For I will fight those who fight you, and I will save your children.

Isaiah 60: 20 (NKJV)
20 Your sun shall no longer go down, Nor shall your moon withdraw itself; For the Lord will be your everlasting light, And the days of your mourning shall be ended.

Matthew 22: 37 - 39 (RSV)
37 And he said to him, "You shall love the Lord your God with all your heart, and with all your soul, and with all your mind. 38 This is the great and first commandment. 39 And a second is like it, You shall love your neighbor as yourself.

Acts 16: 31 (NKJV)
31 So they said, "Believe on the Lord Jesus Christ, and you will be saved, you and your household."

Acts 2: 36 (AMP)
36 Therefore let the whole house of Israel recognize beyond all doubt and acknowledge assuredly that God has made Him both Lord and Christ (the Messiah)—this Jesus Whom you crucified.

Acts 9: 5 (AMP)
5 And Saul said, Who are You, Lord? And He said, I am Jesus, Whom you are persecuting. It is dan-gerous and it will turn out badly for you to keep

kicking against the goad [to offer vain and perilous resistance].

Romans 5: 1 (NKJV)
1 Therefore, having been justified by faith, we have[a] peace with God through our Lord Jesus Christ,

Romans 10: 9 - 10 (NKJV)
9 that if you confess with your mouth the Lord Jesus and believe in your heart that God has raised Him from the dead, you will be saved. 10 For with the heart one believes unto righteousness, and with the mouth confession is made unto salvation.

Romans 14: 8 (GNT)
8 If we live, it is for the Lord that we live, and if we die, it is for the Lord that we die. So whether we live or die, we belong to the Lord.

1 Corinthians 15: 58 (HCSB)
58 Therefore, my dear brothers, be steadfast, immovable, always excelling in the Lord's work, knowing that your labor in the Lord is not in vain.

Colossians 3: 17 (NLT)
17 And whatever you do or say, do it as a representative of the Lord Jesus, giving thanks through him to God the Father.

1 Timothy 6: 15 - 16 (NIV)
15b God, the blessed and only Ruler, the King of kings and Lord of lords, 16 who alone is immortal and who lives in unapproachable light, whom no one has seen or can see. To him be honor and might forever. Amen.

Jude 1: 25 (NIV)
25 to the only God our Savior be glory, majesty, power and authority, through Jesus Christ our Lord, before all ages, now and forevermore! Amen.

Revelation 1: 8 (AMP)
8 I am the Alpha and the Omega [the Beginning and the End]," says the Lord God, "Who is [existing forever] and Who was [continually existing in the past] and Who is to come, the Almighty [the Omnip-otent, the Ruler of all].

LOVE

Proverbs 8: 17 (NKJV)
17 I love those who love me, And those who seek me diligently will find me.

Jeremiah 31: 3 (CEB)
3 the Lord appeared to them from a distance: I have loved you with a love that lasts forever. And so with unfailing love, I have drawn you to myself.

Zephaniah 3: 17 (MEV)
17 The Lord your God is in your midst, a Mighty One, who will save. He will rejoice over you with gladness, He will renew you with His love, He will rejoice over you with singing.

Mark 12: 30 - 31 (NKJV)
30 And you shall love the Lord your God with all your heart, with all your soul, with all your mind, and with all your strength.' This is the first commandment. 31 And the second, like it, is this: 'You shall love your neighbor as yourself.' There is no other commandment greater than these."

John 3: 16 (RSV)

16 For God so loved the world that he gave his only Son, that whoever believes in him should not perish but have eternal life.

John 13: 34 - 35 (NIV)

34 "A new command I give you: Love one another. As I have loved you, so you must love one anoth-er. 35 By this everyone will know that you are my disciples, if you love one another."

John 15: 12 - 14 (NIV)

12 My command is this: Love each other as I have loved you. 13 Greater love has no one than this: to lay down one's life for one's friends. 14 You are my friends if you do what I command.

Romans 5: 8 (NKJV)

8 But God demonstrates His own love toward us, in that while we were still sinners, Christ died for us.

Romans 8: 37 - 39 (MEV)

37 No, in all these things we are more than conquerors through Him who loved us. 38 For I am per-suaded that neither death nor life, neither angels nor principalities nor powers, neither things present nor things to come, 39 neither height nor depth, nor any other created thing, shall be able to separate us from the love of God, which is in Christ Jesus our Lord.

1 Corinthians 13: 13 (NIV)

13 And now these three remain: faith, hope and love. But the greatest of these is love.

Ephesians 3: 17 - 19 (NIV)

17 so that Christ may dwell in your hearts through faith. And I pray that you, being rooted and estab-lished in love, 18 may have power, together with all the Lord's holy people, to grasp how wide and long and high and deep is the love of Christ, 19 and to know this love that surpasses knowledge— that you may be filled to the measure of all the fullness of God.

2 Thessalonians 2: 16 - 17 (CEV)

16 God our Father loves us. He is kind and has given us eternal comfort and a wonderful hope. We pray that our Lord Jesus Christ and God our Father 17 will encourage you and help you always to do and say the right thing.

2 Timothy 1: 7 (NLT)

7 For God has not given us a spirit of fear and timidity, but of power, love, and self-discipline.

1 John 4: 16 - 21 (WEB)

16 We know and have believed the love which God has for us. God is love, and he who remains in love remains in God, and God remains in him. 17 In this love has been made perfect among us, that we may have boldness in the day of judgment, because as he is, even so are we in this world. 18 There is no fear in love; but perfect love casts out fear, because fear has punishment. He who fears is not made perfect in love. 19 We love him, because he first loved us. 20 If a man says, "I love God," and hates his brother, he is a liar; for he who doesn't love his brother whom he has seen, how can he love God whom he has not seen? 21 This commandment we have from him, that he who loves God should also love his brother.

1 John 4: 7 - 8 (HCSB)
7 Dear friends, let us love one another, because love is from God, and everyone who loves has been born of God and knows God. 8 The one who does not love does not know God, because God is love.

LOVE GOD

Deuteronomy 11: 13 - 15 (HCSB)
13 "If you carefully obey my commands I am giving you today, to love the Lord your God and worship Him with all your heart and all your soul, 14 I will provide rain for your land in the proper time, the autumn and spring rains, and you will harvest your grain, new wine, and oil. 15 I will provide grass in your fields for your livestock. You will eat and be satisfied.

Deuteronomy 30: 6 (AMP)
6 "And the Lord your God will circumcise your heart and the hearts of your descendants [that is, He will remove the desire to sin from your heart], so that you will love the Lord your God with all your heart and all your soul, so that you may live [as a recipient of His blessing].

Psalms 37: 4 (AMP)
4 Delight yourself also in the Lord, and He will give you the desires and secret petitions of your heart.

Psalms 91: 14 (NKJV)
14 Because he has set his love upon Me, therefore I will deliver him; I will set him on high, because he has known My name.

Psalms 145: 20 (NLV)
20 The Lord takes care of all who love Him. But He will destroy all the sinful.

Proverbs 8: 17 - 18, 21 (GNT)
17 I love those who love me; whoever looks for me can find me. 18 I have riches and honor to give, prosperity and success. 21 giving wealth to those who love me, filling their houses with treasures.

John 14: 21 (ESV)
21 Whoever has my commandments and keeps them, he it is who loves me. And he who loves me will be loved by my Father, and I will love him and manifest myself to him.

Romans 8: 28 (ESV)
28 And we know that for those who love God all things work together for good, for those who are called according to his purpose.

1 Corinthians 2: 9 - 10 (ESV)
9 But, as it is written, "What no eye has seen, nor ear heard, nor the heart of man imagined, what God has prepared for those who love him"— 10 these things God has revealed to us through the Spirit. For the Spirit searches everything, even the depths of God.

Ephesians 6: 24 (ESV)
24 Grace be with all who love our Lord Jesus Christ with love incorruptible.

James 2: 5 (NIV)
5 Listen, my dear brothers and sisters: Has not God chosen those who are poor in the eyes of the world to be rich in faith and to inherit the kingdom he promised those who love him?

1 John 5: 3 (GNT)
3 For our love for God means that we obey his commands. And his commands are not too hard for us,

LOVING OTHERS

John 13: 34 - 35 (NIV)
34 A new command I give you: Love one another. As I have loved you, so you must love one another. 35 By this everyone will know that you are my disciples, if you love one another.

Romans 12: 9 - 10, 13 (NLT)
9 Don't just pretend to love others. Really love them. Hate what is wrong. Hold tightly to what is good. 10 Love each other with genuine affection, and take delight in honoring each other. 13 When God's people are in need, be ready to help them. Always be eager to practice hospitality.

Galatians 5: 22 - 23 (HCSB)
22 But the fruit of the Spirit is love, joy, peace, patience, kindness, goodness, faith, 23 gentleness, self-control. Against such things there is no law.

Ephesians 4: 1 - 3 (NLT)
1 Therefore I, a prisoner for serving the Lord, beg you to lead a life worthy of your calling, for you have been called by God. 2 Always be humble and gentle. Be patient with each other, making allow-ance for each other's faults because of your love. 3 Make every effort to keep yourselves united in the Spirit, binding yourselves together with peace.

Ephesians 5: 1 - 2 (ESV)
1 Therefore be imitators of God, as beloved children. 2 And walk in love, as Christ loved us and gave himself up for us, a fragrant offering and sacrifice to God.

Colossians 3: 12 - 15 (GNT)
12 You are the people of God; he loved you and chose you for his own. So then, you must clothe yourselves with compassion, kindness, humility, gentleness, and patience. 13 Be tolerant with one another and forgive one another whenever any of you has a complaint against someone else. You must forgive one another just as the Lord has forgiven you. 14 And to all these qualities add love, which binds all things together in perfect unity. 15 The peace that Christ gives is to guide you in the decisions you make; for it is to this peace that God has called you together in the one body. And be thankful.

1 Thessalonians 5: 12 - 15 (NCV)
12 Now, brothers and sisters, we ask you to appreciate those who work hard among you, who lead you in the Lord and teach you. 13 Respect them with a very special love because of the work they do. Live in peace with each other. 14 We ask you, brothers and sisters, to warn those who do not work. Encourage the people who are afraid. Help those who are weak. Be patient with everyone. 15 Be sure that no one pays back wrong for wrong, but always try to do what is good for each other and for all people.

1 John 3: 18 (HCSB)
18 Little children, we must not love with word or speech, but with truth and action.

1 John 4: 7 - 8 (HCSB)
7 Dear friends, let us love one another, because love is from God, and everyone who loves has been born of God and knows God. 8 The one who does not love does not know God, because God is love.

LUST

Exodus 20: 17 (NIV)
17 You shall not covet your neighbor's house. You shall not covet your neighbor's wife, or his male or female servant, his ox or donkey, or anything that belongs to your neighbor.

Proverbs 6: 23 - 29 (NCV)
23 These commands are like a lamp; this teaching is like a light. And the correction that comes from them will help you have life. 24 They will keep you from sinful women and from the pleasing words of another man's unfaithful wife. 25 Don't desire her because she is beautiful. Don't let her capture you by the way she looks at you. 26 A prostitute will treat you like a loaf of bread, and a woman who takes part in adultery may cost you your life. 27 You cannot carry hot coals against your chest without burn-ing your clothes, 28 and you cannot walk on hot coals without burning your feet. 29 The same is true if you have sexual relations with another man's wife. Anyone who does so will be punished.

Matthew 5: 27, 28 (WEB)
27 "You have heard that it was said, 'You shall not commit adultery;' 28 but I tell you that everyone who gazes at a woman to lust after her has committed adultery with her already in his heart.

Romans 13: 14 (NASB)
14 But put on the Lord Jesus Christ, and make no provision for the flesh in regard to its lusts.

Romans 6: 11 - 14 (NASB)
11 Even so consider yourselves to be dead to sin, but alive to God in Christ Jesus. 12 Therefore do not let sin reign in your mortal body so that you obey its lusts, 13 and do not go on presenting the members of your body to sin as instruments of unrighteousness; but present yourselves to God as those alive from the dead, and your members as instruments of righteousness to God. 14 For sin shall not be master over you, for you are not under law but under grace.

Galatians 5: 16 - 17 (NKJV)
16 I say then: Walk in the Spirit, and you shall not fulfill the lust of the flesh. 17 For the flesh lusts against the Spirit, and the Spirit against the flesh; and these are contrary to one another, so that you do not do the things that you wish.

Ephesians 2: 3 - 6 (NKJV)
3 among whom also we all once conducted ourselves in the lusts of our flesh, fulfilling the desires of the flesh and of the mind, and were by nature children of wrath, just as the others. 4 But God, who is rich in mercy, because of His great love with which He loved us, 5 even when we were dead in trespasses, made us alive together with Christ (by grace you have been saved), 6 and raised us up together, and made

us sit together in the heavenly places in Christ Jesus,

2 Timothy 2: 22 (NLT)
22 Run from anything that stimulates youthful lusts. Instead, pursue righteous living, faithfulness, love, and peace. Enjoy the companionship of those who call on the Lord with pure hearts.

Titus 2: 11 - 12 (HCSB)
11 For the grace of God has appeared with salvation for all people, 12 instructing us to deny godless-ness and worldly lusts and to live in a sensible, righteous, and godly way in the present age,

James 4: 1 - 3 (NASB)
1 What is the source of quarrels and conflicts among you? Is not the source your pleasures that wage war in your members? 2 You lust and do not have; so you commit murder. You are envious and can-not obtain; so you fight and quarrel. You do not have because you do not ask. 3 You ask and do not receive, because you ask with wrong motives, so that you may spend it on your pleasures.

1 Peter 1: 14 - 16 (NKJV)
14 as obedient children, not conforming yourselves to the former lusts, as in your ignorance; 15 but as He who called you is holy, you also be holy in all your conduct, 16 because it is written, "Be holy, for I am holy."

2 Peter 1: 3 - 4 (AMP)
3 For His divine power has bestowed upon us all things that [are requisite and suited] to life and godliness, through the [full, personal] knowledge

of Him Who called us by and to His own glory and excellence (virtue). 4 By means of these He has bestowed on us His precious and exceedingly great promises, so that through them you may escape [by flight] from the moral decay (rottenness and corruption) that is in the world because of covetousness (lust and greed), and become sharers (par-takers) of the divine nature.

LYING

Exodus 23: 1 (NLV)
1 Do not tell a lie about someone else. Do not join with the sinful to say something that will hurt some-one.

Leviticus 19: 16 (ESV)
16 You shall not go around as a slanderer among your people, and you shall not stand up against the life of your neighbor: I am the Lord.

Deuteronomy 25: 15 - 16 (GW)
15 Use accurate and honest weights and measures. Then you will live for a long time in the land that the Lord your God is giving you. 16 Everyone who uses dishonest weights and measures is disgusting to the Lord.

Psalms 34: 13 - 15 (NIV)
13 keep your tongue from evil and your lips from telling lies. 14 Turn from evil and do good; seek peace and pursue it. 15 The eyes of the Lord are on the righteous, and his ears are attentive to their cry;

Psalms 58: 3 (NIV)
3 Even from birth the wicked go astray; from the womb they are wayward, spreading lies.

Proverbs 6: 16 - 18 (MEV)

16 These six things the Lord hates, yes, seven are an abomination to him: 17 a proud look, a lying tongue, and hands that shed innocent blood, 18 a heart that devises wicked imaginations, feet that are swift in running to mischief,

Proverbs 11: 1 (ESV)

1 A false balance is an abomination to the Lord, but a just weight is his delight.

Proverbs 14: 5 (MSG)

5 A true witness never lies; a false witness makes a business of it.

Proverbs 19: 5 (NKJV)

5 A false witness will not go unpunished, And he who speaks lies will not escape.

Proverbs 25: 18 (NLT)

18 Telling lies about others is as harmful as hitting them with an ax, wounding them with a sword, or shooting them with a sharp arrow.

Matthew 12: 36 - 37 (NET)

36 I tell you that on the day of judgment, people will give an account for every worthless word they speak. 37 For by your words you will be justified, and by your words you will be condemned.

Luke 6: 31, 45 (NIVUK)

31 Do to others as you would have them do to you. 45 A good man brings good things out of the good stored up in his heart, and an evil man brings evil things out of the evil stored up in his heart. For the mouth speaks what the heart is full of.

Ephesians 4: 25 - 27 (WE)

25 So stop telling lies. Tell the truth to each other. We all are parts of the same body. 26 When you are angry, do not do anything wrong. And do not stay angry after the sun goes down. 27 Do not let the devil control you.

Colossians 3: 9 - 10 (NCV)

9 Do not lie to each other. You have left your old sinful life and the things you did before. 10 You have begun to live the new life, in which you are being made new and are becoming like the One who made you. This new life brings you the true knowledge of God.

1 Thessalonians 4: 6 - 7 (MEV)

6 and that no man take advantage of and defraud his brother in any matter, because the Lord is the avenger in all these things, as we also have forewarned you and testified. 7 For God has not called us to uncleanness, but to holiness.

MARRIAGE

Genesis 2: 18, 22, 25 (NLT)

18 Then the Lord God said, "It is not good for the man to be alone. I will make a helper who is just right for him. 22 Then the Lord God made a woman from the rib, and he brought her to the man. 25 Now the man and his wife were both naked, but they felt no shame.

Genesis 24: 40 (NKJV)

40 But he said to me, 'The Lord, before whom I walk, will send His angel with

you and prosper your way; and you shall take a wife for my son from my family and from my father's house.

1 Samuel 25: 32, 42 (NKJV)
32 Then David said to Abigail: "Blessed is the Lord God of Israel, who sent you this day to meet me! 42 So Abigail rose in haste and rode on a donkey, attended by five of her maidens; and she followed the messengers of David, and became his wife.

Nehemiah 4: 14 (ESV)
14 And I looked and arose and said to the nobles and to the officials and to the rest of the people, "Do not be afraid of them. Remember the Lord, who is great and awesome, and fight for your brothers, your sons, your daughters, your wives, and your homes."

Proverbs 5: 15, 17 - 19 (NIV)
15 Drink water from your own cistern, running water from your own well. 17 Let them be yours alone, never to be shared with strangers. 18 May your fountain be blessed, and may you rejoice in the wife of your youth. 19 A loving doe, a graceful deer— may her breasts satisfy you always, may you ever be intoxicated with her love.

Proverbs 12: 4 (NET)
4 A noble wife is the crown of her husband, but the wife who acts shamefully is like rottenness in his bones.

Proverbs 18: 22 (NET)
22 The one who finds a wife finds what is enjoyable, and receives a pleasurable gift from the Lord.

Proverbs 31: 10 - 11 (NCV)
10 It is hard to find a good wife, because she is worth more than rubies. 11 Her husband trusts her completely. With her, he has everything he needs.

Ecclesiastes 9: 9 (ESV)
9 Enjoy life with the wife whom you love, all the days of your vain[a] life that he has given you under the sun, because that is your portion in life and in your toil at which you toil under the sun.

1 Corinthians 7: 2 - 5, 9 (NET)
2 But because of immoralities, each man should have relations with his own wife and each woman with her own husband. 3 A husband should give to his wife her sexual rights, and likewise a wife to her husband. 4 It is not the wife who has the rights to her own body, but the husband. In the same way, it is not the husband who has the rights to his own body, but the wife. 5 Do not deprive each other, except by mutual agreement for a specified time, so that you may devote yourselves to prayer. Then resume your relationship, so that Satan may not tempt you because of your lack of self-control. 9 But if they do not have self-control, let them get married. For it is better to marry than to burn with sexual desire.

2 Corinthians 6: 14 - 16 (ESV)
14 Do not be unequally yoked with unbelievers. For what partnership has righteousness with lawless-ness? Or what fellowship has light with darkness? 15 What accord has Christ with Belial?[a] Or what portion does a believer share with an unbeliever? 16 What agreement has the temple of God with idols? For we are the temple of the

living God; as God said, "I will make my dwelling among them and walk among them, and I will be their God, and they shall be my people.

Ephesians 5: 21 - 23 (ESV)
21 submitting to one another out of reverence for Christ. 22 Wives, submit to your own husbands, as to the Lord. 23 For the husband is the head of the wife even as Christ is the head of the church, his body, and is himself its Savior.

Ephesians 5: 25, 30, 33 (ESV)
25 Husbands, love your wives, as Christ loved the church and gave himself up for her, 30 because we are members of his body. 33 However, let each one of you love his wife as himself, and let the wife see that she respects her husband.

Colossians 3: 18 - 19 (NLT)
18 Wives, submit to your husbands, as is fitting for those who belong to the Lord. 19 Husbands, love your wives and never treat them harshly.

1 Timothy 5: 8, 14 (GNT)
8 But if any do not take care of their relatives, especially the members of their own family, they have denied the faith and are worse than an unbeliever. 14 So I would prefer that the younger widows get married, have children, and take care of their homes, so as to give our enemies no chance of speak-ing evil of us.

Titus 2: 4 - 5 (AMP)
4 So that they will wisely train the young women to be [a]sane and sober of mind (temperate, disci-plined) and to love their husbands and their children, 5 To be self-controlled, chaste, homemakers, good-natured (kindhearted), adapting and subordinating themselves to their husbands, that the word of God may not be exposed to reproach (blasphemed or discredited).

Hebrews 13: 4 (AMP)
4 Marriage is to be held in honor among all [that is, regarded as something of great value], and the marriage bed undefiled [by immorality or by any sexual sin]; for God will judge the sexually immoral and adulterous.

1 Peter 3: 1 - 2, 7 (NIV)
1 Wives, in the same way submit yourselves to your own husbands so that, if any of them do not be - lieve the word, they may be won over without words by the behavior of their wives, 2 when they see the purity and reverence of your lives. 7 Husbands, in the same way be considerate as you live with your wives, and treat them with respect as the weaker partner and as heirs with you of the gracious gift of life, so that nothing will hinder your prayers.

MATURE

Psalms 92: 12 - 14 (ESV)
12 The righteous flourish like the palm tree and grow like a cedar in Lebanon. 13 They are planted in the house of the Lord; they flourish in the courts of our God. 14 They still bear fruit in old age; they are ever full of sap and green,

2 Corinthians 3: 18 (NIV)
18 And we all, who with unveiled faces contemplate[a] the Lord's glory, are being transformed into his image with

ever-increasing glory, which comes from the Lord, who is the Spirit.

Ephesians 3: 14 - 19 (NET)

14 For this reason I kneel before the Father, 15 from whom every family in heaven and on the earth is named. 16 I pray that according to the wealth of his glory he may grant you to be strengthened with power through his Spirit in the inner person, 17 that Christ may dwell in your hearts through faith, so that, because you have been rooted and grounded in love, 18 you may be able to comprehend with all the saints what is the breadth and length and height and depth, 19 and thus to know the love of Christ that surpasses knowledge, so that you may be filled up to all the fullness of God.

Ephesians 4: 14 - 16 (NLT)

14 Then we will no longer be immature like children. We won't be tossed and blown about by every wind of new teaching. We will not be influenced when people try to trick us with lies so clever they sound like the truth. 15 Instead, we will speak the truth in love, growing in every way more and more like Christ, who is the head of his body, the church. 16 He makes the whole body fit together perfect-ly. As each part does its own special work, it helps the other parts grow, so that the whole body is healthy and growing and full of love.

Philippians 1: 6, 9 - 10 (GNT)

6 And so I am sure that God, who began this good work in you, will carry it on until it is finished on the Day of Christ Jesus. 9 I pray that your love will keep on growing more and more, together with true knowledge

and perfect judgment, 10 so that you will be able to choose what is best. Then you will be free from all impurity and blame on the Day of Christ.

Colossians 1: 9 - 11 (NOG)

9 For this reason we have not stopped praying for you since the day we heard about you. We ask God to fill you with the knowledge of his will through every kind of spiritual wisdom and insight. 10 We ask this so that you will live the kind of lives that prove you belong to the Lord. Then you will want to please him in every way as you grow in producing every kind of good work by this knowledge about God. 11 We ask him to strengthen you by his glorious might with all the power you need to patiently endure everything with joy.

Colossians 3: 16 (NOG)

16 Let Christ's word with all its wisdom and richness live in you. Use psalms, hymns, and spiritual songs to teach and instruct yourselves about God's kindness.[a] Sing to God in your hearts.

1 Timothy 4: 14 - 15 (NIV)

14 Do not neglect your gift, which was given you through prophecy when the body of elders laid their hands on you. 15 Be diligent in these matters; give yourself wholly to them, so that everyone may see your progress.

2 Timothy 3: 16 (ESV)

16 All Scripture is breathed out by God and profitable for teaching, for reproof, for correction, and for training in righteousness,

1 Peter 2: 2 - 3 (NIV)

2 Like newborn babies, crave pure spiritual milk, so that by it you may

grow up in your salvation, 3 now that you have tasted that the Lord is good.

2 Peter 1: 5 - 8 (HCSB)

5 For this very reason, make every effort to supplement your faith with goodness, goodness with knowledge, 6 knowledge with self-control, self-control with endurance, endurance with godliness, 7 godliness with brotherly affection, and brotherly affection with love. 8 For if these qualities are yours and are increasing, they will keep you from being useless or unfruitful in the knowledge of our Lord Jesus Christ.

MENTAL

1 Kings 4: 29 (AMP)

29 And God gave Solomon exceptionally much wisdom and understanding, and breadth of mind like the sand of the seashore.

Psalms 42: 11 (HCSB)

11 Why am I so depressed? Why this turmoil within me? Put your hope in God, for I will still praise Him, my Savior and my God.

Psalms 51: 6 (GNT)

6 Sincerity and truth are what you require; fill my mind with your wisdom.

Psalms 62: 1 - 2 (HCSB)

1 I am at rest in God alone; my salvation comes from Him. 2 He alone is my rock and my salvation, my stronghold; I will never be shaken.

Psalms 104: 34 (NET)

34 May my thoughts be pleasing to him! I will rejoice in the Lord.

Psalms 139: 23 - 24 (GW)

23 Examine me, O God, and know my mind. Test me, and know my thoughts. 24 See whether I am on an evil path. Then lead me on the everlasting path.

Proverbs 12: 25 (NKJV)

25 Anxiety in the heart of man causes depression, But a good word makes it glad.

Proverbs 23: 31 - 33 (NKJV)

31 Do not look on the wine when it is red, When it sparkles in the cup, When it swirls around smooth-ly; 32 At the last it bites like a serpent, And stings like a viper. 33 Your eyes will see strange things, And your heart will utter perverse things.

Isaiah 26: 3 (ESV)

3 You keep him in perfect peace whose mind is stayed on you, because he trusts in you.

Jeremiah 31: 33 (NKJV)

33 But this is the covenant that I will make with the house of Israel after those days, says the Lord: I will put My law in their minds, and write it on their hearts; and I will be their God, and they shall be My people.

Daniel 4: 34, 36 (MEV)

34 But at the end of the days, I, Nebuchadnezzar, lifted up my eyes to heaven, and my understanding returned to me, and I blessed the Most High, and I praised and honored Him who lives forever: For His dominion is an everlasting dominion, and whose

kingdom endures from generation to generation. 36 At the same time my reason returned to me. And for the glory of my kingdom, my honor and splen-dor returned to me. And my counselors and my lords sought me out. Then I was established in my kingdom, and excellent majesty was added to me.

Jonah 2: 6 (CEV)
6 I had sunk down below the underwater mountains; I knew that forever, I would be a prisoner there. But, you, Lord God, rescued me from that pit.

Malachi 4: 2 (GNT)
2 But for you who obey me, my saving power will rise on you like the sun and bring healing like the sun's rays. You will be as free and happy as calves let out of a stall.

Matthew 22: 37 (RSV)
37 And he said to him, "You shall love the Lord your God with all your heart, and with all your soul, and with all your mind.

Romans 12: 2 (NKJV)
2 And do not be conformed to this world, but be transformed by the renewing of your mind, that you may prove what is that good and acceptable and perfect will of God.

1 Corinthians 14: 33 (ESV)
33 For God is not a God of confusion but of peace. As in all the churches of the saints,

Ephesians 1: 18 - 19 (HCSB)
18 I pray that the perception of your mind may be enlightened so you may know what is the hope of His calling, what are the glorious riches of His inheritance among the saints, 19 and what is the im-measurable greatness of His power to us who believe, according to the working of His vast strength.

Philippians 4: 7 - 8 (HCSB)
7 And the peace of God, which surpasses every thought, will guard your hearts and minds in Christ Jesus. 8 Finally brothers, whatever is true, whatever is honorable, whatever is just, whatever is pure, whatever is lovely, whatever is commendable—if there is any moral excellence and if there is any praise—dwell on these things.

2 Timothy 1: 7 (NKJV)
7 For God has not given us a spirit of fear, but of power and of love and of a sound mind.

James 3: 16 - 18 (HCSB)
16 For where envy and selfish ambition exist, there is disorder and every kind of evil. 17 But the wisdom from above is first pure, then peace-loving, gentle, compliant, full of mercy and good fruits, without favoritism and hypocrisy. 18 And the fruit of righteousness is sown in peace by those who cultivate peace.

1 Peter 5: 8 - 10 (ERV)
8 Control yourselves and be careful! The devil is your enemy, and he goes around like a roaring lion looking for someone to attack and eat. 9 Refuse to follow the devil. Stand strong in your faith. You know that your brothers and sisters all over the world are having the same sufferings that you have. 10 Yes, you will suffer for a short time. But after that, God will make everything

right. He will make you strong. He will support you and keep you from falling. He is the God who gives all grace. He chose you to share in his glory in Christ. That glory will continue forever.

3 John 1: 2 (NASB)
2 Beloved, I pray that in all respects you may prosper and be in good health, just as your soul

MERCY

Exodus 33: 19 (NCV)
19 The Lord answered, "I will cause all my goodness to pass in front of you, and I will announce my name, the Lord, so you can hear it. I will show kindness to anyone to whom I want to show kindness, and I will show mercy to anyone to whom I want to show mercy.

Psalms 18: 25 (NKJV)
25 With the merciful You will show Yourself merciful; With a blameless man You will show Yourself blameless;

Psalms 23: 6 (NKJV)
6 Surely goodness and mercy shall follow me All the days of my life; And I will dwell in the house of the Lord Forever.

Psalms 31: 7 - 8 (NKJV)
7 I will be glad and rejoice in Your mercy, For You have considered my trouble; You have known my soul in adversities, 8 And have not shut me up into the hand of the enemy; You have set my feet in a wide place.

Psalms 32: 5 (GNT)
5 Then I confessed my sins to you; I did not conceal my wrongdoings. I decided to confess them to you, and you forgave all my sins.

Psalms 57: 10 (NOG)
10 because your mercy is as high as the heavens. Your truth reaches the skies.

Psalms 86: 5 (NKJV)
5 For You, Lord, are good, and ready to forgive, And abundant in mercy to all those who call upon You.

Psalms 103: 13, 17 (NCV)
13 The Lord has mercy on those who respect him, as a father has mercy on his children. 17 But the Lord's love for those who respect him continues forever and ever, and his goodness continues to their grandchildren

Psalms 138: 8 (NKJV)
8 The Lord will perfect that which concerns me; Your mercy, O Lord, endures forever; Do not forsake the works of Your hands.

Psalms 145: 14 (ESV)
14 The Lord upholds all who are falling and raises up all who are bowed down.

Psalms 145:8 - 9 (NKJV)
8 The Lord is gracious and full of compassion, Slow to anger and great in mercy. 9 The Lord is good to all, And His tender mercies are over all His works.

Proverbs 3: 3 - 4 (NKJV)
3 Let not mercy and truth forsake you; Bind them around your neck, Write them on the tablet of your heart, 4 And

so find favor and high esteem In the sight of God and man.

Proverbs 21: 21 (MEV)
21 He who follows after righteousness and mercy finds life, righteousness, and honor.

Isaiah 30: 18 (GNT)
18 And yet the Lord is waiting to be merciful to you. He is ready to take pity on you because he al-ways does what is right. Happy are those who put their trust in the Lord.

Isaiah 54: 10 (NKJV)
10 For the mountains shall depart And the hills be removed, But My kindness shall not depart from you, Nor shall My covenant of peace be removed," Says the Lord, who has mercy on you.

Lamentations 3: 22 - 25 (NCV)
22 The Lord's love never ends; his mercies never stop. 23 They are new every morning; Lord, your loyalty is great. 24 I say to myself, "The Lord is mine, so I hope in him." 25 The Lord is good to those who hope in him, to those who seek him.

Matthew 5: 7 (NET)
7 Blessed are the merciful, for they will be shown mercy.

Luke 1: 50 (ESV)
50 And his mercy is for those who fear him from generation to generation.

Luke 6: 36 (AMP)
36 So be merciful (sympathetic, tender, responsive, and compassionate) even as your Father is [all these].

2 Corinthians 1: 3 (NCV)
3 Praise be to the God and Father of our Lord Jesus Christ. God is the Father who is full of mercy and all comfort.

Romans 9: 15 - 16 (NLT)
15 For God said to Moses, "I will show mercy to anyone I choose, and I will show compassion to any-one I choose."[a] 16 So it is God who decides to show mercy. We can neither choose it nor work for it.

Hebrews 4: 16 (TLB)
16 So let us come boldly to the very throne of God and stay there to receive his mercy and to find grace to help us in our times of need.

James 3: 17 (NKJV)
17 But the wisdom that is from above is first pure, then peaceable, gentle, willing to yield, full of mercy and good fruits, without partiality and without hypocrisy.

MIRACLE

Joshua 10: 12 - 13 (GNT)
12 On the day that the Lord gave the men of Israel victory over the Amorites, Joshua spoke to the Lord. In the presence of the Israelites he said, "Sun, stand still over Gibeon; Moon, stop over Aijalon Valley." 13 The sun stood still and the moon did not move until the nation had conquered its enemies. This is written in the Book of Jashar. The sun stood still in the middle of the sky and did not go down for a whole day.

Psalms 66: 5 (NLT)

5 Come and see what our God has done, what awesome miracles he performs for people!

Daniel 3: 19 - 30 (NLT)

19 Nebuchadnezzar was so furious with Shadrach, Meshach, and Abednego that his face became distorted with rage. He commanded that the furnace be heated seven times hotter than usual.

20 Then he ordered some of the strongest men of his army to bind Shadrach, Meshach, and Abed-nego and throw them into the blazing furnace. 21 So they tied them up and threw them into the fur-nace, fully dressed in their pants, turbans, robes, and other garments. 22 And because the king, in his anger, had demanded such a hot fire in the furnace, the flames killed the soldiers as they threw the three men in. 23 So Shadrach, Meshach, and Abednego, securely tied, fell into the roaring flames. 24 But suddenly, Nebuchadnezzar jumped up in amazement and exclaimed to his advisers, "Didn't we tie up three men and throw them into the furnace?" "Yes, Your Majesty, we certainly did," they replied. 25 "Look!" Nebuchadnezzar shouted. "I see four men, unbound, walking around in the fire un-harmed! And the fourth looks like a god!" 26 Then Nebuchadnezzar came as close as he could to the door of the flaming furnace and shouted: "Shadrach, Meshach, and Abednego, servants of the Most High God, come out! Come here!" So Shadrach, Meshach, and Abednego stepped out of the fire. 27 Then the high officers, officials, governors, and advisers crowded around them and saw that the fire had not touched them. Not a hair on their heads was singed, and their clothing was not scorched. They didn't even smell of smoke! 28 Then Nebuchadnezzar said, "Praise to the God of Shadrach, Meshach, and Abednego! He sent his angel to rescue his servants who trusted in him. They defied the king's command and were willing to die rather than serve or worship any god except their own God. 29 Therefore, I make this decree: If any people, whatever their race or nation or language, speak a word against the God of Shadrach, Meshach, and Abednego, they will be torn limb from limb, and their houses will be turned into heaps of rubble. There is no other god who can rescue like this!" 30 Then the king promoted Shadrach, Meshach, and Abednego to even higher positions in the prov-ince of Babylon.

Daniel 6: 22 - 23 (NLT)

22 My God sent his angel to shut the lions' mouths so that they would not hurt me, for I have been found innocent in his sight. And I have not wronged you, Your Majesty." 23 The king was overjoyed and ordered that Daniel be lifted from the den. Not a scratch was found on him, for he had trusted in his God.

Matthew 4: 23 (WEB)

23 Jesus went about in all Galilee, teaching in their synagogues, preaching the Good News of the Kingdom, and healing every disease and every sickness among the people.

Matthew 8: 2 - 3 (NET)

2 And a leper approached, and bowed low before him, saying, "Lord, if you are willing, you can make me clean." 3 He stretched out his hand and touched

him saying, "I am willing. Be clean!" Immediately his leprosy was cleansed.

Matthew 9: 27 - 30 (NET)

27 As Jesus went on from there, two blind men followed him, shouting, "Have mercy on us, Son of David!" 28 When he went into the house, the blind men came to him. Jesus said to them, "Do you be-lieve that I am able to do this?" They said to him, "Yes, Lord." 29 Then he touched their eyes saying, "Let it be done for you according to your faith." 30 And their eyes were opened.

Matthew 10: 1 (RSV)

1 And he called to him his twelve disciples and gave them authority over unclean spirits, to cast them out, and to heal every disease and every infirmity.

Matthew 21: 18 - 22 (NLT)

18 In the morning, as Jesus was returning to Jerusalem, he was hungry, 19 and he noticed a fig tree beside the road. He went over to see if there were any figs, but there were only leaves. Then he said to it, "May you never bear fruit again!" And immediately the fig tree withered up. 20 The disciples were amazed when they saw this and asked, "How did the fig tree wither so quickly?" 21 Then Jesus told them, "I tell you the truth, if you have faith and don't doubt, you can do things like this and much more. You can even say to this mountain, 'May you be lifted up and thrown into the sea,' and it will happen. 22 You can pray for anything, and if you have faith, you will receive it."

Mark 1: 40 - 42 (NLT)

40 A man with leprosy came and knelt in front of Jesus, begging to be healed. "If you are willing, you can heal me and make me clean," he said. 41 Moved with compassion, Jesus reached out and touched him. "I am willing," he said. "Be healed!" 42 Instantly the leprosy disappeared, and the man was healed.

Mark 2: 2 - 5, 9 - 12 (ESV)

2 And many were gathered together, so that there was no more room, not even at the door. And he was preaching the word to them. 3 And they came, bringing to him a paralytic carried by four men. 4 And when they could not get near him because of the crowd, they removed the roof above him, and when they had made an opening, they let down the bed on which the paralytic lay. 5 And when Jesus saw their faith, he said to the paralytic, "Son, your sins are forgiven." 9 Which is easier, to say to the paralytic, 'Your sins are forgiven,' or to say, 'Rise, take up your bed and walk'? 10 But that you may know that the Son of Man has authority on earth to forgive sins"—he said to the paralytic— 11 "I say to you, rise, pick up your bed, and go home." 12 And he rose and immediately picked up his bed and went out before them all, so that they were all amazed and glorified God, saying, "We never saw anything like this!"

Mark 11: 13 - 14, 20 - 25 (NCV)

13 13 Seeing a fig tree in leaf from far away, he went to see if it had any figs on it. But he found no figs, only leaves, because it was not the right season for figs. 14 So Jesus said to the tree, "May no one ever eat fruit from you again." And Jesus' followers heard him say this. 20 The next morning as Jesus was passing by with his followers, they saw the fig tree dry and dead, even to the roots. 21 Pe-ter remembered the tree

and said to Jesus, "Teacher, look! The fig tree you cursed is dry and dead!" 22 Jesus answered, "Have faith in God. 23 I tell you the truth, you can say to this mountain, 'Go, fall into the sea.' And if you have no doubts in your mind and believe that what you say will happen, God will do it for you. 24 So I tell you to believe that you have received the things you ask for in prayer, and God will give them to you. 25 When you are praying, if you are angry with someone, forgive him so that your Father in heaven will also forgive your sins.

Mark 16: 17 - 18 (HCSB)

17 And these signs will accompany those who believe: In My name they will drive out demons; they will speak in new languages; 18 they will pick up snakes; if they should drink anything deadly, it will never harm them; they will lay hands on the sick, and they will get well."

Mark 4: 37 - 40 (NIVUK)

37 A furious squall came up, and the waves broke over the boat, so that it was nearly swamped. 38 Jesus was in the stern, sleeping on a cushion. The disciples woke him and said to him, 'Teacher, don't you care if we drown?' 39 He got up, rebuked the wind and said to the waves, 'Quiet! Be still!' Then the wind died down and it was completely calm. 40 He said to his disciples, 'Why are you so afraid? Do you still have no faith?'

Mark 5: 22 - 29, 33 - 36, 41 - 42 (RSV)

22 Then came one of the rulers of the synagogue, Ja'irus by name; and seeing him, he fell at his feet, 23 and besought him, saying, "My little daughter is at the point of death. Come and lay your hands on her, so that she may be made well, and live." 24 And he went with him. And a great crowd followed him and thronged about him. 25 And there was a woman who had had a flow of blood for twelve years, 26 and who had suffered much under many physicians, and had spent all that she had, and was no better but rather grew worse. 27 She had heard the reports about Jesus, and came up behind him in the crowd and touched his garment. 28 For she said, "If I touch even his garments, I shall be made well." 29 And immediately the hemorrhage ceased; and she felt in her body that she was healed of her disease. 33 But the woman, knowing what had been done to her, came in fear and trembling and fell down before him, and told him the whole truth. 34 And he said to her, "Daugh-ter, your faith has made you well; go in peace, and be healed of your disease." 35 While he was still speaking, there came from the ruler's house some who said, "Your daughter is dead. Why trouble the Teacher any further?" 36 But ignoring[a] what they said, Jesus said to the ruler of the synagogue, "Do not fear, only believe." 41 Taking her by the hand he said to her, "Tal'itha cu'mi"; which means, "Little girl, I say to you, arise." 42 And immediately the girl got up and walked (she was twelve years of age), and they were immediately overcome with amazement.

Luke 5: 7 - 9 (NET)

7 So they motioned to their partners in the other boat to come and help them. And they came and filled both boats, so that they were about to sink. 8 But when Simon Peter saw it, he fell down at Je-sus' knees, saying, "Go away from

me, Lord, for I am a sinful man!" 9 For Peter and all who were with him were astonished at the catch of fish that they had taken,

Luke 7: 12 - 15 (WEB)
12 Now when he came near to the gate of the city, behold, one who was dead was carried out, the only son of his mother, and she was a widow. Many people of the city were with her. 13 When the Lord saw her, he had compassion on her, and said to her, "Don't cry." 14 He came near and touched the coffin, and the bearers stood still. He said, "Young man, I tell you, arise!" 15 He who was dead sat up, and began to speak. And he gave him to his mother.

John 4: 47 - 50 (NKJV)
47 When he heard that Jesus had come out of Judea into Galilee, he went to Him and implored Him to come down and heal his son, for he was at the point of death. 48 Then Jesus said to him, "Unless you people see signs and wonders, you will by no means believe." 49 The nobleman said to Him, "Sir, come down before my child dies!" 50 Jesus said to him, "Go your way; your son lives." So the man believed the word that Jesus spoke to him, and he went his way.

John 14: 12 - 14 (RSV)
12 "Truly, truly, I say to you, he who believes in me will also do the works that I do; and greater works than these will he do, because I go to the Father. 13 Whatever you ask in my name, I will do it, that the Father may be glorified in the Son; 14 if you ask anything in my name, I will do it.

John 21: 5 - 6 (NKJV)
5 Then Jesus said to them, "Children, have you any food?" They answered Him, "No." 6 And He said to them, "Cast the net on the right side of the boat, and you will find some." So they cast, and now they were not able to draw it in because of the multitude of fish.

Acts 8: 6 - 8 (NIV)
6 When the crowds heard Philip and saw the signs he performed, they all paid close attention to what he said. 7 For with shrieks, impure spirits came out of many, and many who were paralyzed or lame were healed. 8 So there was great joy in that city.

Acts 10: 38 (NCV)
38 You know about Jesus from Nazareth, that God gave him the Holy Spirit and power. You know how Jesus went everywhere doing good and healing those who were ruled by the devil, because God was with him.

Romans 15: 18 - 19 (GNT)
18 I will be bold and speak only about what Christ has done through me to lead the Gentiles to obey God. He has done this by means of words and deeds, 19 by the power of miracles and wonders, and by the power of the Spirit of God. And so, in traveling all the way from Jerusalem to Illyricum, I have proclaimed fully the Good News about Christ.

1 Corinthians 12: 4, 7, 9 - 11, 31 (GNT)
4 There are different kinds of spiritual gifts, but the same Spirit gives them. 7 The Spirit's presence is shown in some way in each person for the good of all. 9 One and the same Spirit gives

faith to one person, while to another person he gives the power to heal. 10 The Spirit gives one person the power to work miracles; to another, the gift of speaking God's message; and to yet another, the ability to tell the difference between gifts that come from the Spirit and those that do not. To one person he gives the ability to speak in strange tongues, and to another he gives the ability to explain what is said. 11 But it is one and the same Spirit who does all this; as he wishes, he gives a different gift to each per-son. 31 Set your hearts, then, on the more important gifts. Best of all, however, is the following way.

Galatians 3: 5 - 6 (NIV)
5 So again I ask, does God give you his Spirit and work miracles among you by the works of the law, or by your believing what you heard? 6 So also Abraham "believed God, and it was credited to him as righteousness."

James 5: 16 - 18 (MEV)
16 Confess your faults to one another and pray for one another, that you may be healed. The effec-tive, fervent prayer of a righteous man accomplishes much. 17 Elijah was a man subject to natural passions as we are, and he prayed earnestly that it might not rain, and it did not rain on the earth for three years and six months. 18 And he prayed again, and the sky gave rain, and the earth brought forth its fruit.

MONEY

Deuteronomy 8: 18 (NIV)
18 But remember the Lord your God, for it is he who gives you the ability to produce wealth, and so confirms his covenant, which he swore to your ancestors, as it is today.

Deuteronomy 28: 2, 5, 8 (HCSB)
2 All these blessings will come and overtake you, because you obey the Lord your God: 5 Your bas-ket and kneading bowl will be blessed. 8 The Lord will grant you a blessing on your storehouses and on everything you do; He will bless you in the land the Lord your God is giving you.

2 Chronicles 25: 9 (NLT)
9 Amaziah asked the man of God, "But what about all that silver I paid to hire the army of Israel?" The man of God replied, "The Lord is able to give you much more than this!"

2 Chronicles 26: 5 (NLT)
5 Uzziah sought God during the days of Zechariah, who taught him to fear God. And as long as the king sought guidance from the Lord, God gave him success.

Psalms 112: 1 - 3, 5 (NET)
1 Praise the Lord! How blessed is the one who obeys the Lord, who takes great delight in keeping his commands. 2 His descendants will be powerful on the earth; the godly will be blessed. 3 His house contains wealth and riches; his integrity endures. 5 It goes well for the one who generously lends money, and conducts his business honestly.

Psalms 118: 25 (AMP)
25 Save now, we beseech You, O Lord; send now prosperity, O Lord, we beseech You, and give to us success!

Psalms 128: 1 - 2 (GNT)

1 Happy are those who obey the Lord, who live by his commands. 2 Your work will provide for your needs; you will be happy and prosperous.

Proverbs 3: 9 - 10 (NKJV)
9 Honor the Lord with your possessions, And with the firstfruits of all your increase; 10 So your barns will be filled with plenty, And your vats will overflow with new wine.

Proverbs 8: 12, 18 - 19, 21 (NKJV)
12 I, wisdom, dwell with prudence, And find out knowledge and discretion. 18 Riches and honor are with me, Enduring riches and righteousness. 19 My fruit is better than gold, yes, than fine gold, And my revenue than choice silver. 21 That I may cause those who love me to inherit wealth, That I may fill their treasuries.

Proverbs 10: 4 (NET)
4 The one who is lazy becomes poor, but the one who works diligently becomes wealthy.

Proverbs 10: 22 (NLT)
22 The blessing of the Lord makes a person rich, and he adds no sorrow with it.

Proverbs 11: 28 (NET)
28 The one who trusts in his riches will fall, but the righteous will flourish like a green leaf.

Ecclesiastes 4: 6 (GNT)
6 Maybe so, but it is better to have only a little, with peace of mind, than be busy all the time with both hands, trying to catch the wind.

Ecclesiastes 5: 19 (WEB)
19 Every man also to whom God has given riches and wealth, and has given him power to eat of it, and to take his portion, and to rejoice in his labor— this is the gift of God.

Ecclesiastes 10: 19 (NIVUK)
19 A feast is made for laughter,wine makes life merry, and money is the answer for everything.

Isaiah 48: 17 - 18 (AMP)
17 Thus says the Lord, your Redeemer, the Holy One of Israel: I am the Lord your God, Who teach-es you to profit, Who leads you in the way that you should go. 18 Oh, that you had hearkened to My commandments! Then your peace and prosperity would have been like a flowing river, and your righ-teousness [the holiness and purity of the nation] like the [abundant] waves of the sea.

Jeremiah 29: 11- 12 (NIV)
11 For I know the plans I have for you," declares the Lord, "plans to prosper you and not to harm you, plans to give you hope and a future. 12 Then you will call on me and come and pray to me, and I will listen to you.

Malachi 3: 10 - 11 (NASB)
10 Bring the whole tithe into the storehouse, so that there may be food in My house, and test Me now in this," says the Lord of hosts, "if I will not open for you the windows of heaven and pour out for you a blessing until it overflows. 11 Then I will rebuke the devourer for you, so that it will not destroy the fruits of the ground;

nor will your vine in the field cast its grapes," says the Lord of hosts.

Matthew 6: 31 - 33 (NIV)
31 So do not worry, saying, 'What shall we eat?' or 'What shall we drink?' or 'What shall we wear?' 32 For the pagans run after all these things, and your heavenly Father knows that you need them. 33 But seek first his kingdom and his righteousness, and all these things will be given to you as well.

Luke 16: 13 (GNT)
13 No servant can be the slave of two masters; such a slave will hate one and love the other or will be loyal to one and despise the other. You cannot serve both God and money.

Luke 6: 38 (NIVUK)
38 Give, and it will be given to you. A good measure, pressed down, shaken together and running over, will be poured into your lap. For with the measure you use, it will be measured to you.'

Romans 10: 12 (NET)
12 For there is no distinction between the Jew and the Greek, for the same Lord is Lord of all, who richly blesses all who call on him.

2 Corinthians 9: 6- 8 (HCSB)
6 Remember this: The person who sows sparingly will also reap sparingly, and the person who sows generously will also reap generously. 7 Each person should do as he has decided in his heart—not reluctantly or out of necessity, for God loves a cheerful giver. 8 And God is able to make every grace overflow to you, so that in every way,

always having everything you need, you may excel in every good work.

Philippians 4: 19 (NKJV)
19 And my God shall supply all your need according to His riches in glory by Christ Jesus.

1 Timothy 6: 17 - 19 (NIV)
17 Command those who are rich in this present world not to be arrogant nor to put their hope in wealth, which is so uncertain, but to put their hope in God, who richly provides us with everything for our enjoyment. 18 Command them to do good, to be rich in good deeds, and to be generous and willing to share. 19 In this way they will lay up treasure for themselves as a firm foundation for the coming age, so that they may take hold of the life that is truly life.

1 Timothy 6: 9 - 10 (NASB)
9 But those who want to get rich fall into temptation and a snare and many foolish and harmful de - sires which plunge men into ruin and destruction. 10 For the love of money is a root of all [a]sorts of evil, and some by longing for it have wandered away from the faith and pierced themselves with many griefs.

3 John 1: 2 (NASB)
2 Beloved, I pray that in all respects you may prosper and be in good health, just as your soul

NEEDY

Exodus 22: 25 - 26 (NKJV)
25 "If you lend money to any of My people who are poor among you, you

shall not be like a money-lender to him; you shall not charge him interest. 26 If you ever take your neighbor's garment as a pledge, you shall return it to him before the sun goes down.

Leviticus 19: 10 (CEV)
10 Don't strip your grapevines clean or gather the grapes that fall off the vines. Leave them for the poor and for those foreigners who live among you. I am the Lord your God.

Leviticus 23: 22 (NLT)
22 "When you harvest the crops of your land, do not harvest the grain along the edges of your fields, and do not pick up what the harvesters drop. Leave it for the poor and the foreigners living among you. I am the Lord your God."

Psalms 12: 5 (NLT)
5 The Lord replies, "I have seen violence done to the helpless, and I have heard the groans of the poor. Now I will rise up to rescue them, as they have longed for me to do."

Psalms 34: 6 - 7 (NIV)
6 This poor man called, and the Lord heard him; he saved him out of all his troubles. 7 The angel of the Lord encamps around those who fear him, and he delivers them.

Psalms 35: 10 (NIV)
10 My whole being will exclaim, "Who is like you, Lord? You rescue the poor from those too strong for them, the poor and needy from those who rob them."

Psalms 37: 14 - 15 (NIV)
14 The wicked draw the sword and bend the bow to bring down the poor and needy, to slay those whose ways are upright. 15 But their swords will pierce their own hearts, and their bows will be bro-ken.

Psalms 41: 1 (MEV)
1 Blessed are those who consider the poor; the Lord will deliver them in the day of trouble.

Psalms 72: 12 - 13 (NASB)
12 For he will deliver the needy when he cries for help, The afflicted also, and him who has no helper. 13 He will have compassion on the poor and needy, And the lives of the needy he will save.

Psalms 102: 17 (WEB)
17 He has responded to the prayer of the destitute, and has not despised their prayer.

Psalms 113: 7 - 8 (GNT)
7 He raises the poor from the dust; he lifts the needy from their misery 8 and makes them compan-ions of princes, the princes of his people.

Psalms 146: 7 - 9 (NIV)
7 He upholds the cause of the oppressed and gives food to the hungry. The Lord sets prisoners free, the Lord gives sight to the blind, the Lord lifts up those who are bowed down, the Lord loves the righteous. 9 The Lord watches over the foreigner and sustains the fatherless and the widow, but he frustrates the ways of the wicked.

Proverbs 10: 4 (HCSB)
4 Idle hands make one poor, but diligent hands bring riches.

Proverbs 14: 21 (NKJV)
21 He who despises his neighbor sins;
But he who has mercy on the poor,
happy is he.

Proverbs 14: 31 (NIV)
31 Whoever oppresses the poor shows
contempt for their Maker, but whoever
is kind to the needy honors God.

Proverbs 19: 1, 17 (NKJV)
1 Better is the poor who walks in his
integrity Than one who is perverse in
his lips, and is a fool. 17 He who has
pity on the poor lends to the Lord, And
He will pay back what he has given.

Proverbs 20: 13 (NIV)
13 Do not love sleep or you will grow
poor; stay awake and you will have
food to spare.

Proverbs 21: 13 (ESV)
13 Whoever closes his ear to the cry of
the poor will himself call out and not
be answered.

Proverbs 21: 17 (NCV)
17 Whoever loves pleasure will become
poor; whoever loves wine and perfume
will never be rich.

Proverbs 22: 22 - 23 (NET)
22 Do not exploit a poor person
because he is poor and do not crush
the needy in court, 23 for the Lord will
plead their case and will rob those who
are robbing them.

Proverbs 28: 19 (NIV)
19 Those who work their land will
have abundant food, but those who
chase fantasies will have their fill of
poverty.

Proverbs 31: 8 - 9 (ESV)
8 Open your mouth for the mute, for
the rights of all who are destitute. 9
Open your mouth, judge righteously,
defend the rights of the poor and needy.

Proverbs 31: 10, 20 (AMP)
10 A capable, intelligent, and [a]
virtuous woman—who is he who can
find her? She is far more pre-cious than
jewels and her value is far above rubies
or pearls. 20 She opens her hand to
the poor, yes, she reaches out her filled
hands to the needy [whether in body,
mind, or spirit].

Isaiah 58: 7 - 8 (GNT)
7 Share your food with the hungry
and open your homes to the homeless
poor. Give clothes to those who have
nothing to wear, and do not refuse
to help your own relatives. 8 "Then
my favor will shine on you like the
morning sun, and your wounds will
be quickly healed. I will always be
with you to save you; my presence will
protect you on every side.

Matthew 6: 2 - 3 (NIV)
2 So when you give to the needy, do
not announce it with trumpets, as the
hypocrites do in the syna - gogues and
on the streets, to be honored by others.
Truly I tell you, they have received their
reward in full. 3 But when you give to
the needy, do not let your left hand
know what your right hand is doing,

Mark 9: 37 (NIV)
37 Whoever welcomes one of these
little children in my name welcomes
me; and whoever welcomes me does
not welcome me but the one who sent
me.

Luke 3: 11 (TLB)
11 "If you have two coats," he replied, "give one to the poor. If you have extra food, give it away to those who are hungry."

Luke 14: 13 - 14 (HCSB)
13 On the contrary, when you host a banquet, invite those who are poor, maimed, lame, or blind. 14 And you will be blessed, because they cannot repay you; for you will be repaid at the resurrection of the righteous.

Luke 21: 2 - 4 (TLB)
2 Then a poor widow came by and dropped in two small copper coins. 3 "Really," he remarked, "this poor widow has given more than all the rest of them combined. 4 For they have given a little of what they didn't need, but she, poor as she is, has given everything she has."

Acts 20: 35 (TLB)
35 And I was a constant example to you in helping the poor; for I remembered the words of the Lord Jesus, 'It is more blessed to give than to receive.'

1 Corinthians 13: 3 (NIVUK)
3 If I give all I possess to the poor and give over my body to hardship that I may boast, but do not have love, I gain nothing.

2 Corinthians 9: 7 - 9 (TLB)
7 Everyone must make up his own mind as to how much he should give. Don't force anyone to give more than he really wants to, for cheerful givers are the ones God prizes. 8 God is able to make it up to you by giving you everything you need and more so that there will not only be enough for your own needs but plenty left over

to give joyfully to others. 9 It is as the Scriptures say: "The godly man gives generously to the poor. His good deeds will be an honor to him forever."

Galatians 6: 10 (NIV)
10 Therefore, as we have opportunity, let us do good to all people, especially to those who belong to the family of believers.

James 2: 15 - 16 (CEV)
15 If you know someone who doesn't have any clothes or food, 16 you shouldn't just say, "I hope all goes well for you. I hope you will be warm and have plenty to eat." What good is it to say this, unless you do something to help?

James 2: 2 - 4 (NCV)
2 Suppose someone comes into your church meeting wearing nice clothes and a gold ring. At the same time a poor person comes in wearing old, dirty clothes. 3 You show special attention to the one wearing nice clothes and say, "Please, sit here in this good seat." But you say to the poor person, "Stand over there," or, "Sit on the floor by my feet." 4 What are you doing? You are making some peo-ple more important than others, and with evil thoughts you are deciding that one person is better.

James 5: 4 (NLT)
4 For listen! Hear the cries of the field workers whom you have cheated of their pay. The cries of those who harvest your fields have reached the ears of the Lord of Heaven's Armies.

1 John 3: 17 (HCSB)
17 If anyone has this world's goods and sees his brother in need but closes his

eyes to his need— how can God's love reside in him?

NO FEAR

1 Samuel 17: 45 - 47 (NIV)
45 David said to the Philistine, "You come against me with sword and spear and javelin, but I come against you in the name of the Lord Almighty, the God of the armies of Israel, whom you have defied. 46 This day the Lord will deliver you into my hands, and I'll strike you down and cut off your head. This very day I will give the carcasses of the Philistine army to the birds and the wild animals, and the whole world will know that there is a God in Israel. 47 All those gathered here will know that it is not by sword or spear that the Lord saves; for the battle is the Lord's, and he will give all of you into our hands."

2 Kings 6: 16 - 17 (NASB)
16 So he answered, "Do not fear, for those who are with us are more than those who are with them." 17 Then Elisha prayed and said, "O Lord, I pray, open his eyes that he may see." And the Lord opened the servant's eyes and he saw; and behold, the mountain was full of horses and chariots of fire all around Elisha.

Psalms 18: 1 - 2 (NIV)
1 I love you, Lord, my strength. 2 The Lord is my rock, my fortress and my deliverer; my God is my rock, in whom I take refuge, my shield and the horn of my salvation, my stronghold.

Psalms 27: 1 - 3 (NLT)
1 The Lord is my light and my salvation— so why should I be afraid? The Lord is my fortress, pro-tecting me from danger, so why should I tremble? 2 When evil people come to devour me, when my enemies and foes attack me, they will stumble and fall. 3 Though a mighty army surrounds me, my heart will not be afraid. Even if I am attacked, I will remain confident.

Psalms 27: 14 (NLT)
14 Wait patiently for the Lord. Be brave and courageous. Yes, wait patiently for the Lord.

Psalms 31: 24 (NIRV)
24 Be strong, all you who put your hope in the Lord. Never give up.

Proverbs 8: 12, 14 (AMP)
12 I, Wisdom [from God], make prudence my dwelling, and I find out knowledge and discretion. 14 I have counsel and sound knowledge, I have understanding, I have might and power.

Proverbs 28: 1 (CEB)
1 The wicked run away even though no one pursues them, but the righteous are as confident as a lion.

Isaiah 40: 29 - 31 (NET)
29 He gives strength to those who are tired; to the ones who lack power, he gives renewed energy 30 Even youths get tired and weary; even strong young men clumsily stumble. 31 But those who wait for the Lord's help find renewed strength; they rise up as if they had eagles' wings, they run without growing weary, they walk without getting tired.

Isaiah 43: 1 - 2 (NKJV)

1 But now, thus says the Lord, who created you, O Jacob, And He who formed you, O Israel: "Fear not, for I have redeemed you; I have called you by your name; You are Mine. 2 When you pass through the waters, I will be with you; And through the rivers, they shall not overflow you. When you walk through the fire, you shall not be burned, Nor shall the flame scorch you.

Isaiah 50: 7 - 9 (NASB)

7 For the Lord God helps Me, Therefore, I am not disgraced; Therefore, I have set My face like flint, And I know that I will not be ashamed. 8 He who vindicates Me is near; Who will contend with Me? Let us stand up to each other; Who has a case against Me? Let him draw near to Me. 9 Behold, the Lord God helps Me; Who is he who condemns Me? Behold, they will all wear out like a garment; The moth will eat them.

Daniel 3: 17 - 18 (NCV)

17 If you throw us into the blazing furnace, the God we serve is able to save us from the furnace. He will save us from your power, O king. 18 But even if God does not save us, we want you, O king, to know this: We will not serve your gods or worship the gold statue you have set up.

Acts 4: 29 - 31 (ESV)

29 And now, Lord, look upon their threats and grant to your servants to continue to speak your word with all boldness, 30 while you stretch out your hand to heal, and signs and wonders are performed through the name of your holy servant Jesus." 31 And when they had prayed, the place in which they were gathered together was shaken, and they were all filled with the Holy Spirit and continued to speak the word of God with boldness.

Ephesians 6: 10 (GW)

10 Finally, receive your power from the Lord and from his mighty strength.

OBEDIENCE

Joshua 1: 8 (NLT)

8 Study this Book of Instruction continually. Meditate on it day and night so you will be sure to obey everything written in it. Only then will you prosper and succeed in all you do.

Joshua 23: 6 (NLT)

6 "So be very careful to follow everything Moses wrote in the Book of Instruction. Do not deviate from it, turning either to the right or to the left.

1 Samuel 15: 22 (NCV)

22 But Samuel answered, "What pleases the Lord more: burnt offerings and sacrifices or obedience to his voice? It is better to obey than to sacrifice. It is better to listen to God than to offer the fat of sheep.

Ecclesiastes 12: 13 - 14 (NLT)

13 That's the whole story. Here now is my final conclusion: Fear God and obey his commands, for this is everyone's duty. 14 God will judge us for everything we do, including every secret thing, wheth-er good or bad.

Isaiah 1: 19 (ESV)

19 If you are willing and obedient, you shall eat the good of the land;

Isaiah 48: 17 (NIV)
17 This is what the Lord says— your Redeemer, the Holy One of Israel: "I am the Lord your God, who teaches you what is best for you, who directs you in the way you should go.

Jeremiah 7: 23 - 24 (NASB)
23 But this is what I commanded them, saying, 'Obey My voice, and I will be your God, and you will be My people; and you will walk in all the way which I command you, that it may be well with you.' 24 Yet they did not obey or incline their ear, but walked in their own counsels and in the stubbornness of their evil heart, and went backward and not forward.

Matthew 5: 19 (HCSB)
19 Therefore, whoever breaks one of the least of these commands and teaches people to do so will be called least in the kingdom of heaven. But whoever practices and teaches these commands will be called great in the kingdom of heaven.

Matthew 7: 24 - 25 (NCV)
24 "Everyone who hears my words and obeys them is like a wise man who built his house on rock. 25 It rained hard, the floods came, and the winds blew and hit that house. But it did not fall, because it was built on rock.

Luke 5: 5 - 6 (WEB)
5 Simon answered him, "Master, we worked all night, and took nothing; but at your word I will let down the net." 6 When they had done this, they caught a great multitude of fish, and their net was breaking.

John 14: 23 (NET)
23 Jesus replied, "If anyone loves me, he will obey my word, and my Father will love him, and we will come to him and take up residence with him.

John 15: 10 - 11 (NOG)
10 If you obey my commandments, you will live in my love. I have obeyed my Father's command-ments, and in that way I live in his love. 11 I have told you this so that you will be as joyful as I am, and your joy will be complete.

2 Corinthians 10: 5 (WEB)
5 throwing down imaginations and every high thing that is exalted against the knowledge of God, and bringing every thought into captivity to the obedience of Christ;

Hebrews 11: 8 (NIV)
8 By faith Abraham, when called to go to a place he would later receive as his inheritance, obeyed and went, even though he did not know where he was going.

James 1: 25 (NLT)
25 But if you look carefully into the perfect law that sets you free, and if you do what it says and don't forget what you heard, then God will bless you for doing it.

1 John 2: 17 (NCV)
17 The world and everything that people want in it are passing away, but the person who does what God wants lives forever.

1 John 3: 22 (NCV)
22 And God gives us what we ask for because we obey God's commands and do what pleases him.

OLD AGE

Deuteronomy 5: 33 (HCSB)
33 Follow the whole instruction the Lord your God has commanded you, so that you may live, pros-per, and have a long life in the land you will possess.

Proverbs 3: 1 - 2 (NET)
1 My child, do not forget my teaching, but let your heart keep my commandments, 2 for they will provide a long and full life, and they will add well-being to you.

Psalms 91: 16 (NET)
16 I will satisfy him with long life, and will let him see my salvation.

Psalms 92: 12 - 14 (NKJV)
12 The righteous shall flourish like a palm tree, He shall grow like a cedar in Lebanon. 13 Those who are planted in the house of the Lord Shall flourish in the courts of our God. 14 They shall still bear fruit in old age; They shall be fresh and flourishing,

Proverbs 9: 10 - 11 (NKJV)
10 The fear of the Lord is the beginning of wisdom, And the knowledge of the Holy One is under-standing. 11 For by me your days will be multiplied, And years of life will be added to you.

Proverbs 10: 27 (NCV)
27 Whoever respects the Lord will have a long life, but the life of an evil person will be cut short.

Proverbs 16: 31 (ESV)
31 Gray hair is a crown of glory; it is gained in a righteous life.

Proverbs 17: 6 (NET)
6 Grandchildren are like a crown to the elderly, and the glory of children is their parents.

Proverbs 20: 29 (ESV)
29 The glory of young men is their strength, but the splendor of old men is their gray hair.

Isaiah 46: 4 (NIV)
4 Even to your old age and gray hairs I am he, I am he who will sustain you. I have made you and I will carry you; I will sustain you and I will rescue you.

Joel 2: 28 (WEB)
28 It will happen afterward, that I will pour out my Spirit on all flesh; and your sons and your daugh-ters will prophesy. Your old men will dream dreams. Your young men will see visions.

Luke 1: 36 - 37 (AMP)
36 And listen! Your relative Elizabeth in her old age has also conceived a son, and this is now the sixth month with her who was called barren. 37 For with God nothing is ever impossible and no word from God shall be without power or impossible of fulfillment.

Titus 2: 1 - 5 (NET)
1 But as for you, communicate the behavior that goes with sound teaching. 2 Older men are to be temperate, dignified, self-controlled, sound in faith, in love, and in endurance. 3 Older women likewise are to exhibit behavior fitting for those who are holy, not slandering, not slaves to excessive drinking, but teaching what is good. 4 In this way they will train the younger women to love their husbands, to love their children, 5 to be self-controlled,

pure, fulfilling their duties at home, kind, being subject to their own husbands, so that the message of God may not be discredited.

OVERCOMING SIN

Genesis 4: 7 (NKJV)
7 If you do well, will you not be accepted? And if you do not do well, sin lies at the door. And its desire is for you, but you should rule over it.

Psalms 29: 11 (NIV)
11 The Lord gives strength to his people; the Lord blesses his people with peace.

Psalms 32: 5 - 6 (CEV)
5 So I confessed my sins and told them all to you. I said, "I'll tell the Lord each one of my sins." Then you forgave me and took away my guilt. 6 We worship you, Lord, and we should always pray when-ever we find out that we have sinned. Then we won't be swept away by a raging flood.

Psalms 34: 17, 19 (MSG)
17 Is anyone crying for help? God is listening, ready to rescue you. 19 Disciples so often get into trou-ble; still, God is there every time.

Psalms 86: 6 - 7 (HCSB)
6 Lord, hear my prayer; listen to my plea for mercy. 7 I call on You in the day of my distress, for You will answer me.

Psalms 91: 14 - 15 (NKJV)
14 Because he has set his love upon Me, therefore I will deliver him; I will set

him on high, because he has known My name. 15 He shall call upon Me, and I will answer him; I will be with him in trouble; I will deliver him and honor him.

Psalms 103: 4 - 5 (NET)
4 who delivers your life from the Pit, who crowns you with his loyal love and compassion, 5 who sat-isfies your life with good things, so your youth is renewed like an eagle's.

Psalms 119: 11 - 12 (MEV)
11 Your word I have hidden in my heart, that I might not sin against You. 12 Blessed are You, O Lord; teach me Your statutes.

Psalms 138: 8 (AMP)
8 The Lord will perfect that which concerns me; Your mercy and loving-kindness, O Lord, endure for-ever— forsake not the works of Your own hands.

Proverbs 24: 16 (AMP)
16 For a righteous man falls seven times and rises again, but the wicked are overthrown by calamity.

Isaiah 40: 29 (NET)
29 He gives strength to those who are tired; to the ones who lack power, he gives renewed energy.

Jeremiah 29: 12 - 13 (ESV)
12 Then you will call upon me and come and pray to me, and I will hear you. 13 You will seek me and find me, when you seek me with all your heart.

Matthew 11: 28 - 30 (NIV)
28 Come to me, all you who are weary and burdened, and I will give you rest.

29 Take my yoke upon you and learn from me, for I am gentle and humble in heart, and you will find rest for your souls. 30 For my yoke is easy and my burden is light.

Matthew 18: 18 (NASB)

18 Truly I say to you, whatever you bind on earth shall have been bound in heaven; and whatever you loose on earth shall have been loosed in heaven.

Matthew 7: 7 - 11 (WEB)

7 "Ask, and it will be given you. Seek, and you will find. Knock, and it will be opened for you. 8 For everyone who asks receives. He who seeks finds. To him who knocks it will be opened. 9 Or who is there among you who, if his son asks him for bread, will give him a stone? 10 Or if he asks for a fish, who will give him a serpent? 11 If you then, being evil, know how to give good gifts to your children, how much more will your Father who is in heaven give good things to those who ask him!

Mark 11: 23 (NET)

23 I tell you the truth, if someone says to this mountain, 'Be lifted up and thrown into the sea,' and does not doubt in his heart but believes that what he says will happen, it will be done for him.

Luke 10: 19 (WEB)

19 Behold, I give you authority to tread on serpents and scorpions, and over all the power of the ene-my. Nothing will in any way hurt you.

Romans 7: 14 - 25 (NCV)

14 We know that the law is spiritual, but I am not spiritual since sin rules me as if I were its slave. 15 I do not understand the things I do. I do not do what I want to do, and I do the things I hate. 16 And if I do not want to do the hated things I do, that means I agree that the law is good. 17 But I am not really the one who is doing these hated things; it is sin living in me that does them. 18 Yes, I know that noth-ing good lives in me—I mean nothing good lives in the part of me that is earthly and sinful. I want to do the things that are good, but I do not do them. 19 I do not do the good things I want to do, but I do the bad things I do not want to do. 20 So if I do things I do not want to do, then I am not the one doing them. It is sin living in me that does those things. 21 So I have learned this rule: When I want to do good, evil is there with me. 22 In my mind, I am happy with God's law. 23 But I see another law work-ing in my body, which makes war against the law that my mind accepts. That other law working in my body is the law of sin, and it makes me its prisoner. 24 What a miserable man I am! Who will save me from this body that brings me death? 25 I thank God for saving me through Jesus Christ our Lord! So in my mind I am a slave to God's law, but in my sinful self I am a slave to the law of sin.

Romans 8: 1 - 2, 11, 13 - 14 (ESV)

1 There is therefore now no condemnation for those who are in Christ Jesus. 2 For the law of the Spirit of life has set you free in Christ Jesus from the law of sin and death. 11 If the Spirit of him who raised Jesus from the dead dwells in you, he who raised Christ Jesus from the dead will also give life to your mortal bodies through his Spirit who dwells in you. 13 For if

you live according to the flesh you will die, but if by the Spirit you put to death the deeds of the body, you will live. 14 For all who are led by the Spirit of God are sons of God.

Romans 12: 2 (ESV)

2 Do not be conformed to this world, but be transformed by the renewal of your mind, that by testing you may discern what is the will of God, what is good and acceptable and perfect.

1 Corinthians 10: 13 (NLT)

13 The temptations in your life are no different from what others experience. And God is faithful. He will not allow the temptation to be more than you can stand. When you are tempted, he will show you a way out so that you can endure.

2 Corinthians 10: 4 - 5 (NLT)

4 We use God's mighty weapons, not worldly weapons, to knock down the strongholds of human reasoning and to destroy false arguments. 5 We destroy every proud obstacle that keeps people from knowing God. We capture their rebellious thoughts and teach them to obey Christ.

2 Corinthians 12: 9 (NLT)

9 Each time he said, "My grace is all you need. My power works best in weakness." So now I am glad to boast about my weaknesses, so that the power of Christ can work through me.

Galatians 5: 16 - 17 (AMP)

16 But I say, walk and live [habitually] in the [Holy] Spirit [responsive to and controlled and guided by the Spirit]; then you will certainly not gratify the cravings and desires of the flesh (of human nature without God). 17 For the desires of the flesh are opposed to the [Holy] Spirit, and the [desires of the] Spirit are opposed to the flesh (godless human nature); for these are antagonistic to each other [con-tinually withstanding and in conflict with each other], so that you are not free but are prevented from doing what you desire to do.

Philippians 4: 13 (WEB)

13 I can do all things through Christ, who strengthens me.

Hebrews 4: 16 (WEB)

16 Let us therefore draw near with boldness to the throne of grace, that we may receive mercy, and may find grace for help in time of need.

Hebrews 7: 25 (MEV)

25 Therefore He is able to save to the uttermost those who come to God through Him, because He at all times lives to make intercession for them.

James 4: 8 (NCV)

8 Come near to God, and God will come near to you. You sinners, clean sin out of your lives. You who are trying to follow God and the world at the same time, make your thinking pure.

James 5: 16 (NLT)

16 Confess your sins to each other and pray for each other so that you may be healed. The earnest prayer of a righteous person has great power and produces wonderful results.

PARENTS

Exodus 20: 12 (MEV)
12 Honor your father and your mother, that your days may be long in the land which the Lord your God is giving you.

Deuteronomy 11: 18 - 21 (GW)
18 Take these words of mine to heart and keep them in mind. Write them down, tie them around your wrist, and wear them as headbands as a reminder. 19 Teach them to your children, and talk about them when you're at home or away, when you lie down or get up. 20 Write them on the doorframes of your houses and on your gates. 21 Then you and your children will live for a long time in this land that the Lord swore to give to your ancestors—as long as there's a sky above the earth.

Proverbs 1: 8 - 9 (RSV)
8 Hear, my son, your father's instruction, and reject not your mother's teaching; 9 for they are a fair garland for your head, and pendants for your neck.

Proverbs 13: 24 (NET)
24 The one who spares his rod hates his child, but the one who loves his child is diligent in disciplin-ing him.

Proverbs 17: 6 (GW)
6 Grandchildren are the crown of grandparents, and parents are the glory of their children.

Proverbs 22: 6 (NET)
6 Train a child in the way that he should go, and when he is old he will not turn from it.

Proverbs 29: 15, 17 (WEB)
15 The rod of correction gives wisdom, but a child left to himself causes shame to his mother. 17 Cor-rect your son, and he will give you peace; yes, he will bring delight to your soul.

Ephesians 6: 4 (RSV)
4 Fathers, do not provoke your children to anger, but bring them up in the discipline and instruction of the Lord.

Colossians 3: 21 (WEB)
21 Fathers, don't provoke your children, so that they won't be discouraged.

PATIENCE

Psalms 27: 14 (NIV)
14 Wait for the Lord; be strong and take heart and wait for the Lord.

Psalms 37: 34 (NLV)
34 Wait for the Lord. Keep His way. And He will give you a high place to receive the land. When the sinful are cut off, you will see it.

Psalms 37: 7, 9 (NKJV)
7 Rest in the Lord, and wait patiently for Him; Do not fret because of him who prospers in his way, Be-cause of the man who brings wicked schemes to pass. 9 For evildoers shall be cut off; But those who wait on the Lord, They shall inherit the earth.

Psalms 40: 1 (GNT)
1 I waited patiently for the Lord's help; then he listened to me and heard my cry.

Proverbs 25: 15 (ISV)
15 Through patience a ruler may be persuaded; a gentle word can break a bone.

Ecclesiastes 7: 8 - 9 (ISV)
8 The conclusion of something is better than its beginning, and a patient attitude is more valuable than a proud one. 9 Never be in a hurry to become internally angry, since anger settles down in the lap of fools.

Isaiah 40: 31 (ESV)
31 but they who wait for the Lord shall renew their strength; they shall mount up with wings like ea-gles; they shall run and not be weary; they shall walk and not faint.

Lamentations 3: 25 - 26 (ESV)
25 The Lord is good to those who wait for him, to anyone who seeks help from him. 26 It is good to continue to hope and wait silently for the Lord to save us.

Habakkuk 2: 3 (NIV)
3 For the revelation awaits an appointed time; it speaks of the end and will not prove false. Though it linger, wait for it; it will certainly come and will not delay.

Luke 8: 15 (NIVUK)
15 And as for that in the good soil, they are those who, hearing the word, hold it fast in an honest and good heart, and bring forth fruit with patience.

Luke 21: 17 - 19 (NASB)
17 and you will be hated by all because of My name. 18 Yet not a hair of your head will perish. 19 By your endurance you will gain your lives.

Romans 5: 3 - 5 (NCV)
3 We also have joy with our troubles, because we know that these troubles produce patience. 4 And patience produces character, and character produces hope. 5 And this hope will never disappoint us, because God has poured out his love to fill our hearts. He gave us his love through the Holy Spirit, whom God has given to us.

Romans 8: 24 - 25 (NASB)
24 For in hope we have been saved, but hope that is seen is not hope; for who hopes for what he already sees? 25 But if we hope for what we do not see, with perseverance we wait eagerly for it.

Romans 15: 5 (NASB)
5 Now may the God who gives perseverance and encouragement grant you to be of the same mind with one another according to Christ Jesus,

Galatians 5: 22 (NCV)
22 But the Spirit produces the fruit of love, joy, peace, patience, kindness, goodness, faithfulness,

Galatians 6: 9 (MEV)
9 And let us not grow weary in doing good, for in due season we shall reap, if we do not give up.

Colossians 1: 11 - 12 (ESV)
11 May you be strengthened with all power, according to his glorious might, for all endurance and patience with joy, 12 giving thanks to the Father, who has qualified you to share in the inheritance of the saints in light.

Hebrews 6: 12, 15 (NET)
12 so that you may not be sluggish, but imitators of those who through faith

and perseverance inherit the promises. 15 And so by persevering, Abraham inherited the promise.

Hebrews 10: 36 - 37 (NLT)
36 Patient endurance is what you need now, so that you will continue to do God's will. Then you will receive all that he has promised. 37 "For in just a little while, the Coming One will come and not delay.

James 1: 2, 4 (NKJV)
2 My brethren, count it all joy when you fall into various trials, 4 But let patience have its perfect work, that you may be perfect and complete, lacking nothing.

James 1: 19 - 20 (NCV)
19 My dear brothers and sisters, always be willing to listen and slow to speak. Do not become angry easily, 20 because anger will not help you live the right kind of life God wants.

1 Peter 2: 19 - 20 (NLT)
19 For God is pleased when, conscious of his will, you patiently endure unjust treatment. 20 Of course, you get no credit for being patient if you are beaten for doing wrong. But if you suffer for doing good and endure it patiently, God is pleased with you.

PEACE

Psalms 4: 8 (NKJV)
8 I will both lie down in peace, and sleep; For You alone, O Lord, make me dwell in safety.

Psalms 29: 11 (HCSB)
11 The Lord gives His people strength; the Lord blesses His people with peace.

Psalms 37: 37 (NKJV)
37 Mark the blameless man, and observe the upright; For the future of that man is peace.

Psalms 46: 8 - 9 (NCV)
8 Come and see what the Lord has done, the amazing things he has done on the earth. 9 He stops wars everywhere on the earth. He breaks all bows and spears and burns up the chariots with fire.

Psalms 147: 14 (NIV)
14 He grants peace to your borders and satisfies you with the finest of wheat.

Psalms 119: 165 (NIV)
165 Great peace have those who love your law, and nothing can make them stumble.

Proverbs 3: 1 - 2 (NIV)
1 My son, do not forget my teaching, but keep my commands in your heart, 2 for they will prolong your life many years and bring you peace and prosperity.

Proverbs 3: 13, 17 (NIV)
13 Blessed are those who find wisdom, those who gain understanding, 17 Her ways are pleasant ways, and all her paths are peace.

Proverbs 29: 9 (AMP)
9 If a wise man has an argument with a foolish man, the fool only rages or laughs, and there is no rest.

Ecclesiastes 4: 6 (GNT)
6 Maybe so, but it is better to have only a little, with peace of mind, than be busy all the time with both hands, trying to catch the wind.

Ecclesiastes 10: 4 (NLT)
4 If your boss is angry at you, don't quit! A quiet spirit can overcome even great mistakes.

Isaiah 26: 3 (ESV)
3 You keep him in perfect peace whose mind is stayed on you, because he trusts in you.

Isaiah 32: 16 - 18 (NIV)
16 The Lord's justice will dwell in the desert, his righteousness live in the fertile field. 17 The fruit of that righteousness will be peace; its effect will be quietness and confidence forever. 18 My people will live in peaceful dwelling places, in secure homes, in undisturbed places of rest.

Isaiah 48: 22 (NCV)
22 "There is no peace for evil people," says the Lord.

Isaiah 52: 7 (AMP)
7 How beautiful upon the mountains are the feet of him who brings good tidings, who publishes peace, who brings good tidings of good, who publishes salvation, who says to Zion, Your God reigns!

Isaiah 55: 12 (MEV)
12 For you shall go out with joy, and be led out with peace; the mountains and the hills shall break forth into singing before you, and all the trees of the field shall clap their hands.

Isaiah 57: 19 (NCV)
19 I will give peace, real peace, to those far and near, and I will heal them," says the Lord.

Mark 4: 39 (NIVUK)
39 He got up, rebuked the wind and said to the waves, 'Quiet! Be still!' Then the wind died down and it was completely calm.

Mark 5: 34 (NKJV)
34 He said to her, "Daughter, your faith has made you well. Go in peace, and be cured of your disease."

Luke 11: 21 (NIV)
21 When a strong man, fully armed, guards his own house, his possessions are safe.

John 14: 27 (GNT)
27 "Peace is what I leave with you; it is my own peace that I give you. I do not give it as the world does. Do not be worried and upset; do not be afraid.

Romans 5: 1 (NET)
1 Therefore, since we have been declared righteous by faith, we have peace with God through our Lord Jesus Christ,

Romans 12: 18 (NIV)
18 If it is possible, as far as it depends on you, live at peace with everyone.

Romans 14: 17 - 19 (NIV)
17 For the kingdom of God is not a matter of eating and drinking, but of righteousness, peace and joy in the Holy Spirit, 18 because anyone who serves Christ in this way is pleasing to God and receives human approval. 19 Let us therefore make every effort to

do what leads to peace and to mutual edifi-cation.

1 Corinthians 14: 33 (NCV)
33 God is not a God of confusion but a God of peace. As is true in all the churches of God's people,

Galatians 5: 22 (MEV)
22 But the fruit of the Spirit is love, joy, peace, patience, gentleness, goodness, faith,

Philippians 4: 6 - 9 (NLT)
6 Don't worry about anything; instead, pray about everything. Tell God what you need, and thank him for all he has done. 7 Then you will experience God's peace, which exceeds anything we can under-stand. His peace will guard your hearts and minds as you live in Christ Jesus. 8 And now, dear broth-ers and sisters, one final thing. Fix your thoughts on what is true, and honorable, and right, and pure, and lovely, and admirable. Think about things that are excellent and worthy of praise. 9 Keep putting into practice all you learned and received from me— everything you heard from me and saw me do-ing. Then the God of peace will be with you.

1 Timothy 2: 1 - 2 (NET)
1 First of all, then, I urge that requests, prayers, intercessions, and thanks be offered on behalf of all people, 2 even for kings and all who are in authority, that they may lead a peaceful and quiet life in all godliness and dignity.

Hebrews 13: 20 - 21 (NIV)
20 Now may the God of peace, who through the blood of the eternal covenant brought back from the dead our Lord Jesus, that great Shepherd of the sheep, 21 equip you with everything good for doing his will, and may he work in us what is pleasing to him, through Jesus Christ, to whom be glory for ever and ever. Amen.

James 3: 17 - 18 (NIV)
17 But the wisdom that comes from heaven is first of all pure; then peace-loving, considerate, sub-missive, full of mercy and good fruit, impartial and sincere. 18 Peacemakers who sow in peace reap a harvest of righteousness.

PERSEVERANCE

2 Chronicles 5: 13 - 14 (NCV)
13 Those who blew the trumpets and those who sang together sounded like one person as they praised and thanked the Lord. They sang as others played their trumpets, cymbals, and other in-struments. They praised the Lord with this song: "He is good; his love continues forever." Then the Temple of the Lord was filled with a cloud. 14 The priests could not continue their work because of the cloud, because the Lord's glory filled the Temple of God.

Psalms 31:24 (NIRV)
Be strong, all you who put your hope in the Lord. Never give up.

Psalms 147: 10 - 11 (ESV)
10 His delight is not in the strength of the horse, nor his pleasure in the legs of a man, 11 but the Lord takes pleasure in those who fear him, in those who hope in his steadfast love.

Psalms 149: 1 - 6 (NCV)

1 Praise the Lord! Sing a new song to the Lord; sing his praise in the meeting of his people. 2 Let the Israelites be happy because of God, their Maker. Let the people of Jerusalem rejoice because of their King. 3 They should praise him with dancing. They should sing praises to him with tambourines and harps. 4 The Lord is pleased with his people; he saves the humble. 5 Let those who worship him rejoice in his glory. Let them sing for joy even in bed! 6 Let them shout his praise with their two-edged swords in their hands.

Ecclesiastes 7.8,9 (CEV)

Something completed is better than something just begun; patience is better than too much pride.
Only fools get angry quickly and hold a grudge.

Isaiah 40.31 (ESV)

but they who wait for the Lord shall renew their strength; they shall mount up with wings like eagles; they shall run and not be weary; they shall walk and not faint.

Lamentations 3.25,26 (ESV)

The Lord is good to those who wait for him, to the soul who seeks him. It is good that one should wait quietly for the salvation of the Lord.

Luke 8.15 (NIV)

But the seed on good soil stands for those with a noble and good heart, who hear the word, retain it, and by persevering produce a crop.

Luke 11.5,7,8,9,10 (NET)

5 Then he said to them, "Suppose one of you has a friend, and you go to him at midnight and say to him, 'Friend, lend me three loaves of bread, 7 Then he will reply from inside, 'Do not bother me. The door is already shut, and my children and I are in bed. I cannot get up and give you anything.' 8 I tell you, even though the man inside will not get up and give him anything because he is his friend, yet because of the first man's sheer persistence he will get up and give him whatever he needs. 9 "So I tell you: Ask, and it will be given to you; seek, and you will find; knock, and the door will be opened for you. 10 For everyone who asks receives, and the one who seeks finds, and to the one who knocks, the door will be opened.

Luke 18.1 (NIV)

Then Jesus told his disciples a parable to show them that they should always pray and not give up.

Luke 21.17,18,19 (NASB)

17 and you will be hated by all because of My name. 18 Yet not a hair of your head will perish. 19 By your endurance you will gain your lives.

Romans 8: 8 - 9 (ESV)\

8 Those who are in the flesh cannot please God. 9 You, however, are not in the flesh but in the Spirit, if in fact the Spirit of God dwells in you. Anyone who does not have the Spirit of Christ does not be-long to him.

Romans 8.24,25 (NASB)

For in hope we have been saved, but hope that is seen is not hope; for who hopes for what he al-ready sees? 25 But if we hope for what we do not see, with perseverance we wait eagerly for it.

Romans 15.5 (NASB)

Now may the God [a]who gives perseverance and encouragement grant you to be of the same mind with one another according to Christ Jesus,

1 Corinthians 1: 21 (NLT)

21 Since God in his wisdom saw to it that the world would never know him through human wisdom, he has used our foolish preaching to save those who believe.

1 Corinthians 12: 18 (NKJV)

18 But now God has set the members, each one of them, in the body just as He pleased.

Galatians 6.9 (WEB)

Let us not be weary in doing good, for we will reap in due season, if we don't give up. Habakkuk

Colossians 1: 9 - 10 (NLT)

9 So we have not stopped praying for you since we first heard about you. We ask God to give you complete knowledge of his will and to give you spiritual wisdom and understanding. 10 Then the way you live will always honor and please the Lord, and your lives will produce every kind of good fruit. All the while, you will grow as you learn to know God better and better.

Colossians 1:11,12 (ESV)

11 May you be strengthened with all power, according to his glorious might, for all endurance and patience with joy, 12 giving thanks to the Father, who has qualified you to share in the inheritance of the saints in light.

1 Thessalonians 4: 1 - 3 (NIV)

1 As for other matters, brothers and sisters, we instructed you how to live in order to please God, as in fact you are living. Now we ask you and urge you in the Lord Jesus to do this more and more. 2 For you know what instructions we gave you by the authority of the Lord Jesus. 3 It is God's will that you should be sanctified: that you should avoid sexual immorality;

1 Thessalonians 5.21 (WEB)

Test all things, and hold firmly that which is good.

1 Timothy 2: 1 - 4 (NCV)

1 First, I tell you to pray for all people, asking God for what they need and being thankful to him.
2 Pray for rulers and for all who have authority so that we can have quiet and peaceful lives full of worship and respect for God. 3 This is good, and it pleases God our Savior, 4 who wants all people to be saved and to know the truth.

Hebrews 6.12,15 (NET)

12 so that you may not be sluggish, but imitators of those who through faith and perseverance inherit the promises. 15 And so by persevering, Abraham inherited the promise.

Hebrews 10: 36,37 (NLT)

36 Patient endurance is what you need now, so that you will continue to do God's will. Then you will receive all that he has promised. 37 "For in just a little while, the Coming One will come and not delay.

James 1: 2,3,4 (NKJV)

2 My brethren, count it all joy when you fall into various trials, 3 knowing

that the testing of your faith produces patience. 4 But let patience have its perfect work, that you may be perfect and complete, lacking nothing.

James 5:10,11 (WEB)

10 Take, brothers, for an example of suffering and of patience, the prophets who spoke in the name of the Lord. 11 Behold, we call them blessed who endured. You have heard of the patience of Job, and have seen the Lord in the outcome, and how the Lord is full of compassion and mercy.

1 Peter 2: 5 (NLT)

5 And you are living stones that God is building into his spiritual temple. What's more, you are his holy priests. Through the mediation of Jesus Christ, you offer spiritual sacrifices that please God.

1 Peter 2: 19 - 20 (NLT)

19 For God is pleased when, conscious of his will, you patiently endure unjust treatment. 20 Of course, you get no credit for being patient if you are beaten for doing wrong. But if you suffer for doing good and endure it patiently, God is pleased with you.

1 John 3: 22 - 23 (WEB)

22 and whatever we ask, we receive from him, because we keep his commandments and do the things that are pleasing in his sight. 23 This is his commandment, that we should believe in the name of his Son, Jesus Christ, and love one another, even as he commanded.

Revelation 4: 11 (NLT)

11 You are worthy, O Lord our God, to receive glory and honor and power. For you created all things, and they exist because you created what you pleased.

POOR

Exodus 22: 25 - 26 (NKJV)

25 "If you lend money to any of My people who are poor among you, you shall not be like a money-lender to him; you shall not charge him interest. 26 If you ever take your neighbor's garment as a pledge, you shall return it to him before the sun goes down.

Leviticus 19: 10 (CEV)

10 Don't strip your grapevines clean or gather the grapes that fall off the vines. Leave them for the poor and for those foreigners who live among you. I am the Lord your God.

Psalms 12: 5 (NLT)

5 The Lord replies, "I have seen violence done to the helpless, and I have heard the groans of the poor. Now I will rise up to rescue them, as they have longed for me to do."

Psalms 37: 14 - 15 (NIV)

14 The wicked draw the sword and bend the bow to bring down the poor and needy, to slay those whose ways are upright. 15 But their swords will pierce their own hearts, and their bows will be bro-ken.

Psalms 41: 1 (MEV)

1 Blessed are those who consider the poor; the Lord will deliver them in the day of trouble.

Psalms 72: 12 - 13 (NASB)

12 For he will deliver the needy when he cries for help, The afflicted also, and him who has no helper. 13 He will have compassion on the poor and needy, And the lives of the needy he will save.

Psalms 102: 17 (WEB)
17 He has responded to the prayer of the destitute, and has not despised their prayer.

Psalms 113: 7 - 8 (GNT)
7 He raises the poor from the dust; he lifts the needy from their misery 8 and makes them compan-ions of princes, the princes of his people.

Proverbs 10: 4 (HCSB)
4 Idle hands make one poor, but diligent hands bring riches.

Proverbs 14: 31 (NIV)
31 Whoever oppresses the poor shows contempt for their Maker, but whoever is kind to the needy honors God.

Proverbs 19: 1, 17 (NKJV)
1 Better is the poor who walks in his integrity Than one who is perverse in his lips, and is a fool. 17 He who has pity on the poor lends to the Lord, And He will pay back what he has given.

Proverbs 21: 13 (ESV)
13 Whoever closes his ear to the cry of the poor will himself call out and not be answered.

Proverbs 22: 22 - 23 (NET)
22 Do not exploit a poor person because he is poor and do not crush the needy in court, 23 for the Lord will plead their case and will rob those who are robbing them.

Proverbs 28: 19 (NIV)
19 Those who work their land will have abundant food, but those who chase fantasies will have their fill of poverty.

Proverbs 31: 8 - 9 (ESV)
8 Open your mouth for the mute, for the rights of all who are destitute. 9 Open your mouth, judge righteously, defend the rights of the poor and needy.

Isaiah 58: 7 - 8 (GNT)
7 Share your food with the hungry and open your homes to the homeless poor. Give clothes to those who have nothing to wear, and do not refuse to help your own relatives. 8 "Then my favor will shine on you like the morning sun, and your wounds will be quickly healed. I will always be with you to save you; my presence will protect you on every side.

Matthew 6: 2 - 3 (NIV)
2 So when you give to the needy, do not announce it with trumpets, as the hypocrites do in the syna - gogues and on the streets, to be honored by others. Truly I tell you, they have received their reward in full. 3 But when you give to the needy, do not let your left hand know what your right hand is doing,

Luke 3: 11 (TLB)
11 "If you have two coats," he replied, "give one to the poor. If you have extra food, give it away to those who are hungry."

Luke 14: 13 - 14 (HCSB)
13 On the contrary, when you host a banquet, invite those who are poor, maimed, lame, or blind.
14 And you will be blessed, because they cannot repay you; for you will be repaid at the resurrection of the righteous.

Acts 20: 35 (TLB)
35 And I was a constant example to you in helping the poor; for I remembered

the words of the Lord Jesus, 'It is more blessed to give than to receive.'

2 Corinthians 9: 7 - 9 (TLB)

7 Everyone must make up his own mind as to how much he should give. Don't force anyone to give more than he really wants to, for cheerful givers are the ones God prizes. 8 God is able to make it up to you by giving you everything you need and more so that there will not only be enough for your own needs but plenty left over to give joyfully to others. 9 It is as the Scriptures say: "The godly man gives generously to the poor. His good deeds will be an honor to him forever."

James 2: 15 - 16 (CEV)

15 If you know someone who doesn't have any clothes or food, 16 you shouldn't just say, "I hope all goes well for you. I hope you will be warm and have plenty to eat." What good is it to say this, unless you do something to help?

James 2: 2 - 4 (NCV)

2 Suppose someone comes into your church meeting wearing nice clothes and a gold ring. At the same time a poor person comes in wearing old, dirty clothes. 3 You show special attention to the one wearing nice clothes and say, "Please, sit here in this good seat." But you say to the poor person, "Stand over there," or, "Sit on the floor by my feet." 4 What are you doing? You are making some peo-ple more important than others, and with evil thoughts you are deciding that one person is better.

1 John 3: 17 (HCSB)

17 If anyone has this world's goods and sees his brother in need but closes his eyes to his need— how can God's love reside in him?

POWER

1 Samuel 17: 45 - 47 (NIV)

45 David said to the Philistine, "You come against me with sword and spear and javelin, but I come against you in the name of the Lord Almighty, the God of the armies of Israel, whom you have defied. 46 This day the Lord will deliver you into my hands, and I'll strike you down and cut off your head. This very day I will give the carcasses of the Philistine army to the birds and the wild animals, and the whole world will know that there is a God in Israel. 47 All those gathered here will know that it is not by sword or spear that the Lord saves; for the battle is the Lord's, and he will give all of you into our hands."

2 Kings 6: 16 - 17 (MEV)

16 And he said, "Do not be afraid, for there are more with us than with them." 17 Then Elisha prayed, "Lord, open his eyes and let him see." So the Lord opened the eyes of the young man, and he saw that the mountain was full of horses and chariots of fire surrounding Elisha.

Psalms 18: 29, 32 - 34, 39 (NIV)

29 With your help I can advance against a troop[a]; with my God I can scale a wall. 32 It is God who arms me with strength and keeps my way secure. 33 He makes my feet like the feet of a deer; he causes me to stand on the heights. 34 He trains my hands for battle; my arms can bend a bow of bronze. 39 You

armed me with strength for battle; you humbled my adversaries before me.

Psalms 68: 35 (NIV)
35 You, God, are awesome in your sanctuary; the God of Israel gives power and strength to his peo-ple. Praise be to God!

Proverbs 18: 21 (HCSB)
21 Life and death are in the power of the tongue, and those who love it will eat its fruit.

Proverbs 28: 1 (CEB)
1 The wicked run away even though no one pursues them, but the righteous are as confident as a lion.

Isaiah 40: 29 - 31 (NET)
29 He gives strength to those who are tired; to the ones who lack power, he gives renewed energy. 30 Even youths get tired and weary; even strong young men clumsily stumble. 31 But those who wait for the Lord's help find renewed strength; they rise up as if they had eagles' wings, they run without growing weary, they walk without getting tired.

Jeremiah 12: 5 (MEV)
5 If you have run with the footmen, and they have wearied you, then how can you contend with hors-es? And if in the land of peace in which you trusted, they wearied you, then how will you do in the thicket of the Jordan?

Matthew 11: 12 (MEV)
12 From the days of John the Baptist until now, the kingdom of heaven has forcefully advanced, and the strong take it by force.

Matthew 18: 18 (NASB)
18 Truly I say to you, whatever you bind on earth shall have been bound in heaven; and whatever you loose on earth shall have been loosed in heaven.

Matthew 28: 18 (NCV)
18 Then Jesus came to them and said, "All power in heaven and on earth is given to me.

Luke 10: 19 (GW)
19 I have given you the authority to trample snakes and scorpions and to destroy the enemy's power. Nothing will hurt you.

Acts 1: 8 (WEB)
8 But you will receive power when the Holy Spirit has come upon you. You will be witnesses to me in Jerusalem, in all Judea and Samaria, and to the uttermost parts of the earth.

1 Corinthians 2: 4 - 5 (NCV)
4 My teaching and preaching were not with words of human wisdom that persuade people but with proof of the power that the Spirit gives. 5 This was so that your faith would be in God's power and not in human wisdom.

Ephesians 1: 18 - 20 (HCSB)
18 I pray that the perception of your mind may be enlightened so you may know what is the hope of His calling, what are the glorious riches of His inheritance among the saints, 19 and what is the im-measurable greatness of His power to us who believe, according to the working of His vast strength.

Ephesians 3: 16 - 17, 20 (HCSB)
16 I pray that He may grant you, according to the riches of His glory,

to be strengthened with power in the inner man through His Spirit, 17 and that the Messiah may dwell in your hearts through faith. I pray that you, being rooted and firmly established in love, 20 Now to Him who is able to do above and beyond all that we ask or think according to the power that works in us—

Ephesians 6: 10 (ASV)
10 Finally, be strong in the Lord, and in the strength of his might.

Ephesians 6: 13 - 18 (GNT)
13 So put on God's armor now! Then when the evil day comes, you will be able to resist the enemy's attacks; and after fighting to the end, you will still hold your ground. 14 So stand ready, with truth as a belt tight around your waist, with righteousness as your breastplate, 15 and as your shoes the read-iness to announce the Good News of peace. 16 At all times carry faith as a shield; for with it you will be able to put out all the burning arrows shot by the Evil One. 17 And accept salvation as a helmet, and the word of God as the sword which the Spirit gives you. 18 Do all this in prayer, asking for God's help. Pray on every occasion, as the Spirit leads. For this reason keep alert and never give up; pray always for all God's people.

Philippians 4: 12 - 13 (NKJV)
12 I know how to be abased, and I know how to abound. Everywhere and in all things I have learned both to be full and to be hungry, both to abound and to suffer need. 13 I can do all things through Christ who strengthens me.

Colossians 1: 16 - 17 (RSV)

16 for in him all things were created, in heaven and on earth, visible and invisible, whether thrones or dominions or principalities or authorities—all things were created through him and for him. 17 He is before all things, and in him all things hold together.

2 Timothy 1: 7 - 8 (NKJV)
7 For God has not given us a spirit of fear, but of power and of love and of a sound mind. 8 Therefore do not be ashamed of the testimony of our Lord, nor of me His prisoner, but share with me in the suf-ferings for the gospel according to the power of God,

1 Peter 3: 22 (GNT)
22 who has gone to heaven and is at the right side of God, ruling over all angels and heavenly au-thorities and powers.

PRAISE

2 Samuel 22: 49 - 50 (NKJV)
49 He delivers me from my enemies. You also lift me up above those who rise against me; You have delivered me from the violent man. 50 Therefore I will give thanks to You, O Lord, among the Gen-tiles, And sing praises to Your name.

1 Chronicles 16: 25 - 26 (NCV)
25 The Lord is great; he should be praised. He should be respected more than all the gods. 26 All the gods of the nations are only idols, but the Lord made the skies.

Psalms 16: 7 - 9 (CEV)
7 I praise you, Lord, for being my guide. Even in the darkest night, your

teachings fill my mind. 8 I will always look to you, as you stand beside me and protect me from fear. 9 With all my heart, I will celebrate, and I can safely rest.

Psalms 28: 7 (NKJV)

7 The Lord is my strength and my shield; My heart trusted in Him, and I am helped; Therefore my heart greatly rejoices, And with my song I will praise Him.

Psalms 30: 11 - 12 (NIV)

11 You turned my wailing into dancing; you removed my sackcloth and clothed me with joy, 12 that my heart may sing your praises and not be silent. Lord my God, I will praise you forever.

Psalms 33: 1 - 3 (NCV)

1 Sing to the Lord, you who do what is right; honest people should praise him. 2 Praise the Lord on the harp; make music for him on a ten-stringed lyre. 3 Sing a new song to him; play well and joyfully.

Psalms 34: 1 - 4 (ESV)

1 I will bless the Lord at all times; his praise shall continually be in my mouth. 2 My soul makes its boast in the Lord; let the humble hear and be glad. 3 Oh, magnify the Lord with me, and let us exalt his name together! 4 I sought the Lord, and he answered me and delivered me from all my fears.

Psalms 96: 1 - 4 (NCV)

1 Sing to the Lord a new song; sing to the Lord, all the earth. 2 Sing to the Lord and praise his name; every day tell how he saves us. 3 Tell the nations of his glory; tell all peoples the miracles he does, 4 because the Lord is great; he

should be praised at all times. He should be honored more than all the gods,

Psalms 100: 4 (WEB)

4 Enter into his gates with thanksgiving, into his courts with praise. Give thanks to him, and bless his name.

Psalms 103: 1 - 5 (NKJV)

1 Bless the Lord, O my soul; And all that is within me, bless His holy name!2 Bless the Lord, O my soul, And forget not all His benefits: 3 Who forgives all your iniquities, Who heals all your diseases, 4 Who redeems your life from destruction, Who crowns you with lovingkindness and tender mercies, 5 Who satisfies your mouth with good things, So that your youth is renewed like the eagle's.

Psalms 103: 20 - 22 (NIV)

20 Praise the Lord, you his angels, you mighty ones who do his bidding, who obey his word. 21 Praise the Lord, all his heavenly hosts, you his servants who do his will. 22 Praise the Lord, all his works everywhere in his dominion. Praise the Lord, my soul.

Psalms 149: 3, 6 (NCV)

1 Praise the Lord! It is good to sing praises to our God; it is good and pleasant to praise him.3 They should praise him with dancing. They should sing praises to him with tambourines and harps. 6 Let them shout his praise with their two-edged swords in their hands.

Proverbs 27: 2 (HCSB)

2 Let another praise you, and not your own mouth— a stranger, and not your own lips.

Isaiah 42: 8 - 10 (GNT)
8 "I alone am the Lord your God. No other god may share my glory; I will not let idols share my praise The things I predicted have now come true. Now I will tell you of new things even before they begin to happen." 10 Sing a new song to the Lord; sing his praise, all the world! Praise him, you that sail the sea; praise him, all creatures of the sea! Sing, distant lands and all who live there!

Jeremiah 17: 14 (NIV)
14 Heal me, Lord, and I will be healed; save me and I will be saved, for you are the one I praise.

Jeremiah 33: 11 (NKJV)
11 the voice of joy and the voice of gladness, the voice of the bridegroom and the voice of the bride, the voice of those who will say: "Praise the Lord of hosts, For the Lord is good, For His mercy en-dures forever"— and of those who will bring the sacrifice of praise into the house of the Lord. For I will cause the captives of the land to return as at the first,' says the Lord.

Joel 2: 26 (NIV)
26 You will have plenty to eat, until you are full, and you will praise the name of the Lord your God, who has worked wonders for you; never again will my people be shamed.

Acts 16: 25 - 26 (CEV)
25 About midnight Paul and Silas were praying and singing praises to God, while the other prisoners listened. 26 Suddenly a strong earthquake shook the jail to its foundations. The doors opened, and the chains fell from all the prisoners.

Philippians 4: 8 (NLT)
8 And now, dear brothers and sisters, one final thing. Fix your thoughts on what is true, and honor-able, and right, and pure, and lovely, and admirable. Think about things that are excellent and worthy of praise.

James 5: 11 (NIRV)
11 As you know, we think that people who don't give up are blessed. You have heard that Job was pa-tient. And you have seen what the Lord finally did for him. The Lord is full of tender mercy and loving concern.

PRAYER

Psalms 18: 6 -7 (NKJV)
6 In my distress I called upon the Lord, And cried out to my God; He heard my voice from His temple, And my cry came before Him, even to His ears. 7 Then the earth shook and trembled; The founda-tions of the hills also quaked and were shaken, Because He was angry.

Psalms 34: 15, 17 (NKJV)
15 The eyes of the Lord are on the righteous, And His ears are open to their cry. 17 The righteous cry out, and the Lord hears, And delivers them out of all their troubles.

Psalms 50: 14 - 15 (NLT)
14 Make thankfulness your sacrifice to God, and keep the vows you made to the Most High. 15 Then call on me when you are in trouble, and I will rescue you, and you will give me glory.

Psalms 55: 17 (NLT)
17 Morning, noon, and night I cry out in my distress, and the Lord hears my voice.

Psalms 66: 18 (CEV)
18 If my thoughts had been sinful, he would have refused to hear me.

Psalms 91: 15 (NKJV)
15 He shall call upon Me, and I will answer him; I will be with him in trouble; I will deliver him and hon-or him.

Psalms 102: 17 (ESV)
17 he regards the prayer of the destitute and does not despise their prayer.

Psalms 116: 2 (NLT)
2 Because he bends down to listen, I will pray as long as I have breath!

Psalms 145: 18 - 19 (NRSV)
18 The Lord is near to all who call on him, to all who call on him in truth. 19 He fulfills the desire of all who fear him; he also hears their cry, and saves them.

Proverbs 15: 8 (NLV)
8 The Lord hates the gifts of the sinful, but the prayer of the faithful is His joy.

Isaiah 58: 9 - 10 (ISV)
9 Then you'll call, and the Lord will answer; you'll cry for help, and he'll respond, 'Here I am.' "If you do away with the yoke among you, and pointing fingers and malicious talk; 10 if you pour yourself out for the hungry and satisfy the needs of afflicted souls, then your light will rise in darkness, and your night will be like noonday.

Isaiah 59: 1 - 2 (NLT)
1 Listen! The Lord's arm is not too weak to save you, nor is his ear too deaf to hear you call. 2 It's your sins that have cut you off from God. Because of your sins, he has turned away and will not listen anymore.

Isaiah 65: 24 (NLT)
24 I will answer them before they even call to me. While they are still talking about their needs, I will go ahead and answer their prayers!

Jeremiah 29: 11 - 13 (NLT)
11 For I know the plans I have for you," says the Lord. "They are plans for good and not for disaster, to give you a future and a hope. 12 In those days when you pray, I will listen. 13 If you look for me wholeheartedly, you will find me.

Jeremiah 33: 3 (NLT)
3 Ask me and I will tell you remarkable secrets you do not know about things to come.

Matthew 6: 6 - 13 (HCSB)
6 But when you pray, go into your private room, shut your door, and pray to your Father who is in secret. And your Father who sees in secret will reward you. 7 When you pray, don't babble like the idolaters, since they imagine they'll be heard for their many words. 8 Don't be like them, because your Father knows the things you need before you ask Him. 9 "Therefore, you should pray like this:
Our Father in heaven, Your name be honored as holy. 10 Your kingdom come. Your will be done on earth as it is in heaven. 11 Give us today our daily bread.12 And forgive us our debts, as we also have forgiven our debtors. 13

And do not bring us into temptation, but deliver us from the evil one. [For Yours is the kingdom and the power and the glory forever. Amen.]

Matthew 18: 19 - 20 (CEV)
19 I promise that when any two of you on earth agree about something you are praying for, my Father in heaven will do it for you. 20 Whenever two or three of you come together in my name, I am there with you.

Matthew 26: 41 (HCSB)
41 Stay awake and pray, so that you won't enter into temptation. The spirit is willing, but the flesh is weak.

Mark 11: 23 - 24 (NET)
23 I tell you the truth, if someone says to this mountain, 'Be lifted up and thrown into the sea,' and does not doubt in his heart but believes that what he says will happen, it will be done for him. 24 For this reason I tell you, whatever you pray and ask for, believe that you have received it, and it will be yours.

Luke 18: 1 (ISV)
1 Jesus told his disciples a parable about their need to pray all the time and never give up.

John 14: 13 - 14 (NCV)
13 And if you ask for anything in my name, I will do it for you so that the Father's glory will be shown through the Son. 14 If you ask me for anything in my name, I will do it.

John 15: 7 (CEB)
7 If you remain in me and my words remain in you, ask for whatever you want and it will be done for you.

John 16: 23 - 24 (HCSB)
23 In that day you will not ask Me anything. "I assure you: Anything you ask the Father in My name, He will give you. 24 Until now you have asked for nothing in My name. Ask and you will receive, so that your joy may be complete.

Philippians 4: 6 - 7 (AMP)
6 Do not fret or have any anxiety about anything, but in every circumstance and in everything, by prayer and petition (definite requests), with thanksgiving, continue to make your wants known to God. (AMP) 7 Then you will experience God's peace, which exceeds anything we can understand. His peace will guard your hearts and minds as you live in Christ Jesus. (NLT)

1 Timothy 2: 1 - 2 (ESV)
1 First of all, then, I urge that supplications, prayers, intercessions, and thanksgivings be made for all people, 2 for kings and all who are in high positions, that we may lead a peaceful and quiet life, godly and dignified in every way.

Hebrews 4: 16 (TLB)
16 So let us come boldly to the very throne of God and stay there to receive his mercy and to find grace to help us in our times of need.

James 1: 5 - 8 (NCV)
5 But if any of you needs wisdom, you should ask God for it. He is generous to everyone and will give you wisdom without criticizing you. 6 But when you ask God, you must believe and not doubt. Anyone who doubts is like a wave in the sea, blown up and down by the wind. 7-8 Such doubters are

thinking two different things at the same time, and they cannot decide about anything they do. They should not think they will receive anything from the Lord.

James 5: 14 - 17 (NKJV)
14 Is anyone among you sick? Let him call for the elders of the church, and let them pray over him, anointing him with oil in the name of the Lord. 15 And the prayer of faith will save the sick, and the Lord will raise him up. And if he has committed sins, he will be forgiven. 16 Confess your trespasses to one another, and pray for one another, that you may be healed. The effective, fervent prayer of a righteous man avails much. 17 Elijah was a man with a nature like ours, and he prayed earnestly that it would not rain; and it did not rain on the land for three years and six months.

1 Peter 3: 7 (GNT)
7 In the same way you husbands must live with your wives with the proper understanding that they are more delicate than you. Treat them with respect, because they also will receive, together with you, God's gift of life. Do this so that nothing will interfere with your prayers.

1 John 3: 21 - 22 (ESV)
21 Beloved, if our heart does not condemn us, we have confidence before God; 22 and whatever we ask we receive from him, because we keep his commandments and do what pleases him.

1 John 5: 14 - 15 (ESV)
14 And this is the confidence that we have toward him, that if we ask anything according to his will he hears us. 15 And if we know that he hears us in whatever we ask, we know that we have the requests that we have asked of him.

PRIDE

1 Samuel 2: 3 (TLB)
3 Quit acting so proud and arrogant! The Lord knows what you have done, And he will judge your deeds.

Psalms 18: 26 - 27 (NIV)
26 to the pure you show yourself pure, but to the devious you show yourself shrewd. 27 You save the humble but bring low those whose eyes are haughty.

Proverbs 8: 13 (NET)
13 The fear of the Lord is to hate evil; I hate arrogant pride and the evil way and perverse utterances.

Proverbs 16: 18 - 19 (NET)
18 Pride goes before destruction, and a haughty spirit before a fall. 19 It is better to be lowly in spirit with the afflicted than to share the spoils with the proud.

Proverbs 16: 5 (NET)
5 The Lord abhors every arrogant person; rest assured that they will not go unpunished.

Proverbs 21: 4 (HCSB)
4 The lamp that guides the wicked— haughty eyes and an arrogant heart—is sin.

Proverbs 26 : 12 (NIV)
12 Do you see a person wise in their own eyes? There is more hope for a fool than for them.

Proverbs 27: 2 (NCV)
2 Don't praise yourself. Let someone else do it. Let the praise come from a stranger and not from your own mouth.

Mark 7: 21 - 23 (NIV)
21 For it is from within, out of a person's heart, that evil thoughts come—sexual immorality, theft, mur-der, 22 adultery, greed, malice, deceit, lewdness, envy, slander, arrogance and folly. 23 All these evils come from inside and defile a person.

Mark 9: 35 (NIVUK)
35 Sitting down, Jesus called the Twelve and said, 'Anyone who wants to be first must be the very last, and the servant of all.'

Luke 14: 10 - 11 (ESV)
10 But when you are invited, go and sit in the lowest place, so that when your host comes he may say to you, 'Friend, move up higher.' Then you will be honored in the presence of all who sit at table with you. 11 For everyone who exalts himself will be humbled, and he who humbles himself will be exalt-ed."

Romans 12: 3, 16 (AMP)
3 For by the grace (unmerited favor of God) given to me I warn everyone among you not to estimate and think of himself more highly than he ought [not to have an exaggerated opinion of his own impor-tance], but to rate his ability with sober judgment, each according to the degree of faith apportioned by God to him. 16 Live in harmony with one another; do not be haughty (snobbish, high-minded, exclusive), but readily adjust yourself to [people, things] and give yourselves to humble tasks. Never

overestimate yourself or be wise in your own conceits.

2 Corinthians 10: 17 - 18 (GW)
17 "Whoever brags should brag about what the Lord has done." 18 It isn't the person who makes his own recommendation who receives approval, but the person whom the Lord recommends.

Galatians 6: 3 - 5 (NET)
3 For if anyone thinks he is something when he is nothing, he deceives himself. 4 Let each one ex-amine his own work. Then he can take pride in himself and not compare himself with someone else. 5 For each one will carry his own load.

James 4: 6, 10 (NCV)
6 But God gives us even more grace, as the Scripture says, "God is against the proud, but he gives grace to the humble." 10 Humble yourself in the Lord's presence, and he will honor you.

PRISONERS

Genesis 39: 21 (NET)
21 But the Lord was with Joseph and showed him kindness. He granted him favor in the sight of the prison warden.

Job 42: 10 (AMP)
10 And the Lord turned the captivity of Job and restored his fortunes, when he prayed for his friends; also the Lord gave Job twice as much as he had before.

Psalms 69: 33 (GNT)
33 The Lord listens to those in need and does not forget his people in prison.

Psalms 107: 14 (NLT)
14 He led them from the darkness and deepest gloom; he snapped their chains.

Psalms 126: 4 - 5 (AMP)
4 Turn to freedom our captivity and restore our fortunes, O Lord, as the streams in the South (the Negeb) [are restored by the torrents]. 5 They who sow in tears shall reap in joy and singing.

Psalms 146: 7 (GW)
7 He brings about justice for those who are oppressed. He gives food to those who are hungry. The Lord sets prisoners free.

Isaiah 49: 24 - 25 (ESV)
24 Can the prey be taken from the mighty, or the captives of a tyrant be rescued? 25 For thus says the Lord: "Even the captives of the mighty shall be taken, and the prey of the tyrant be rescued, for I will contend with those who contend with you, and I will save your children.

Isaiah 61: 1 - 2 (MEV)
1 The Spirit of the Lord God is upon me because the Lord has anointed me to preach good news to the poor; He has sent me to heal the broken-hearted, to proclaim liberty to the captives, and the opening of the prison to those who are bound; 2 to proclaim the acceptable year of the Lord and the day of vengeance of our God; to comfort all who mourn,

Jeremiah 30: 16 - 17 (NET)
16 But all who destroyed you will be destroyed. All your enemies will go into exile. Those who plundered you will be plundered. I will cause those who pillaged you to be pillaged. 17 Yes, I will re-store you to health. I will heal your wounds. I, the Lord, affirm it! For you have been called an outcast, Zion, whom no one cares for.

Matthew 25: 36, 39, 40 (WEB)
36 I was naked and you clothed me. I was sick and you visited me. I was in prison and you came to me.' 39 When did we see you sick or in prison and come to you?' 40 "The King will answer them, 'Most certainly I tell you, because you did it to one of the least of these my brothers, you did it to me.'

Hebrews 13: 3 (NET)
3 Remember those in prison as though you were in prison with them, and those ill-treated as though you too felt their torment.

PROSPERITY

Deuteronomy 28: 2, 5, 8 (GW)
2 These are all the blessings that will come to you and stay close to you because you obey the Lord your God: 5 The grain you harvest and the bread you bake will be blessed. 8 The Lord will bless your barns and everything you do. The Lord your God will bless you in the land that he is giving you.

Deuteronomy 8: 18 (NIV)
18 But remember the Lord your God, for it is he who gives you the ability to produce wealth, and so confirms

his covenant, which he swore to your ancestors, as it is today.

Joshua 1: 8 (NLT)

8 Study this Book of Instruction continually. Meditate on it day and night so you will be sure to obey everything written in it. Only then will you prosper and succeed in all you do.

2 Chronicles 25: 9 (NLT)

9 Amaziah asked the man of God, "But what about all that silver I paid to hire the army of Israel?" The man of God replied, "The Lord is able to give you much more than this!"

Psalms 1: 1 - 3 (NIV)

1 Blessed is the one who does not walk in step with the wicked or stand in the way that sinners take or sit in the company of mockers, 2 but whose delight is in the law of the Lord, and who meditates on his law day and night. 3 That person is like a tree planted by streams of water, which yields its fruit in season and whose leaf does not wither— whatever they do prospers.

Psalms 35: 27 (AMP)

27 Let those who favor my righteous cause and have pleasure in my uprightness shout for joy and be glad and say continually, Let the Lord be magnified, Who takes pleasure in the prosperity of His servant.

Psalms 41: 1 (ERV)

1 Those who help the poor succeed will get many blessings. When trouble comes, the Lord will save them.

Psalms 85: 12 (RSV)

12 Yea, the Lord will give what is good, and our land will yield its increase.

Psalms 92: 13 - 14 (NASB)

13 Planted in the house of the Lord, They will flourish in the courts of our God. 14 They will still yield fruit in old age; They shall be full of sap and very green,

Psalms 112: 1 - 3 (TLB)

1 Praise the Lord! For all who fear God and trust in him are blessed beyond expression. Yes, happy is the man who delights in doing his commands. 2 His children shall be honored everywhere, for good men's sons have a special heritage. 3 He himself shall be wealthy, and his good deeds will never be forgotten.

Psalms 118: 25 (AMP)

25 Save now, we beseech You, O Lord; send now prosperity, O Lord, we beseech You, and give to us success!

Proverbs 3: 9 - 10 (NKJV)

9 Honor the Lord with your possessions, And with the firstfruits of all your increase; 10 So your barns will be filled with plenty, And your vats will overflow with new wine.

Proverbs 8: 12, 18 - 19, 21 (WEB)

12 I, wisdom, have made prudence my dwelling. Find out knowledge and discretion. 18 With me are riches, honor, enduring wealth, and prosperity. 19 My fruit is better than gold, yes, than fine gold; my yield than choice silver. 21 That I may give wealth to those who love me. I fill their treasuries.

Proverbs 10: 4 (HCSB)

4 Idle hands make one poor, but diligent hands bring riches.

Proverbs 10: 22 (NLT)
22 The blessing of the Lord makes a person rich, and he adds no sorrow with it.

Proverbs 11: 25 (NIV)
25 A generous person will prosper; whoever refreshes others will be refreshed.

Proverbs 13: 11 (CEV)
11 Money wrongly gotten will disappear bit by bit; money earned little by little will grow and grow.

Proverbs 14: 23 (NIV)
23 All hard work brings a profit, but mere talk leads only to poverty.

Proverbs 22: 4 (ESV)
4 The reward for humility and fear of the Lord is riches and honor and life.

Proverbs 28: 22 (NIV)
22 The stingy are eager to get rich and are unaware that poverty awaits them.

Ecclesiastes 5: 9 (WEB)
9 Moreover the profit of the earth is for all. The king profits from the field.

Isaiah 48: 17 (AMP)
17 This is what the Lord, your Redeemer, the Holy One of Israel says, "I am the Lord your God, who teaches you to profit (benefit), Who leads you in the way that you should go.

Jeremiah 29: 11 (GNT)
11 I alone know the plans I have for you, plans to bring you prosperity and not disaster, plans to bring about the future you hope for.

Malachi 3: 10 - 11 (NASB)
10 Bring the whole tithe into the storehouse, so that there may be food in My house, and test Me now in this," says the Lord of hosts, "if I will not open for you the windows of heaven and pour out for you a blessing until it overflows. 11 Then I will rebuke the devourer for you, so that it will not destroy the fruits of the ground; nor will your vine in the field cast its grapes," says the Lord of hosts.

Luke 6: 38 (NIVUK)
38 Give, and it will be given to you. A good measure, pressed down, shaken together and running over, will be poured into your lap. For with the measure you use, it will be measured to you.

Luke 15: 31 (NIV)
31 'My son,' the father said, 'you are always with me, and everything I have is yours.

Romans 10: 12 (NET)
12 For there is no distinction between the Jew and the Greek, for the same Lord is Lord of all, who richly blesses all who call on him.

2 Corinthians 9: 6 - 8 (TLB)
6 But remember this—if you give little, you will get little. A farmer who plants just a few seeds will get only a small crop, but if he plants much, he will reap much. 7 Everyone must make up his own mind as to how much he should give. Don't force anyone to give more than he really wants to, for cheerful givers are the ones God prizes. 8 God is able to make it up to you by giving you everything you need and more so that there will not only be enough for

your own needs but plenty left over to give joyfully to others.

1 Timothy 6: 17 - 19 (NIV)
17 Command those who are rich in this present world not to be arrogant nor to put their hope in wealth, which is so uncertain, but to put their hope in God, who richly provides us with everything for our enjoyment. 18 Command them to do good, to be rich in good deeds, and to be generous and willing to share. 19 In this way they will lay up treasure for themselves as a firm foundation for the coming age, so that they may take hold of the life that is truly life.

3 John 1: 2 (NASB)
2 Beloved, I pray that in all respects you may prosper and be in good health, just as your soul prospers.

PROTECTOR

Exodus 23: 20 - 23 (GNT)
20 "I will send an angel ahead of you to protect you as you travel and to bring you to the place which I have prepared. 21 Pay attention to him and obey him. Do not rebel against him, for I have sent him, and he will not pardon such rebellion. 22 But if you obey him and do everything I command, I will fight against all your enemies. 23 My angel will go ahead of you and take you into the land of the Amorites, the Hittites, the Perizzites, the Canaanites, the Hivites, and the Jebusites, and I will destroy them.

Deuteronomy 1: 30 (NLT)
30 The Lord your God is going ahead of you. He will fight for you, just as you saw him do in Egypt.

Deuteronomy 33: 27 (NKJV)
27 The eternal God is your refuge, And underneath are the everlasting arms; He will thrust out the enemy from before you, And will say, 'Destroy!'

1 Samuel 2: 8 - 9 (RSV)
8 He raises up the poor from the dust; he lifts the needy from the ash heap, to make them sit with princes and inherit a seat of honor. For the pillars of the earth are the Lord's, and on them he has set the world. 9 "He will guard the feet of his faithful ones; but the wicked shall be cut off in darkness; for not by might shall a man prevail.

Psalms 3: 3 (HCSB)
3 But You, Lord, are a shield around me, my glory, and the One who lifts up my head.

Psalms 9: 9 (NLT)
9 The Lord is a shelter for the oppressed, a refuge in times of trouble.

Psalms 20: 2, 6 (MEV)
2 may He send you help from the sanctuary, and strengthen you from Zion; 6 Now I know that the Lord saves His anointed; He will answer him from His holy heaven with the saving strength of His right hand.

Psalms 27: 5 (ERV)
5 He will protect me when I am in danger. He will hide me in his tent. He will take me up to his place of safety.

Psalms 34: 7 (RSV)
7 The angel of the Lord encamps around those who fear him, and delivers them.

Psalms 34: 19 (MEV)
19 Many are the afflictions of the righteous, but the Lord delivers him out of them all.

Psalms 61: 2 - 4 (GNT)
2 In despair and far from home I call to you! Take me to a safe refuge, 3 for you are my protector, my strong defense against my enemies. 4 Let me live in your sanctuary all my life; let me find safety under your wings.

Psalms 91: 4, 14 - 15 (NKJV)
4 He shall cover you with His feathers, And under His wings you shall take refuge; His truth shall be your shield and buckler. 14 Because he has set his love upon Me, therefore I will deliver him; I will set him on high, because he has known My name. 15 He shall call upon Me, and I will answer him; I will be with him in trouble; I will deliver him and honor him.

Psalms 105: 12, 14 (GNT)
12 God's people were few in number, strangers in the land of Canaan. 14 But God let no one oppress them; to protect them, he warned the kings:

Psalms 118: 5 - 10 (NIV)
5 When hard pressed, I cried to the Lord; he brought me into a spacious place. 6 The Lord is with me; I will not be afraid. What can mere mortals do to me? 7 The Lord is with me; he is my helper. I look in triumph on my enemies. 8 It is better to take refuge in the Lord than to trust in humans. 9 It is better to take refuge in the Lord than to trust in princes. 10 All the nations surrounded me, but in the name of the Lord I cut them down.

Psalms 121: 1 - 3 (GNT)
1 I look to the mountains; where will my help come from? 2 My help will come from the Lord, who made heaven and earth. 3 He will not let you fall; your protector is always awake.

Psalms 121: 6 - 8 (NASB)
6 The sun will not smite you by day, Nor the moon by night. 7 The Lord will protect you from all evil; He will keep your soul. 8 The Lord will guard your going out and your coming in From this time forth and forever.

Psalms 138: 7 (NIV)
7 Though I walk in the midst of trouble, you preserve my life. You stretch out your hand against the anger of my foes; with your right hand you save me.

Proverbs 1: 33 (RSV)
33 but he who listens to me will dwell secure and will be at ease, without dread of evil.

Proverbs 18: 10 (NLV)
10 The name of the Lord is a strong tower. The man who does what is right runs into it and is safe.

Isaiah 43: 2 (NLT)
2 When you go through deep waters, I will be with you. When you go through rivers of difficulty, you will not drown. When you walk through the fire of oppression, you will not be burned up; the flames will not consume you.

Isaiah 54: 15 (GW)
15 If anyone attacks you, it will not be my doing. Whoever attacks you will be defeated by you.

2 Timothy 3: 11 (NET)
11 as well as the persecutions and sufferings that happened to me in Antioch, in Iconium, and in Lys-tra. I endured these persecutions and the Lord delivered me from them all.

PROVISION

Deuteronomy 28: 2, 5, 8 (GW)
2 These are all the blessings that will come to you and stay close to you because you obey the Lord your God: 5 The grain you harvest and the bread you bake will be blessed. 8 The Lord will bless your barns and everything you do. The Lord your God will bless you in the land that he is giving you.

Deuteronomy 8: 18 (NIV)
18 But remember the Lord your God, for it is he who gives you the ability to produce wealth, and so confirms his covenant, which he swore to your ancestors, as it is today.

Psalms 34: 9 - 10 (RSV)
9 O fear the Lord, you his saints, for those who fear him have no want! 10 The young lions suffer want and hunger; but those who seek the Lord lack no good thing.

Psalms 37: 18 - 19 (CEV)
18 Those who obey the Lord are daily in his care, and what he has given them will be theirs forever. 19 They won't be in trouble when times are bad, and they will have plenty when food is scarce.

Psalms 84: 11 - 12 (NASB)
11 For the Lord God is a sun and shield; The Lord gives grace and glory; No good thing does He with-hold from those who walk uprightly. 12 O Lord of hosts, How blessed is the man who trusts in You!

Psalms 128: 1 - 2 (NLT)
1 How joyful are those who fear the Lord— all who follow his ways! 2 You will enjoy the fruit of your labor. How joyful and prosperous you will be!

Psalms 147: 14 (NIV)
14 He grants peace to your borders and satisfies you with the finest of wheat.

Proverbs 3: 9 - 10 (NKJV)
9 Honor the Lord with your possessions, And with the firstfruits of all your increase; 10 So your barns will be filled with plenty, And your vats will overflow with new wine.

Proverbs 8: 12, 18 - 19, 21 (AMP)
Ecclesiastes 5: 19 (WEB)
19 Every man also to whom God has given riches and wealth, and has given him power to eat of it, and to take his portion, and to rejoice in his labor— this is the gift of God.

Proverbs 10: 22, 25, 27 (NLT)
22 The blessing of the Lord makes a person rich, and he adds no sorrow with it. 25 When the storms of life come, the wicked are whirled away, but the godly have a lasting foundation. 27 Fear of the Lord lengthens one's life, but the years of the wicked are cut short.

Proverbs 12: 11 (NIV)
11 Those who work their land will have abundant food, but those who chase fantasies have no sense.

Proverbs 27: 18 (NIV)
18 The one who guards a fig tree will eat its fruit, and whoever protects their master will be honored.

Joel 2: 26 (ESV)
26 You shall eat in plenty and be satisfied, and praise the name of the Lord your God, who has dealt wondrously with you. And my people shall never again be put to shame.

Malachi 3: 10 - 11 (NASB)
10 Bring the whole tithe into the storehouse, so that there may be food in My house, and test Me now in this," says the Lord of hosts, "if I will not open for you the windows of heaven and pour out for you a blessing until it overflows. 11 Then I will rebuke the devourer for you, so that it will not destroy the fruits of the ground; nor will your vine in the field cast its grapes," says the Lord of hosts.

Matthew 6: 31 - 33 (NIV)
31 So do not worry, saying, 'What shall we eat?' or 'What shall we drink?' or 'What shall we wear?' 32 For the pagans run after all these things, and your heavenly Father knows that you need them. 33 But seek first his kingdom and his righteousness, and all these things will be given to you as well.

Luke 6: 38 (NIVUK)
38 Give, and it will be given to you. A good measure, pressed down, shaken together and running over, will be poured into your lap. For with the measure you use, it will be measured to you.

Luke 15: 29, 31 (NIVUK)
29 But he answered his father, "Look! All these years I've been slaving for you

and never disobeyed your orders. Yet you never gave me even a young goat so I could celebrate with my friends.

Romans 8: 32 (WEB)
32 He who didn't spare his own Son, but delivered him up for us all, how would he not also with him freely give us all things?

Romans 10: 12 (NET)
12 For there is no distinction between the Jew and the Greek, for the same Lord is Lord of all, who richly blesses all who call on him.

2 Corinthians 9: 6 - 8 (GNT)
6 Remember that the person who plants few seeds will have a small crop; the one who plants many seeds will have a large crop. 7 You should each give, then, as you have decided, not with regret or out of a sense of duty; for God loves the one who gives gladly. 8 And God is able to give you more than you need, so that you will always have all you need for yourselves and more than enough for every good cause.

Philippians 4: 19 (NKJV)
19 And my God shall supply all your need according to His riches in glory by Christ Jesus.

1 Timothy 6: 17 - 19 (NIV)
17 Command those who are rich in this present world not to be arrogant nor to put their hope in wealth, which is so uncertain, but to put their hope in God, who richly provides us with everything for our enjoyment. 18 Command them to do good, to be rich in good deeds, and to be generous and willing to share. 19 In this way they will lay up treasure for themselves as a

firm foundation for the coming age, so that they may take hold of the life that is truly life.

RECEIVE

Genesis 26: 12 (NKJV)
12 Then Isaac sowed in that land, and reaped in the same year a hundredfold; and the Lord blessed him.

Psalms 24: 4 - 5 (ESV)
4 He who has clean hands and a pure heart, who does not lift up his soul to what is false and does not swear deceitfully. 5 He will receive blessing from the Lord and righteousness from the God of his salvation.

Proverbs 4: 10 (MEV)
10 Hear, my son, and receive my sayings, and the years of your life will be many.

Proverbs 8: 10 - 11 (WEB)
10 Receive my instruction rather than silver; knowledge rather than choice gold. 11 For wisdom is bet-ter than rubies. All the things that may be desired can't be compared to it.

Matthew 7: 7 - 10 (WEB)
7 "Ask, and it will be given you. Seek, and you will find. Knock, and it will be opened for you. 8 For everyone who asks receives. He who seeks finds. To him who knocks it will be opened. 9 Or who is there among you who, if his son asks him for bread, will give him a stone? 10 Or if he asks for a fish, who will give him a serpent?

Matthew 10: 8 (NASB)
8 Heal the sick, raise the dead, cleanse the lepers, cast out demons. Freely you received, freely give.

Mark 11: 22 - 24 (NCV)
22 Jesus answered, "Have faith in God. 23 I tell you the truth, you can say to this mountain, 'Go, fall into the sea.' And if you have no doubts in your mind and believe that what you say will happen, God will do it for you. 24 So I tell you to believe that you have received the things you ask for in prayer, and God will give them to you.

Luke 18: 41 - 42 (NLT)
41 "What do you want me to do for you?" "Lord," he said, "I want to see!" 42 And Jesus said, "All right, receive your sight! Your faith has healed you."

John 1: 12 (NKJV)
12 But as many as received Him, to them He gave the right to become children of God, to those who believe in His name:

John 16: 23 - 24 (ESV)
23 In that day you will ask nothing of me. Truly, truly, I say to you, whatever you ask of the Father in my name, he will give it to you. 24 Until now you have asked nothing in my name. Ask, and you will receive, that your joy may be full.

Acts 1: 8 (NIV)
8 But you will receive power when the Holy Spirit comes on you; and you will be my witnesses in Je-rusalem, and in all Judea and Samaria, and to the ends of the earth.

Acts 8: 17 (NIV)
17 Then Peter and John placed their hands on them, and they received the Holy Spirit.

Romans 8: 32 (NKJV)
32 He who did not spare His own Son, but delivered Him up for us all, how shall He not with Him also freely give us all things?

Galatians 3: 2 (AMP)
2 Let me ask you this one question: Did you receive the [Holy] Spirit as the result of obeying the Law and doing its works, or was it by hearing [the message of the Gospel] and believing [it]? [Was it from observing a law of rituals or from a message of faith?]

Ephesians 6: 8 (WEB)
8 knowing that whatever good thing each one does, he will receive the same again from the Lord, whether he is bound or free.

Colossians 3: 25 (WEB)
25 But he who does wrong will receive again for the wrong that he has done, and there is no partiality.

Hebrews 10: 35 - 37 (ISV)
35 So don't lose your confidence, since it holds a great reward for you. 36 For you need endurance, so that after you have done God's will you can receive what he has promised. 37 For "in a very little while the one who is coming will return — he will not delay;

James 1: 6 - 7 (NKJV)
6 But let him ask in faith, with no doubting, for he who doubts is like a wave of the sea driven and tossed by the wind. 7 For let not that man

suppose that he will receive anything from the Lord;

James 4: 3 (NKJV)
3 You ask and do not receive, because you ask amiss, that you may spend it on your pleasures.

2 Peter 1: 3 - 4 (NKJV)
3 as His divine power has given to us all things that pertain to life and godliness, through the knowl-edge of Him who called us by glory and virtue, 4 by which have been given to us exceedingly great and precious promises, that through these you may be partakers of the divine nature, having escaped the corruption that is in the world through lust.

1 John 2: 27 (NIVUK)
27 As for you, the anointing you received from him remains in you, and you do not need anyone to teach you. But as his anointing teaches you about all things and as that anointing is real, not counter-feit – just as it has taught you, remain in him.

1 John 3: 22 - 23 (WEB)
22 and whatever we ask, we receive from him, because we keep his commandments and do the things that are pleasing in his sight. 23 This is his commandment, that we should believe in the name of his Son, Jesus Christ, and love one another, even as he commanded.

RESCUE

1 Samuel 30: 17 - 19 (NIV)
17 David fought them from dusk until the evening of the next day, and none

of them got away, except four hundred young men who rode off on camels and fled. 18 David recovered everything the Amale-kites had taken, including his two wives. 19 Nothing was missing: young or old, boy or girl, plunder or anything else they had taken. David brought everything back.

2 Samuel 22: 17 - 18 (NKJV)

17 He sent from above, He took me, He drew me out of many waters. 18 He delivered me from my strong enemy, From those who hated me; For they were too strong for me.

Psalms 37: 23 - 24 (HCSB)

23 A man's steps are established by the Lord, and He takes pleasure in his way. 24 Though he falls, he will not be overwhelmed, because the Lord holds his hand.

Psalms 50: 15 (GW)

15 Call on me in times of trouble. I will rescue you, and you will honor me.

Psalms 91: 15 (NKJV)

15 He shall call upon Me, and I will answer him; I will be with him in trouble; I will deliver him and hon-or him.

Psalms 107: 20, 28 - 29 (NLT)

20 He sent out his word and healed them, snatching them from the door of death. 28 "Lord, help!" they cried in their trouble, and he saved them from their distress. 29 He calmed the storm to a whis-per and stilled the waves.

Psalms 113: 7 (ESV)

7 He raises the poor from the dust and lifts the needy from the ash heap,

Psalms 118: 5 (HCSB)

5 I called to the Lord in distress; the Lord answered me and put me in a spacious place.

Psalms 138: 3, 7 - 8 (NKJV)

3 In the day when I cried out, You answered me, And made me bold with strength in my soul. 7 Though I walk in the midst of trouble, You will revive me; You will stretch out Your hand Against the wrath of my enemies, And Your right hand will save me. 8 The Lord will perfect that which concerns me; Your mercy, O Lord, endures forever; Do not forsake the works of Your hands.

Psalms 145: 14, 19 (MEV)

14 The Lord upholds all who fall, and raises up all who are bowed down. 19 He will fulfill the desire of those who fear Him; He also will hear their cry and will save them.

Isaiah 46: 4 (NIV)

4 Even to your old age and gray hairs I am he, I am he who will sustain you. I have made you and I will carry you; I will sustain you and I will rescue you.

Malachi 4: 2 (NLT)

2 "But for you who fear my name, the Sun of Righteousness will rise with healing in his wings. And you will go free, leaping with joy like calves let out to pasture.

Luke 4: 18 - 19 (HCSB)

The Spirit of the Lord is on Me, because He has anointed Me to preach good news to the poor. He has sent Me to proclaim freedom to the captives and recovery of sight to the blind, to set free the op-pressed, 19 to proclaim the year of the Lord's favor.

Romans 8: 2 (RSV)
2 For the law of the Spirit of life in Christ Jesus has set me free from the law of sin and death.

1 Corinthians 10: 13 (MEV)
13 No temptation has taken you except what is common to man. God is faithful, and He will not per-mit you to be tempted above what you can endure, but will with the temptation also make a way to escape, that you may be able to bear it.

2 Timothy 3: 11 (NET)
11 as well as the persecutions and sufferings that happened to me in Antioch, in Iconium, and in Lystra. I endured these persecutions and the Lord delivered me from them all.

Revelation 12: 10 - 11 (NET)
10 Then I heard a loud voice in heaven saying, "The salvation and the power and the kingdom of our God, and the ruling authority of his Christ, have now come, because the accuser of our brothers and sisters, the one who accuses them day and night before our God, has been thrown down. 11 But they overcame him by the blood of the Lamb and by the word of their testimony, and they did not love their lives so much that they were afraid to die.

REST

Genesis 2: 2 (RSV)
2 And on the seventh day God finished his work which he had done, and he rested on the seventh day from all his work which he had done.

Exodus 23: 12 (NKJV)
12 Six days you shall do your work, and on the seventh day you shall rest, that your ox and your don-key may rest, and the son of your female servant and the stranger may be refreshed.

1 Kings 5: 4 (NLT)
4 But now the Lord my God has given me peace on every side; I have no enemies, and all is well.

Psalms 23: 2 (CEB)
2 He lets me rest in grassy meadows; he leads me to restful waters;

Psalms 29: 11 (NIV)
11 The Lord gives strength to his people; the Lord blesses his people with peace.

Psalms 62: 1 (EXB)
1 I ·find rest [wait quietly] in God; only he can ·save me [give me victory].

Psalms 91: 1 (NIVUK)
1 Whoever dwells in the shelter of the Most High will rest in the shadow of the Almighty.

Psalms 116: 7 (NLT)
7 Let my soul be at rest again, for the Lord has been good to me.

Proverbs 6: 10 - 11 (HCSB)
10 A little sleep, a little slumber, a little folding of the arms to rest, 11 and your poverty will come like a robber, your need, like a bandit.

Proverbs 19: 23 (ESV)
23 The fear of the Lord leads to life, and whoever has it rests satisfied; he will not be visited by harm.

Isaiah 14: 3 (NKJV)
3 It shall come to pass in the day the Lord gives you rest from your sorrow, and from your fear and the hard bondage in which you were made to serve,

Isaiah 26: 3 (ESV)
3 You keep him in perfect peace whose mind is stayed on you, because he trusts in you.

Isaiah 30: 15 (CEB)
15 Therefore, the Lord God, the holy one of Israel, says: In return and rest you will be saved; quiet-ness and trust will be your strength

Isaiah 32: 18 (NIV)
18 My people will live in peaceful dwelling places, in secure homes, in undisturbed places of rest.

Jeremiah 6: 16 (NIV)
16 This is what the Lord says: "Stand at the crossroads and look; ask for the ancient paths, ask where the good way is, and walk in it, and you will find rest for your souls.

Jeremiah 31: 25 (EXB)
25 I will ·give rest [satisfy] and ·strength to [replenish] those who ·are weak [languish] and ·tired [faint].

Zephaniah 3: 17 (AMP)
17 The Lord your God is in the midst of you, a Mighty One, a Savior [Who saves]! He will rejoice over you with joy; He will rest [in silent satisfaction] and in His love He will be silent and make no mention [of past sins, or even recall them]; He will exult over you with singing.

Matthew 11: 28 - 29 (MEV)
28 Come to Me, all you who labor and are heavily burdened, and I will give you rest. 29 Take My yoke upon you, and learn from Me. For I am meek and lowly in heart, and you will find rest for your souls.

2 Corinthians 12: 9 (CEB)
9 He said to me, "My grace is enough for you, because power is made perfect in weakness." So I'll gladly spend my time bragging about my weaknesses so that Christ's power can rest on me.

2 Thessalonians 3: 16 (NASB)
16 Now may the Lord of peace Himself continually grant you peace in every circumstance. The Lord be with you all!

Hebrews 4: 1 (CEV)
1 The promise to enter the place of rest is still good, and we must take care that none of you miss out.

1 Peter 4: 14 (NKJV)
14 If you are reproached for the name of Christ, blessed are you, for the Spirit of glory and of God rests upon you. On their part He is blasphemed, but on your part He is glorified.

RESTORATION

1 Samuel 30: 17 - 19 (NIV)
17 David fought them from dusk until the evening of the next day, and none of them got away, except four hundred young men who rode off on camels and fled. 18 David recovered everything the Amale-kites had taken, including his two wives. 19 Nothing was missing:

young or old, boy or girl, plunder or anything else they had taken. David brought everything back.

1 Kings 13: 6 (RSV)

6 And the king said to the man of God, "Entreat now the favor of the Lord your God, and pray for me, that my hand may be restored to me." And the man of God entreated the Lord; and the king's hand was restored to him, and became as it was before.

Nehemiah 1: 9 (NASB)

9 but if you return to Me and keep My commandments and do them, though those of you who have been scattered were in the most remote part of the heavens, I will gather them from there and will bring them to the place where I have chosen to cause My name to dwell.

Job 42: 10 (AMP)

10 The Lord restored the fortunes of Job when he prayed for his friends, and the Lord gave Job twice as much as he had before.

Psalms 41: 3 (GNT)

3 The Lord will help them when they are sick and will restore them to health.

Psalms 51: 12 (TLB)

12 Restore to me again the joy of your salvation, and make me willing to obey you.

Psalms 80: 3 (GW)

3 O God, restore us and smile on us so that we may be saved.

Isaiah 38: 15 - 16 (HCSB)

15 What can I say? He has spoken to me, and He Himself has done it. I walk

along slowly all my years because of the bitterness of my soul, 16 Lord, because of these promises people live, and in all of them is the life of my spirit as well; You have restored me to health and let me live.

Jeremiah 33: 11 (NLT)

11 the sounds of joy and laughter. The joyful voices of bridegrooms and brides will be heard again, along with the joyous songs of people bringing thanksgiving offerings to the Lord. They will sing, 'Give thanks to the Lord of Heaven's Armies, for the Lord is good. His faithful love endures forever!' For I will restore the prosperity of this land to what it was in the past, says the Lord.

Daniel 4: 34, 36 (ISV)

34 When that period of time was over, I, Nebuchadnezzar, lifted my eyes to heaven and my sanity returned to me. I blessed the Most High, praising and honoring the one who lives forever: For his sovereignty is eternal, and his kingdom continues from generation to generation. 36 At that moment I recovered my sanity, and my honor and majesty returned to me, for the sake of my kingdom. My advisors and officials sought me out, my throne was restored, and even more greatness than I had before was added to me.

Joel 2: 24 - 26 (NKJV)

24 The threshing floors shall be full of wheat, And the vats shall overflow with new wine and oil. 25 "So I will restore to you the years that the swarming locust has eaten, The crawling locust, The con-suming locust, And the chewing locust, My

great army which I sent among you. 26 You shall eat in plenty and be satisfied, And praise the name of the Lord your God, Who has dealt wondrously with you; And My people shall never be put to shame.

Zechariah 9: 12 (AMP)

12 Return to the stronghold [of security and prosperity], you prisoners of hope; even today do I de-clare that I will restore double your former prosperity to you.

REWARD

2 Chronicles 15: 7 (NIV)

7 But as for you, be strong and do not give up, for your work will be rewarded.

Psalms 19: 7 - 9, 11 (CEV)

7 The Law of the Lord is perfect; it gives us new life. His teachings last forever, and they give wisdom to ordinary people. 8 The Lord's instruction is right; it makes our hearts glad. His commands shine brightly, and they give us light. 9 Worshiping the Lord is sacred; he will always be worshiped. All of his decisions are correct and fair. 11 By your teachings, Lord, I am warned; by obeying them, I am greatly rewarded.

Psalms 58: 11 (NLT)

11 Then at last everyone will say, "There truly is a reward for those who live for God; surely there is a God who judges justly here on earth."

Psalms 127: 3 (NIV)

3 Children are a heritage from the Lord, offspring a reward from him.

Proverbs 13: 13 (CEV)

13 If you reject God's teaching, you will pay the price; if you obey his commands, you will be reward-ed.

Proverbs 21: 14 (KJV)

14 A gift in secret pacifieth anger: and a reward in the bosom strong wrath.

Proverbs 24: 14 (MEV)

14 so shall the knowledge of wisdom be to your soul; when you have found it, then there will be a reward, and your expectation will not be cut off.

Proverbs 25: 21 - 22 (NIV)

21 If your enemy is hungry, give him food to eat; if he is thirsty, give him water to drink. 22 In doing this, you will heap burning coals on his head, and the Lord will reward you.

Ecclesiastes 4: 9 (ASV)

9 Two are better than one, because they have a good reward for their labor.

Isaiah 3: 11 (NKJV)

11 Woe to the wicked! It shall be ill with him, For the reward of his hands shall be given him.

Jeremiah 17: 10 (RSV)

10 I the Lord search the mind and try the heart, to give every man according to his ways, according to the fruit of his doings.

Matthew 6: 3 - 4 (MEV)

3 But when you do your charitable deeds, do not let your left hand know what your right hand is doing, 4 that your charitable deeds may be in secret. And your Father who sees in secret will Himself reward you openly.

Matthew 6: 6 (MEV)
6 But you, when you pray, enter your closet, and when you have shut your door, pray to your Father who is in secret. And your Father who sees in secret will reward you openly.

Mark 9: 41 (NASB)
41 For whoever gives you a cup of water to drink because of your name as followers of Christ, truly I say to you, he will not lose his reward.

Luke 6: 35 (MEV)
35 But love your enemies, and do good, and lend, hoping for nothing in return. Then your reward will be great, and you will be the sons of the Highest. For He is kind to the unthankful and the evil.

1 Corinthians 3: 8 (NIVUK)
8 The one who plants and the one who waters have one purpose, and they will each be rewarded according to their own labour.

Ephesians 6: 8 (WEB)
8 knowing that whatever good thing each one does, he will receive the same again from the Lord, whether he is bound or free.

1 Timothy 5: 18 (MEV)
18 For the Scripture says, "You shall not muzzle the ox that treads out the grain," and, "The laborer is worthy of his reward."

Hebrews 10: 35 (WEB)
35 Therefore don't throw away your boldness, which has a great reward.

Hebrews 11: 6 (CEB)
6 It's impossible to please God without faith because the one who draws near to God must believe that he exists and that he rewards people who try to find him.

RIGHTEOUSNESS

Psalms 5: 12 (NIV)
12 Surely, Lord, you bless the righteous; you surround them with your favor as with a shield.

Psalms 23: 3 (ESV)
3 He restores my soul. He leads me in paths of righteousness for his name's sake.

Psalms 34: 17, 19 (NKJV)
17 The righteous cry out, and the Lord hears, And delivers them out of all their troubles. 19 Many are the afflictions of the righteous, But the Lord delivers him out of them all.

Psalms 103: 17 - 18 (GW)
17 But from everlasting to everlasting, the Lord's mercy is on those who fear him. His righteousness belongs to their children and grandchildren, 18 to those who are faithful to his promise, to those who remember to follow his guiding principles.

Proverbs 8: 1, 8 (AMP)
12 "I, wisdom, dwell with prudence, and I find knowledge and discretion. 18 Riches and honor are with me, enduring wealth and righteousness.

Proverbs 8: 12, 18 (ESV)
12 "I, wisdom, dwell with prudence, and I find knowledge and discretion.

18 Riches and honor are with me, enduring wealth and righteousness.

Proverbs 11: 28 (NET)
28 The one who trusts in his riches will fall, but the righteous will flourish like a green leaf.

Proverbs 12: 10 (NIV)
10 The righteous care for the needs of their animals, but the kindest acts of the wicked are cruel.

Proverbs 13: 21 (GNT)
21 Trouble follows sinners everywhere, but righteous people will be rewarded with good things.

Isaiah 3: 10 (NKJV)
10 Say to the righteous that it shall be well with them, For they shall eat the fruit of their doings.

Isaiah 32: 17 - 18 (NKJV)
17 The work of righteousness will be peace, And the effect of righteousness, quietness and assur-ance forever. 18 My people will dwell in a peaceful habitation, In secure dwellings, and in quiet resting places,

Isaiah 41: 10 (NIV)
10 So do not fear, for I am with you do not be dismayed, for I am your God. I will strengthen you and help you; I will uphold you with my righteous right hand.

Hosea 10: 12 (NLT)
12 I said, 'Plant the good seeds of righteousness, and you will harvest a crop of love. Plow up the hard ground of your hearts, for now is the time to seek the Lord, that he may come and shower right-teousness upon you.'

Matthew 5: 6 (ASV)
6 Blessed are they that hunger and thirst after righteousness: for they shall be filled.

Matthew 6: 33 (NIV)
33 But seek first his kingdom and his righteousness, and all these things will be given to you as well.

Romans 1: 17 (NIV)
17 For in the gospel the righteousness of God is revealed—a righteousness that is by faith from first to last, just as it is written: "The righteous will live by faith."

Romans 6: 16 - 18 (NIV)
16 Don't you know that when you offer yourselves to someone as obedient slaves, you are slaves of the one you obey—whether you are slaves to sin, which leads to death, or to obedience, which leads to righteousness? 17 But thanks be to God that, though you used to be slaves to sin, you have come to obey from your heart the pattern of teaching that has now claimed your allegiance. 18 You have been set free from sin and have become slaves to righteousness.

Romans 8: 10 (NIV)
10 But if Christ is in you, then even though your body is subject to death because of sin, the Spirit gives life because of righteousness.

2 Corinthians 5: 21 (RSV)
21 For our sake he made him to be sin who knew no sin, so that in him we might become the right-teousness of God.

Galatians 3: 6 - 7 (GNT)
6 Consider the experience of Abraham; as the scripture says, "He believed God, and because of his faith God accepted him as righteous." 7 You should realize, then, that the real descendants of Abraham are the people who have faith.

Ephesians 5: 9 - 10 (WEB)
9 for the fruit of the Spirit is in all goodness and righteousness and truth, 10 proving what is well pleasing to the Lord.

Ephesians 6: 13 - 14 (GNT)
13 So put on God's armor now! Then when the evil day comes, you will be able to resist the enemy's attacks; and after fighting to the end, you will still hold your ground. 14 So stand ready, with truth as a belt tight around your waist, with righteousness as your breastplate,

Philippians 3: 8 - 9 (NLT)
8 Yes, everything else is worthless when compared with the infinite value of knowing Christ Jesus my Lord. For his sake I have discarded everything else, counting it all as garbage, so that I could gain Christ 9 and become one with him. I no longer count on my own righteousness through obeying the law; rather, I become righteous through faith in Christ. For God's way of making us right with himself depends on faith.

James 1: 19 - 20 (WEB)
19 So, then, my beloved brothers, let every man be swift to hear, slow to speak, and slow to anger; 20 for the anger of man doesn't produce the righteousness of God.

1 Peter 3: 12, 14 (NIV)
12 For the eyes of the Lord are on the righteous and his ears are attentive to their prayer, but the face of the Lord is against those who do evil." 14 But even if you should suffer for what is right, you are blessed. "Do not fear their threats; do not be frightened."

SADNESS

Psalms 6: 7 - 9 (GW)
7 My eyes blur from grief. They fail because of my enemies. 8 Get away from me, all you troublemak-ers, because the Lord has heard the sound of my crying. 9 The Lord has heard my plea for mercy. The Lord accepts my prayer.

Psalms 30: 11 - 12 (NKJV)
11 You have turned for me my mourning into dancing; You have put off my sackcloth and clothed me with gladness, 12 To the end that my glory may sing praise to You and not be silent. O Lord my God, I will give thanks to You forever.

Psalms 34: 18 (NKJV)
18 The Lord is near to those who have a broken heart, And saves such as have a contrite spirit.

Psalms 42: 11 (GNT)
11 Why am I so sad? Why am I so troubled? I will put my hope in God, and once again I will praise him, my savior and my God.

Psalms 119: 28 (NIV)
28 My soul is weary with sorrow; strengthen me according to your word.

Psalms 126: 5 - 6 (NIV)
5 Those who sow with tears will reap with songs of joy. 6 Those who go out weeping, carrying seed to sow, will return with songs of joy, carrying sheaves with them.

Proverbs 25: 25 (NIV)
25 Like cold water to a weary soul is good news from a distant land.

Isaiah 61: 1 - 2 (ESV)
1 The Spirit of the Lord God is upon me, because the Lord has anointed me to bring good news to the poor; he has sent me to bind up the brokenhearted, to proclaim liberty to the captives, and the open-ing of the prison to those who are bound; 2 to proclaim the year of the Lord's favor, and the day of vengeance of our God; to comfort all who mourn;

Jeremiah 31: 25 (NASB)
25 For I satisfy the weary ones and refresh everyone who languishes.

Matthew 5: 3 - 4 (MEV)
3 "Blessed are the poor in spirit, for theirs is the kingdom of heaven. 4 Blessed are those who mourn, for they shall be comforted.

John 11: 33 (GNT)
33 Jesus saw her weeping, and he saw how the people with her were weeping also; his heart was touched, and he was deeply moved.

1 Peter 3: 14 (NIV)
14 But even if you should suffer for what is right, you are blessed. "Do not fear their threats; do not be frightened."

SALVATION

Psalms 91: 16 (NKJV)
With long life I will satisfy him, And show him My salvation.

Isaiah 1: 18 - 19 (ESV)
18 "Come now, let us reason together, says the Lord: though your sins are like scarlet, they shall be as white as snow; though they are red like crimson, they shall become like wool.19 If you are willing and obedient, you shall eat the good of the land;

Lamentations 3: 26 (ESV)
26 It is good that one should wait quietly for the salvation of the Lord.

Joel 2: 32 (NIV)
And everyone who calls on the name of the Lord will be saved; for on Mount Zion and in Jerusa-lem there will be deliverance, as the Lord has said, even among the survivors whom the Lord calls.

John 1: 12 - 13 (NLT)
12 But to all who believed him and accepted him, he gave the right to become children of God.
13 They are reborn—not with a physical birth resulting from human passion or plan, but a birth that comes from God.

John 6: 43 - 44 (RSV)
43 Jesus answered them, "Do not murmur among yourselves. 44 No one can come to me unless the Father who sent me draws him; and I will raise him up at the last day.

John 10: 9 - 10 (NLV)
9 Yes, I am the gate. Those who come in through me will be saved. They will come and go freely and will find good pastures.

Acts 2: 21 (MEV)
21 And whoever calls on the name of the Lord shall be saved.

Acts 4: 12 (RSV)
12 And there is salvation in no one else, for there is no other name under heaven given among men by which we must be saved.

John 14: 6 (NLT)
6 Jesus told him, "I am the way, the truth, and the life. No one can come to the Father except through me.

Acts 16: 31 (NET)
31 They replied, "Believe in the Lord Jesus and you will be saved, you and your household."

Romans 3: 23 (NLT)
23 For everyone has sinned; we all fall short of God's glorious standard.

Romans 4: 5 (NLT)
5 But people are counted as righteous, not because of their work, but because of their faith in God who forgives sinners.

Romans 5: 8 (NLT)
8 But God showed his great love for us by sending Christ to die for us while we were still sinners.

Romans 6: 23 (NLT)
23 For the wages of sin is death, but the free gift of God is eternal life through Christ Jesus our Lord.

Romans 10: 9 - 10, 13 (NIV)
9 If you declare with your mouth, "Jesus is Lord," and believe in your heart that God raised him from the dead, you will be saved. 10 For it is with your heart that you believe and are justified, and it is with your mouth that you profess your faith and are saved. 13 for, "Everyone who calls on the name of the Lord will be saved."

2 Corinthians 5: 17, 21 (MEV)
17 Therefore, if any man is in Christ, he is a new creature. Old things have passed away. Look, all things have become new. 21 God made Him who knew no sin to be sin for us, that we might become the righteousness of God in Him.

2 Corinthians 6: 2 (NIV)
2 For he says, "In the time of my favor I heard you, and in the day of salvation I helped you." I tell you, now is the time of God's favor, now is the day of salvation.

Ephesians 2: 8 (NIV)
8 For it is by grace you have been saved, through faith—and this is not from yourselves, it is the gift of God—

1 Timothy 2: 3 - 4 (NLT)
3 This is good and pleases God our Savior, 4 who wants everyone to be saved and to understand the truth.

Titus 3: 5 (NCV)
5 he saved us because of his mercy. It was not because of good deeds we did to be right with him. He saved us through the washing that made us new people through the Holy Spirit.

SATISFACTION

Psalms 63: 5 (NLT)
5 You satisfy me more than the richest feast. I will praise you with songs of joy.

Psalms 90: 14 (RSV)
14 Satisfy us in the morning with thy steadfast love, that we may rejoice and be glad all our days.

Psalms 91: 16 (NIV)
16 With long life I will satisfy him and show him my salvation."

Psalms 103: 5 (NIV)
5 who satisfies your desires with good things so that your youth is renewed like the eagle's.

Psalms 107: 9 (RSV)
9 For he satisfies him who is thirsty, and the hungry he fills with good things.

Psalms 145: 16 (NIV)
16 You open your hand and satisfy the desires of every living thing.

Psalms 147: 14 (NIV)
14 He grants peace to your borders and satisfies you with the finest of wheat.

Isaiah 58: 10 - 11 (NIV)
10 and if you spend yourselves in behalf of the hungry and satisfy the needs of the oppressed, then your light will rise in the darkness, and your night will become like the noonday. 11 The Lord will guide you always; he will satisfy your needs in a sun-scorched land and will strengthen your frame. You will be like a well-watered garden, like a spring whose waters never fail.

Joel 2: 19, 26 (NKJV)
19 The Lord will answer and say to His people, "Behold, I will send you grain and new wine and oil, And you will be satisfied by them; I will no longer make you a reproach among the nations. 26 You shall eat in plenty and be satisfied, And praise the name of the Lord your God, Who has dealt won-drously with you; And My people shall never be put to shame.

Matthew 5: 6 (ESV)
6 Blessed are those who hunger and thirst for righteousness, for they shall be satisfied.

Romans 8: 32 (NKJV)
32 He who did not spare His own Son, but delivered Him up for us all, how shall He not with Him also freely give us all things?

SAVIOR

Matthew 1: 21 (NIV)
21 She will give birth to a son, and you are to give him the name Jesus, because he will save his peo-ple from their sins.

Luke 2: 10 - 11 (ESV)
10 And the angel said to them, "Fear not, for behold, I bring you good news of great joy that will be for all the people. 11 For unto you is born this day in the city of David a Savior, who is Christ the Lord.

Luke 19: 10 (NKJV)
10 for the Son of Man has come to seek and to save that which was lost.

John 3: 16 (RSV)
16 For God so loved the world that he gave his only Son, that whoever believes in him should not perish but have eternal life.

John 10: 9 (NIV)
9 I am the gate; whoever enters through me will be saved. They will come in and go out, and find pasture.

John 14: 6 (NLT)
6 Jesus told him, "I am the way, the truth, and the life. No one can come to the Father except through me.

Acts 13: 23 (NIV)
23 From this man's descendants God has brought to Israel the Savior Jesus, as he promised.

Romans 10: 9 (NIV)
9 If you declare with your mouth, "Jesus is Lord," and believe in your heart that God raised him from the dead, you will be saved.

Ephesians 2: 8 - 9 (NIV)
8 For it is by grace you have been saved, through faith—and this is not from yourselves, it is the gift of God— 9 not by works, so that no one can boast.

Ephesians 5: 23 (GW)
23 The husband is the head of his wife as Christ is the head of the church. It is his body, and he is its Savior.

1 Thessalonians 5: 9 (NCV)
9 God did not choose us to suffer his anger but to have salvation through our Lord Jesus Christ.

1 Timothy 1: 15 (NIV)
15 Here is a trustworthy saying that deserves full acceptance: Christ Jesus came into the world to save sinners—of whom I am the worst.

Titus 3: 5 (NCV)
5 he saved us because of his mercy. It was not because of good deeds we did to be right with him. He saved us through the washing that made us new people through the Holy Spirit.

SERVE

Deuteronomy 11: 13 - 15 (NIV)
13 So if you faithfully obey the commands I am giving you today—to love the Lord your God and to serve him with all your heart and with all your soul— 14 then I will send rain on your land in its sea-son, both autumn and spring rains, so that you may gather in your grain, new wine and olive oil. 15 I will provide grass in the fields for your cattle, and you will eat and be satisfied.

Psalms 34: 22 (GW)
22 The Lord protects the souls of his servants. All who take refuge in him will never be condemned.

Psalms 35: 27 (NKJV)
Let them shout for joy and be glad, Who favor my righteous cause; And let them say continually, "Let the Lord be magnified, Who has pleasure in the prosperity of His servant."

Psalms 101: 6 (NOG)
6 My eyes will be watching the faithful people in the land so that they may live

with me. The person who lives with integrity will serve me.

Matthew 4: 10 (WEB)
10 Then Jesus said to him, "Get behind me, Satan! For it is written, 'You shall worship the Lord your God, and you shall serve him only.'"

Matthew 6: 24 (NIV)
24 "No one can serve two masters. Either you will hate the one and love the other, or you will be de-voted to the one and despise the other. You cannot serve both God and money.

Luke 22: 26 - 27 (NLT)
26 But among you it will be different. Those who are the greatest among you should take the lowest rank, and the leader should be like a servant. 27 Who is more important, the one who sits at the table or the one who serves? The one who sits at the table, of course. But not here! For I am among you as one who serves.

John 12: 26 (WEB)
26 If anyone serves me, let him follow me. Where I am, there will my servant also be. If anyone serves me, the Father will honor him.

Romans 7: 6 (GNT)
6 Now, however, we are free from the Law, because we died to that which once held us prisoners. No longer do we serve in the old way of a written law, but in the new way of the Spirit.

Galatians 5: 13 (NLT)
13 For you have been called to live in freedom, my brothers and sisters. But don't use your freedom to satisfy your sinful nature. Instead, use your freedom to serve one another in love.

SEXUAL BEHAVIOR

Leviticus 18: 6, 20 (NCV)
6 You must never have sexual relations with your close relatives. I am the Lord. 20 You must not have sexual relations with your neighbor's wife and make yourself unclean with her.

Proverbs 5: 15 - 21 (NIV)
15 Drink water from your own cistern, running water from your own well. 16 Should your springs overflow in the streets, your streams of water in the public squares? 17 Let them be yours alone, never to be shared with strangers. 18 May your fountain be blessed, and may you rejoice in the wife of your youth. 19 A loving doe, a graceful deer— may her breasts satisfy you always, may you ever be intoxicated with her love. 20 Why, my son, be intoxicated with another man's wife? Why embrace the bosom of a wayward woman? 21 For your ways are in full view of the Lord, and he examines all your paths.

Proverbs 6: 24 - 29 (NIV)
24 keeping you from your neighbor's wife, from the smooth talk of a wayward woman. 25 Do not lust in your heart after her beauty or let her captivate you with her eyes. 26 For a prostitute can be had for a loaf of bread, but another man's wife preys on your very life. 27 Can a man scoop fire into his lap without his clothes being burned? 28 Can a man walk on hot coals without his feet being scorched? 29 So is he who

sleeps with another man's wife; no one who touches her will go unpunished.

Matthew 15: 19 (ESV)
19 For out of the heart come evil thoughts, murder, adultery, sexual immorality, theft, false witness, slander.

Romans 1: 26 - 27 (CEV)
26 God let them follow their own evil desires. Women no longer wanted to have sex in a natural way, and they did things with each other that were not natural. 27 Men behaved in the same way. They stopped wanting to have sex with women and had strong desires for sex with other men. They did shameful things with each other, and what has happened to them is punishment for their foolish deeds.

1 Corinthians 5: 9 - 10 (HCSB)
9 I wrote to you in a letter not to associate with sexually immoral people. 10 I did not mean the immor-al people of this world or the greedy and swindlers or idolaters; otherwise you would have to leave the world.

1 Corinthians 6: 9 - 11, 13 (NET)
9 Do you not know that the unrighteous will not inherit the kingdom of God? Do not be deceived! The sexually immoral, idolaters, adulterers, passive homosexual partners, practicing homosexuals, 10 thieves, the greedy, drunkards, the verbally abusive, and swindlers will not inherit the kingdom of God. 11 Some of you once lived this way. But you were washed, you were sanctified, you were jus-tified in the name of the Lord Jesus Christ and by the Spirit of our God. 13 "Food is for the stomach and the stomach is for

food, but God will do away with both." The body is not for sexual immorality, but for the Lord, and the Lord for the body.

1 Corinthians 6: 18 - 20 (MEV)
18 Escape from sexual immorality. Every sin that a man commits is outside the body. But he who commits sexual immorality sins against his own body. 19 What? Do you not know that your body is the temple of the Holy Spirit, who is in you, whom you have received from God, and that you are not your own? 20 You were bought with a price. Therefore glorify God in your body and in your spirit, which are God's.

1 Corinthians 7: 1, 8 - 9 (RSV)
1 Now concerning the matters about which you wrote. It is well for a man not to touch a woman. 8 To the unmarried and the widows I say that it is well for them to remain single as I do. 9 But if they can-not exercise self-control, they should marry. For it is better to marry than to be aflame with passion.

1 Corinthians 10: 13 (MEV)
13 No temptation has taken you except what is common to man. God is faithful, and He will not per-mit you to be tempted above what you can endure, but will with the temptation also make a way to escape, that you may be able to bear it.

Galatians 5: 19 (NCV)
19 The wrong things the sinful self does are clear: being sexually unfaithful, not being pure, taking part in sexual sins,

Colossians 3: 5 - 6 (NKJV)
5 Therefore put to death your members which are on the earth: fornication,

uncleanness, passion, evil desire, and covetousness, which is idolatry. 6 Because of these things the wrath of God is coming upon the sons of disobedience,

1 Thessalonians 4: 3, 5 (NET)
3 For this is God's will: that you become holy, that you keep away from sexual immorality, 5 not in lustful passion like the Gentiles who do not know God.

Hebrews 13: 4 (NKJV)
4 Marriage is honorable among all, and the bed undefiled; but fornicators and adulterers God will judge.

SIN

Genesis 4: 7 (NIRV)
7 Do what is right and then you will be accepted. If you don't do what is right, sin is waiting at your door to grab you. It desires to control you. But you must rule over it.

Psalms 25: 8 (ERV)
8 The Lord is good and does what is right. He shows sinners the right way to live.

Psalms 32: 5 (ERV)
5 But then I decided to confess my sins to the Lord. I stopped hiding my guilt and told you about my sins. And you forgave them all! Selah

Psalms 38: 5 (NIVUK)
5 My wounds fester and are loathsome because of my sinful folly.

Psalms 66: 18 (GNT)
18 If I had ignored my sins, the Lord would not have listened to me.

Psalms 103: 10 (NKJV)
10 He has not dealt with us according to our sins, Nor punished us according to our iniquities.

Proverbs 21: 4 (ERV)
4 Proud looks and proud thoughts are sins. They show a person is evil.

Proverbs 28: 13 (MEV)
13 He who covers his sins will not prosper, but whoever confesses and forsakes them will have mer-cy.

Proverbs 29: 22 (NIV)
22 An angry person stirs up conflict, and a hot-tempered person commits many sins.

Isaiah 53: 6 (GNT)
6 All of us were like sheep that were lost, each of us going his own way. But the Lord made the pun-ishment fall on him, the punishment all of us deserved.

Ezekiel 36: 25 - 26 (NIV)
25 I will sprinkle clean water on you, and you will be clean; I will cleanse you from all your impurities and from all your idols. 26 I will give you a new heart and put a new spirit in you; I will remove from you your heart of stone and give you a heart of flesh.

Matthew 6: 15 (NIV)
15 But if you do not forgive others their sins, your Father will not forgive your sins.

John 1: 29 (MEV)
29 The next day John saw Jesus coming toward him and said, "Look, the Lamb of God, who takes away the sin of the world.

Acts 13: 38 (NCV)
38 Brothers, understand what we are telling you: You can have forgiveness of your sins through Je-sus. The law of Moses could not free you from your sins. But through Jesus everyone who believes is free from all sins.

Romans 3: 23 (ESV)
23 for all have sinned and fall short of the glory of God,

Romans 6: 1 - 2, 7 (ESV)
1 What shall we say then? Are we to continue in sin that grace may abound? 2 By no means! How can we who died to sin still live in it? 7 For one who has died has been set free from sin.

Romans 6: 12 - 14 (ESV)
12 Let not sin therefore reign in your mortal body, to make you obey its passions. 13 Do not present your members to sin as instruments for unrighteousness, but present yourselves to God as those who have been brought from death to life, and your members to God as instruments for righteousness. 14 For sin will have no dominion over you, since you are not under law but under grace.

Hebrews 1: 3 (GNT)
3 He reflects the brightness of God's glory and is the exact likeness of God's own being, sustaining the universe with his powerful word. After achieving forgiveness for the sins of all human beings, he sat down in heaven at the right side of God, the Supreme Power.

James 1: 5 (NIV)
5 If any of you lacks wisdom, you should ask God, who gives generously to all without finding fault, and it will be given to you.

James 4: 17 (NIV)
17 If anyone, then, knows the good they ought to do and doesn't do it, it is sin for them.

James 5: 15 (NIV)
15 And the prayer offered in faith will make the sick person well; the Lord will raise them up. If they have sinned, they will be forgiven.

1 Peter 2: 24 (NIV)
24 "He himself bore our sins" in his body on the cross, so that we might die to sins and live for righ-teousness; "by his wounds you have been healed."

1 Peter 4: 8 (NIV)
8 Above all, love each other deeply, because love covers over a multitude of sins.

1 John 1: 9 (NLT)
9 But if we confess our sins to him, he is faithful and just to forgive us our sins and to cleanse us from all wickedness.

1 John 3: 5, 8 (NLT)
5 And you know that Jesus came to take away our sins, and there is no sin in him. 8 But when people keep on sinning, it shows that they belong to the devil, who has been sinning since the beginning. But the Son of God came to destroy the works of the devil.

SLAVES

Proverbs 22: 7 (AMP)
7 The rich rule over the poor, and the borrower is servant to the lender.

John 8: 34 -36 (NIV)
34 Jesus replied, "Very truly I tell you, everyone who sins is a slave to sin. 35 Now a slave has no permanent place in the family, but a son belongs to it forever. 36 So if the Son sets you free, you will be free indeed.

Romans 6: 6 - 7 (NIV)
6 For we know that our old self was crucified with him so that the body ruled by sin might be done away with, that we should no longer be slaves to sin— 7 because anyone who has died has been set free from sin.

Romans 6: 16 - 18 (NIV)
16 Don't you know that when you offer yourselves to someone as obedient slaves, you are slaves of the one you obey—whether you are slaves to sin, which leads to death, or to obedience, which leads to righteousness? 17 But thanks be to God that, though you used to be slaves to sin, you have come to obey from your heart the pattern of teaching that has now claimed your allegiance. 18 You have been set free from sin and have become slaves to righteousness.

1 Corinthians 9: 19 - 22 (RSV)
19 For though I am free from all men, I have made myself a slave to all, that I might win the more. 20 To the Jews I became as a Jew, in order to win Jews; to those under the law I became as one under the law—though not being myself under the law—that I might win those under the law. 21 To those outside the law I became as one outside the law—not being without law toward God but under the law of Christ—that I might win those outside the law. 22 To the weak I became weak, that I might win the weak. I have become all things to all men, that I might by all means save some.

SLEEP

Psalms 3: 5 (NLT)
5 I lay down and slept, yet I woke up in safety, for the Lord was watching over me.

Psalms 4: 8 (NLV)
8 I will lie down and sleep in peace. O Lord, You alone keep me safe.

Psalms 127: 2 (ERV)
2 It is a waste of time to get up early and stay up late, trying to make a living. The Lord provides for those he loves, even while they are sleeping.

Proverbs 3: 13, 21, 23 - 24 (NIV)
13 Blessed are those who find wisdom, those who gain understanding, 21 My son, do not let wisdom and understanding out of your sight, preserve sound judgment and discretion; 23 Then you will go on your way in safety, and your foot will not stumble. 24 When you lie down, you will not be afraid; when you lie down, your sleep will be sweet.

Proverbs 6: 9 - 11 (NIV)
9 How long will you lie there, you sluggard? When will you get up from

your sleep? 10 A little sleep, a little slumber, a little folding of the hands to rest— 11 and poverty will come on you like a thief and scarcity like an armed man.

Proverbs 20: 13 (NIV)
13 Do not love sleep or you will grow poor; stay awake and you will have food to spare.

Ecclesiastes 5: 12 (NASB)
12 The sleep of the working man is pleasant, whether he eats little or much; but the full stomach of the rich man does not allow him to sleep.

Jeremiah 31: 25 - 26 (NLT)
25 For I have given rest to the weary and joy to the sorrowing." 26 At this, I woke up and looked around. My sleep had been very sweet.

1 Thessalonians 5: 6 (EXB)
6 So we should not be like other people who are sleeping, but we should be ·alert and ·have self-con-trol.

SLOTHFULNESS

Proverbs 6: 6 (ISV)
6 Go to the ant, you lazy man! Observe its ways and become wise.

Proverbs 10: 4 (NET)
4 The one who is lazy becomes poor, but the one who works diligently becomes wealthy.

Proverbs 10: 26 (CJB)
26 Like vinegar to the teeth and smoke to the eyes is a lazy person to his employer.

Proverbs 12: 24 (CEV)
24 Work hard, and you will be a leader; be lazy, and you will end up a slave.

Proverbs 13: 4 (NIV)
4 A sluggard's appetite is never filled, but the desires of the diligent are fully satisfied.

Proverbs 20: 4 (NLT)
4 Those too lazy to plow in the right season will have no food at the harvest.

Proverbs 24: 33 - 34 (NCV)
33 You sleep a little; you take a nap. You fold your hands and lie down to rest. 34 Soon you will be as poor as if you had been robbed; you will have as little as if you had been held up.

Proverbs 28: 19 (AMP)
19 He who cultivates his land will have plenty of bread, but he who follows worthless people and pur-suits will have poverty enough.

Romans 12: 11 (CJB)
11 Don't be lazy when hard work is needed, but serve the Lord with spiritual fervor.

Ephesians 4: 28 (WEB)
28 Let him who stole steal no more; but rather let him labor, producing with his hands something that is good, that he may have something to give to him who has need.

1 Thessalonians 4: 11 - 12 (GW)
11 Also, make it your goal to live quietly, do your work, and earn your own living, as we ordered you. 12 Then your way of life will win respect from those outside the church, and you won't

have to depend on anyone else for what you need.

2 Thessalonians 3: 10 - 12 (TLB)
10 Even while we were still there with you, we gave you this rule: "He who does not work shall not eat." 11 Yet we hear that some of you are living in laziness, refusing to work, and wasting your time in gossiping. 12 In the name of the Lord Jesus Christ we appeal to such people—we command them— to quiet down, get to work, and earn their own living.

Hebrews 6: 11 - 12 (NIV)
11 We want each of you to show this same diligence to the very end, so that what you hope for may be fully realized. 12 We do not want you to become lazy, but to imitate those who through faith and patience inherit what has been promised.

SOUND MIND

1 Kings 4: 29 (AMP)
29 And God gave Solomon exceptionally much wisdom and understanding, and breadth of mind like the sand of the seashore.

Psalms 42: 11 (HCSB)
11 Why am I so depressed? Why this turmoil within me? Put your hope in God, for I will still praise Him, my Savior and my God.

Psalms 51: 6 (GNT)
6 Sincerity and truth are what you require; fill my mind with your wisdom.

Psalms 62: 1 - 2 (HCSB)
1 I am at rest in God alone; my salvation comes from Him. 2 He alone is my rock and my salvation, my stronghold; I will never be shaken.

Psalms 104: 34 (NET)
34 May my thoughts be pleasing to him! I will rejoice in the Lord.

Psalms 139: 23 - 24 (GW)
23 Examine me, O God, and know my mind. Test me, and know my thoughts. 24 See whether I am on an evil path. Then lead me on the everlasting path.

Proverbs 12: 25 (NKJV)
25 Anxiety in the heart of man causes depression, But a good word makes it glad.

Proverbs 23: 31 - 33 (NKJV)
31 Do not look on the wine when it is red, When it sparkles in the cup, When it swirls around smooth-ly; 32 At the last it bites like a serpent, And stings like a viper. 33 Your eyes will see strange things, And your heart will utter perverse things.

Isaiah 26: 3 (ESV)
3 You keep him in perfect peace whose mind is stayed on you, because he trusts in you.

Jeremiah 31: 33 (NKJV)
33 But this is the covenant that I will make with the house of Israel after those days, says the Lord: I will put My law in their minds, and write it on their hearts; and I will be their God, and they shall be My people.

Daniel 4: 34, 36 (MEV)

34 But at the end of the days, I, Nebuchadnezzar, lifted up my eyes to heaven, and my understanding returned to me, and I blessed the Most High, and I praised and honored Him who lives forever: For His dominion is an everlasting dominion, and whose kingdom endures from generation to generation. 36 At the same time my reason returned to me. And for the glory of my kingdom, my honor and splen-dor returned to me. And my counselors and my lords sought me out. Then I was established in my kingdom, and excellent majesty was added to me.

Jonah 2: 6 (CEV)

6 I had sunk down below the underwater mountains; I knew that forever, I would be a prisoner there. But, you, Lord God, rescued me from that pit.

Malachi 4: 2 (GNT)

2 But for you who obey me, my saving power will rise on you like the sun and bring healing like the sun's rays. You will be as free and happy as calves let out of a stall.

Matthew 22: 37 (RSV)

37 And he said to him, "You shall love the Lord your God with all your heart, and with all your soul, and with all your mind.

Romans 12: 2 (NKJV)

2 And do not be conformed to this world, but be transformed by the renewing of your mind, that you may prove what is that good and acceptable and perfect will of God.

1 Corinthians 14: 33 (ESV)

33 For God is not a God of confusion but of peace. As in all the churches of the saints,

Ephesians 1: 18 - 19 (HCSB)

18 I pray that the perception of your mind may be enlightened so you may know what is the hope of His calling, what are the glorious riches of His inheritance among the saints, 19 and what is the im-measurable greatness of His power to us who believe, according to the working of His vast strength.

Philippians 4: 7 - 8 (HCSB)

7 And the peace of God, which surpasses every thought, will guard your hearts and minds in Christ Jesus. 8 Finally brothers, whatever is true, whatever is honorable, whatever is just, whatever is pure, whatever is lovely, whatever is commendable—if there is any moral excellence and if there is any praise—dwell on these things.

2 Timothy 1: 7 (NKJV)

7 For God has not given us a spirit of fear, but of power and of love and of a sound mind.

James 3: 16 - 18 (HCSB)

16 For where envy and selfish ambition exist, there is disorder and every kind of evil. 17 But the wisdom from above is first pure, then peace-loving, gentle, compliant, full of mercy and good fruits, without favoritism and hypocrisy. 18 And the fruit of righteousness is sown in peace by those who cultivate peace.

1 Peter 5: 8 - 10 (ERV)

8 Control yourselves and be careful! The devil is your enemy, and he goes around like a roaring lion looking for

someone to attack and eat. 9 Refuse to follow the devil. Stand strong in your faith. You know that your brothers and sisters all over the world are having the same sufferings that you have. 10 Yes, you will suffer for a short time. But after that, God will make everything right. He will make you strong. He will support you and keep you from falling. He is the God who gives all grace. He chose you to share in his glory in Christ. That glory will continue forever.

3 John 1: 2 (NASB)
2 Beloved, I pray that in all respects you may prosper and be in good health, just as your soul

SPEAKING

1 Samuel 2: 3 (NKJV)
3 Talk no more so very proudly; Let no arrogance come from your mouth, For the Lord is the God of knowledge; And by Him actions are weighed.

Psalms 37: 30 (NIRV)
30 The mouths of those who do what is right speak words of wisdom. They say what is honest.

Psalms 103: 20 - 22 (ISV)
20 Bless the Lord, you angels who belong to him, you mighty warriors who carry out his commands, who are obedient to the sound of his words. 21 Bless the Lord, all his heavenly armies, his ministers who do his will. 22 Bless the Lord, all his creation, in all the places of his dominion. Bless the Lord, my soul.

Psalms 141: 1 - 2 (MEV)
1 Lord, I cry unto You; make haste to me; give ear to my voice, when I cry unto You. 2 Let my prayer be set forth before You as incense, and the lifting up of my hands as the evening sacrifice.

Proverbs 12: 18 (MEV)
18 There is one who speaks like the piercings of a sword, but the tongue of the wise is health.

Proverbs 18: 4 (MEV)
4 The words of a man's mouth are as deep waters, and the wellspring of wisdom as a flowing brook.

Proverbs 15: 1 (NIV)
1 A gentle answer turns away wrath, but a harsh word stirs up anger.

Proverbs 16: 24 (ESV)
24 Gracious words are like a honeycomb, sweetness to the soul and health to the body.

Proverbs 17: 27 - 28 (NET)
27 The truly wise person restrains his words, and the one who stays calm is discerning. 28 Even a fool who remains silent is considered wise, and the one who holds his tongue is deemed discerning.

Proverbs 18: 20 - 21 (MEV)
20 A man's stomach will be satisfied with the fruit of his mouth; and with the increase of his lips will he be filled. 21 Death and life are in the power of the tongue, and those who love it will eat its fruit.

Ecclesiastes 3: 7 (WEB)
7 a time to tear, and a time to sew; a time to keep silence, and a time to speak;

Isaiah 55: 11 (NKJV)
11 So shall My word be that goes forth from My mouth; It shall not return to Me void, But it shall ac-complish what I please, And it shall prosper in the thing for which I sent it.

Matthew 12: 34 - 37 (NIV)
34 You brood of vipers, how can you who are evil say anything good? For the mouth speaks what the heart is full of. 35 A good man brings good things out of the good stored up in him, and an evil man brings evil things out of the evil stored up in him. 36 But I tell you that everyone will have to give account on the day of judgment for every empty word they have spoken. 37 For by your words you will be acquitted, and by your words you will be condemned.

Mark 4: 39 (GW)
39 Then he got up, ordered the wind to stop, and said to the sea, "Be still, absolutely still!" The wind stopped blowing, and the sea became very calm.

Mark 11: 23 (ISV)
23 I tell all of you with certainty, if anyone says to this mountain, 'Be lifted up and thrown into the sea,' if he doesn't doubt in his heart but believes that what he says will happen, it will be done for him.

Luke 12: 12 (AMP)
12 For the Holy Spirit will teach you in that very hour and moment what [you] ought to say.

Luke 17: 6 (CEB)
6 The Lord replied, "If you had faith the size of a mustard seed, you could say to this mulberry tree, 'Be uprooted

and planted in the sea,' and it would obey you.

Romans 10: 8 - 10 (NKJV)
8 But what does it say? "The word is near you, in your mouth and in your heart" (that is, the word of faith which we preach): 9 that if you confess with your mouth the Lord Jesus and believe in your heart that God has raised Him from the dead, you will be saved. 10 For with the heart one believes unto righteousness, and with the mouth confession is made unto salvation.

2 Corinthians 4: 13 (NIV)
13 It is written: "I believed; therefore I have spoken." Since we have that same spirit of faith, we also believe and therefore speak,

Ephesians 6: 10 - 11, 17 (NIV)
10 Finally, be strong in the Lord and in his mighty power. 11 Put on the full armor of God, so that you can take your stand against the devil's schemes. 17 Take the helmet of salvation and the sword of the Spirit, which is the word of God.

Hebrews 10: 23 (NCV)
23 Let us hold firmly to the hope that we have confessed, because we can trust God to do what he promised.

Hebrews 11: 3 (NET)
3 By faith we understand that the worlds were set in order at God's command, so that the visible has its origin in the invisible.

James 1: 26 (GW)
26 If a person thinks that he is religious but can't control his tongue, he is

fooling himself. That per-son's religion is worthless.

1 Peter 3: 9 - 12 (NIV)

9 Do not repay evil with evil or insult with insult. On the contrary, repay evil with blessing, because to this you were called so that you may inherit a blessing. 10 For, "Whoever would love life and see good days must keep their tongue from evil and their lips from deceitful speech. 11 They must turn from evil and do good; they must seek peace and pursue it. 12 For the eyes of the Lord are on the righteous and his ears are attentive to their prayer, but the face of the Lord is against those who do evil.

STEWARDSHIP

Leviticus 23: 22 (NLT)

22 When you harvest the crops of your land, do not harvest the grain along the edges of your fields, and do not pick up what the harvesters drop. Leave it for the poor and the foreigners living among you. I am the Lord your God.

Psalms 41: 1 - 2 (MEV)

1 Blessed are those who consider the poor; the Lord will deliver them in the day of trouble. 2 The Lord will preserve them and keep them alive, and they will be blessed on the earth, and You will not deliver them to the will of their enemies.

Psalms 112: 5, 9 (CEV)

5 Life will go well for those who freely lend and are honest in business. 9 They will always be remem-bered and

greatly praised, because they were kind and freely gave to the poor.

Proverbs 22: 9 (CEV)

9 The Lord blesses everyone who freely gives food to the poor.

Isaiah 58: 7 - 11 (ERV)

7 I want you to share your food with the hungry. I want you to find the poor who don't have homes and bring them into your own homes. When you see people who have no clothes, give them your clothes! Don't hide from your relatives when they need help." 8 If you do these things, your light will begin to shine like the light of dawn. Then your wounds will heal. Your "Goodness" will walk in front of you, and the Glory of the Lord will come following behind you. 9 Then you will call to the Lord, and he will answer you. You will cry out to him, and he will say, "Here I am." Stop causing trouble and putting burdens on people. Stop saying things to hurt people or accusing them of things they didn't do. 10 Feel sorry for hungry people and give them food. Help those who are troubled and satisfy their needs. Then your light will shine in the darkness. You will be like the bright sunshine at noon. 11 The Lord will always lead you and satisfy your needs in dry lands. He will give strength to your bones. You will be like a garden that has plenty of water, like a spring that never goes dry.

Malachi 3: 10 - 11 (NASB)

10 Bring the whole tithe into the storehouse, so that there may be food in My house, and test Me now in this," says the Lord of hosts, "if I will not open for you the windows of heaven and pour out for you a blessing until

it overflows. 11 Then I will rebuke the devourer for you, so that it will not destroy the fruits of the ground; nor will your vine in the field cast its grapes," says the Lord of hosts.

Matthew 5: 41 - 42 (MEV)

41 And whoever compels you to go a mile, go with him two. 42 Give to him who asks you, and from him who would borrow from you do not turn away.

Matthew 6: 1 - 4 (WEB)

1 Be careful that you don't do your charitable giving before men, to be seen by them, or else you have no reward from your Father who is in heaven. 2 Therefore when you do merciful deeds, don't sound a trumpet before yourself, as the hypocrites do in the synagogues and in the streets, that they may get glory from men. Most certainly I tell you, they have received their reward. 3 But when you do merciful deeds, don't let your left hand know what your right hand does, 4 so that your merciful deeds may be in secret, then your Father who sees in secret will reward you openly.

Matthew 25: 34 - 40 (ESV)

34 Then the King will say to those on his right, 'Come, you who are blessed by my Father, inherit the kingdom prepared for you from the foundation of the world. 35 For I was hungry and you gave me food, I was thirsty and you gave me drink, I was a stranger and you welcomed me, 36 I was naked and you clothed me, I was sick and you visited me, I was in prison and you came to me.' 37 Then the righteous will answer him, saying, 'Lord, when did we see you hungry and feed you, or thirsty

and give you drink? 38 And when did we see you a stranger and welcome you, or naked and clothe you? 39 And when did we see you sick or in prison and visit you?' 40 And the King will answer them, 'Truly, I say to you, as you did it to one of the least of these my brothers, you did it to me.'

Luke 16: 10 - 13 (NIVUK)

10 'Whoever can be trusted with very little can also be trusted with much, and whoever is dishonest with very little will also be dishonest with much. 11 So if you have not been trustworthy in handling worldly wealth, who will trust you with true riches? 12 And if you have not been trustworthy with someone else's property, who will give you property of your own? 13 'No one can serve two masters. Either you will hate the one and love the other, or you will be devoted to the one and despise the other. You cannot serve both God and Money.'

2 Corinthians 8: 9, 12 - 14 (NIV)

9 For you know the grace of our Lord Jesus Christ, that though he was rich, yet for your sake he became poor, so that you through his poverty might become rich. 12 For if the willingness is there, the gift is acceptable according to what one has, not according to what one does not have. 13 Our desire is not that others might be relieved while you are hard pressed, but that there might be equality. 14 At the present time your plenty will supply what they need, so that in turn their plenty will supply what you need. The goal is equality,

2 Corinthians 9: 6 - 8 (GNT)

6 Remember that the person who plants few seeds will have a small crop; the one who plants many seeds will

have a large crop. 7 You should each give, then, as you have decided, not with regret or out of a sense of duty; for God loves the one who gives gladly. 8 And God is able to give you more than you need, so that you will always have all you need for yourselves and more than enough for every good cause.

James 2: 14 - 16 (ISV)
14 What good does it do, my brothers, if someone claims to have faith but does not prove it with actions? This kind of faith cannot save him, can it? 15 Suppose a brother or sister does not have any clothes or daily food 16 and one of you tells them, "Go in peace! Stay warm and eat heartily." If you do not provide for their bodily needs, what good does it do?

STRENGTH

Joshua 1: 7 (NIV)
7 "Be strong and very courageous. Be careful to obey all the law my servant Moses gave you; do not turn from it to the right or to the left, that you may be successful wherever you go.

Nehemiah 8: 10 (ESV)
10 Then he said to them, "Go your way. Eat the fat and drink sweet wine and send portions to anyone who has nothing ready, for this day is holy to our Lord. And do not be grieved, for the joy of the Lord is your strength."

Psalms 18: 1 - 3 (NIV)
1 I love you, Lord, my strength. 2 The Lord is my rock, my fortress and my deliverer; my God is my rock, in whom I take refuge, my shield and the horn of my salvation, my stronghold. 3 I called to the Lord, who is worthy of praise, and I have been saved from my enemies.

Psalms 18: 29, 32 - 34, 39 (NIV)
29 With your help I can advance against a troop; with my God I can scale a wall. 32 It is God who arms me with strength and keeps my way secure. 33 He makes my feet like the feet of a deer; he causes me to stand on the heights. 34 He trains my hands for battle; my arms can bend a bow of bronze. 39 You armed me with strength for battle; you humbled my adversaries before me.

Psalms 27: 1 (MEV)
1 The Lord is my light and my salvation; whom will I fear? The Lord is the strength of my life; of whom will I be afraid?

Psalms 27: 14 (NKJV)
14 Wait on the Lord; Be of good courage, And He shall strengthen your heart; Wait, I say, on the Lord!

Psalms 29: 11 (RSV)
11 May the Lord give strength to his people! May the Lord bless his people with peace!

Psalms 31: 24 (NET)
24 Be strong and confident, all you who wait on the Lord!

Psalms 119: 28 (NIV)
28 My soul is weary with sorrow; strengthen me according to your word.

Proverbs 8: 12, 14 (AMP)
12 I, Wisdom [from God], make prudence my dwelling, and I find out knowledge and discretion. 14 I have

counsel and sound knowledge, I have understanding, I have might and power.

Proverbs 24: 5 (RSV)
5 A wise man is mightier than a strong man, and a man of knowledge than he who has strength;

Proverbs 28: 1 (CEB)
1 The wicked run away even though no one pursues them, but the righteous are as confident as a lion.

Isaiah 41: 10, 13 (ESV)
10 fear not, for I am with you; be not dismayed, for I am your God; I will strengthen you, I will help you, I will uphold you with my righteous right hand. 13 For I, the Lord your God, hold your right hand; it is I who say to you, "Fear not, I am the one who helps you."

Jeremiah 12: 5 (NASB)
5 If you have run with footmen and they have tired you out, Then how can you compete with horses? If you fall down in a land of peace, How will you do in the thicket of the Jordan?

Daniel 10:17 (NIV)
17 How can I, your servant, talk with you, my lord? My strength is gone and I can hardly breathe.

2 Corinthians 12: 9 - 10 (NKJV)
9 And He said to me, "My grace is sufficient for you, for My strength is made perfect in weakness." Therefore most gladly I will rather boast in my infirmities, that the power of Christ may rest upon me. 10 Therefore I take pleasure in infirmities, in reproaches, in needs, in persecutions, in distresses,

for Christ's sake. For when I am weak, then I am strong.

Ephesians 3: 16 - 17, 20 (NET)
16 I pray that according to the wealth of his glory he may grant you to be strengthened with power through his Spirit in the inner person, 17 that Christ may dwell in your hearts through faith, so that, because you have been rooted and grounded in love, 20 Now to him who by the power that is work-ing within us is able to do far beyond all that we ask or think,

Ephesians 6: 10, 13 - 14 (WEB)
10 Finally, be strong in the Lord, and in the strength of his might. 13 Therefore put on the whole armor of God, that you may be able to withstand in the evil day, and, having done all, to stand. 14 Stand therefore, having the utility belt of truth buckled around your waist, and having put on the breastplate of righteousness,

Philippians 4: 12 - 13 (WEB)
12 I know how to be humbled, and I know also how to abound. In everything and in all things I have learned the secret both to be filled and to be hungry, both to abound and to be in need. 13 I can do all things through Christ, who strengthens me.

TIME

Psalms 62: 8 (NKJV)
8 Trust in Him at all times, you people; Pour out your heart before Him; God is a refuge for us.

Psalms 118: 24 - 25 (NKJV)

24 This is the day the Lord has made; We will rejoice and be glad in it. 25 Save now, I pray, O Lord; O Lord, I pray, send now prosperity.

Psalms 119: 126 (NRSV)

126 It is time for the Lord to act, for your law has been broken.

Psalms 145: 15 (AMP)

15 The eyes of all wait for You [looking, watching, and expecting] and You give them their food in due season.

Ecclesiastes 3: 1 - 3 (GNV)

1 To all things there is an appointed time, and a time to every purpose under the heaven. 2 A time to be born, and a time to die: a time to plant, and a time to pluck up that which is planted. 3 A time to slay, and a time to heal: a time to break down, and a time to build.

Ecclesiastes 9: 12 (RSV)

12 For man does not know his time. Like fish which are taken in an evil net, and like birds which are caught in a snare, so the sons of men are snared at an evil time, when it suddenly falls upon them.

Luke 18: 1 (ISV)

1 Jesus told his disciples a parable about their need to pray all the time and never give up.

Acts 17: 26 (NIRV)

26 From one man he made all the people of the world. Now they live all over the earth. He decided exactly when they should live. And he decided exactly where they should live.

2 Corinthians 6: 1 - 3 (NIV)

1 As God's co-workers we urge you not to receive God's grace in vain. 2 For he says, "In the time of my favor I heard you, and in the day of salvation I helped you." I tell you, now is the time of God's favor, now is the day of salvation. 3 We put no stumbling block in anyone's path, so that our ministry will not be discredited.

Galatians 6: 9 (MEV)

9 And let us not grow weary in doing good, for in due season we shall reap, if we do not give up.

Ephesians 6: 18 (WEB)

18 with all prayer and requests, praying at all times in the Spirit, and being watchful to this end in all perseverance and requests for all the saints:

2 Thessalonians 3: 16 (ASV)

16 Now the Lord of peace himself give you peace at all times in all ways. The Lord be with you all.

Hebrews 4: 16 (TLB)

16 So let us come boldly to the very throne of God and stay there to receive his mercy and to find grace to help us in our times of need.

Hebrews 13: 8 (LEB)

8 Jesus Christ is the same yesterday and today and forever.

1 Peter 5: 6 (NKJV)

Therefore humble yourselves under the mighty hand of God, that He may exalt you in due time,

TRUST

Psalms 27: 14 (NET)
14 Rely on the Lord! Be strong and confident! Rely on the Lord!

Psalms 28: 7 (NIV)
7 The Lord is my strength and my shield; my heart trusts in him, and he helps me. My heart leaps for joy, and with my song I praise him.

Psalms 32: 10 (NIRV)
10 Sinful people have all kinds of trouble. But the Lord's faithful love is all around those who trust in him.

Psalms 34: 19 (CEB)
19 The righteous have many problems, but the Lord delivers them from every one.

Psalms 37: 4 - 6 (NIV)
4 Take delight in the Lord, and he will give you the desires of your heart. 5 Commit your way to the Lord; trust in him and he will do this: 6 He will make your righteous reward shine like the dawn, your vindication like the noonday sun.

Psalms 46: 1 - 2 (ERV)
1 God is our protection and source of strength. He is always ready to help us in times of trouble. 2 So we are not afraid when the earth quakes and the mountains fall into the sea.

Psalms 50: 15 (NET)
15 Pray to me when you are in trouble! I will deliver you, and you will honor me!

Psalms 62: 5 (NLT)
5 Let all that I am wait quietly before God, for my hope is in him.

Psalms 62: 8 (NCV)
8 People, trust God all the time. Tell him all your problems, because God is our protection. Selah

Psalms 84: 11 - 12 (NET)
11 For the Lord God is our sovereign protector. The Lord bestows favor and honor; he withholds no good thing from those who have integrity. 12 O Lord who rules over all, how blessed are those who trust in you!

Psalms 143: 8 (HCSB)
8 Let me experience Your faithful love in the morning, for I trust in You. Reveal to me the way I should go because I long for You.

Psalms 145: 15 - 16 (CEB)
15 All eyes look to you, hoping, and you give them their food right on time, 16 opening your hand and satisfying the desire of every living thing.

Proverbs 3: 5 - 6 (NET)
5 Trust in the Lord with all your heart, and do not rely on your own understanding. 6 Acknowledge him in all your ways, and he will make your paths straight.

Isaiah 40: 31 (HCSB)
31 but those who trust in the Lord will renew their strength; they will soar on wings like eagles; they will run and not grow weary; they will walk and not faint.

Isaiah 41: 10 (NIV)
10 So do not fear, for I am with you; do not be dismayed, for I am your God. I will strengthen you and help you; I will uphold you with my righteous right hand.

Habakkuk 2: 3 (NIV)
3 For the revelation awaits an appointed time; it speaks of the end and will not prove false. Though it linger, wait for it; it will certainly come and will not delay.

Matthew 6: 31 - 32 (ERV)
31 "Don't worry and say, 'What will we eat?' or 'What will we drink?' or 'What will we wear?' 32 That's what those people who don't know God are always thinking about. Don't worry, because your Father in heaven knows that you need all these things.

Luke 16: 10 - 12 (CJB)
10 Someone who is trustworthy in a small matter is also trustworthy in large ones, and someone who is dishonest in a small matter is also dishonest in large ones. 11 So if you haven't been trustworthy in handling worldly wealth, who is going to trust you with the real thing? 12 And if you haven't been trust-worthy with what belongs to someone else, who will give you what ought to belong to you?

John 14: 1 (CJB)
1 Don't let yourselves be disturbed. Trust in God and trust in me.

Romans 8: 31, 35, 37 (AMP)
31 What then shall we say to [all] this? If God is for us, who [can be] against us? [Who can be our foe, if God is on our side?] 35 Who shall ever separate us from Christ's love? Shall suffering and affliction and tribulation? Or calamity and distress? Or persecution or hunger or destitution or peril or sword? 37 Yet amid all these things we are more than conquerors [a]and gain a surpassing victory through Him Who loved us.

1 Corinthians 10: 13 (MEV)
13 No temptation has taken you except what is common to man. God is faithful, and He will not per-mit you to be tempted above what you can endure, but will with the temptation also make a way to escape, that you may be able to bear it.

1 Peter 5: 7 (TLB)
7 Let him have all your worries and cares, for he is always thinking about you and watching every-thing that concerns you.

WARFARE

Psalms 91: 1 - 16 (NIVUK)
1 Whoever dwells in the shelter of the Most High will rest in the shadow of the Almighty. 2 I will say of the Lord, "He is my refuge and my fortress, my God, in whom I trust." 3 Surely he will save you from the fowler's snare and from the deadly pestilence. 4 He will cover you with his feathers, and under his wings you will find refuge; his faithfulness will be your shield and rampart. 5 You will not fear the terror of night, nor the arrow that flies by day, 6 nor the pestilence that stalks in the darkness, nor the plague that destroys at midday. 7 A thousand may fall at your side, ten thousand at your right hand, but it will not come near you. 8

You will only observe with your eyes and see the punishment of the wicked. 9 If you say, "The Lord is my refuge," and you make the Most High your dwelling, 10 no harm will overtake you, no disaster will come near your tent. 11 For he will command his angels con-cerning you to guard you in all your ways; 12 they will lift you up in their hands, so that you will not strike your foot against a stone. 13 You will tread on the lion and the cobra; you will trample the great lion and the serpent. 14 "Because he loves me," says the Lord, "I will rescue him; I will protect him, for he acknowledges my name. 15 He will call on me, and I will answer him; I will be with him in trouble, I will deliver him and honor him. 16 With long life I will satisfy him and show him my salvation."

Proverbs 26: 2 (NKJV)
2 Like a flitting sparrow, like a flying swallow, So a curse without cause shall not alight.

Jeremiah 23: 29 (NLT)
29 Does not my word burn like fire?" says the Lord. "Is it not like a mighty hammer that smashes a rock to pieces?

Matthew 11: 12 (AMP)
12 From the days of John the Baptist until now the kingdom of heaven suffers violent assault, and violent men seize it by force [as a precious prize].

Matthew 12: 29 (WEB)
29 Or how can one enter into the house of the strong man, and plunder his goods, unless he first bind the strong man? Then he will plunder his house.

Matthew 18: 18 (NIV)

18 "Truly I tell you, whatever you bind on earth will be bound in heaven, and whatever you loose on earth will be loosed in heaven.

Mark 11: 23 (NET)
23 I tell you the truth, if someone says to this mountain, 'Be lifted up and thrown into the sea,' and does not doubt in his heart but believes that what he says will happen, it will be done for him.

Mark 16: 18 (NCV)
18 They will pick up snakes and drink poison without being hurt. They will touch the sick, and the sick will be healed.

Luke 10: 19 (GW)
19 I have given you the authority to trample snakes and scorpions and to destroy the enemy's power. Nothing will hurt you.

Romans 12: 21 (NIV)
21 Do not be overcome by evil, but overcome evil with good.

2 Corinthians 10: 3 - 5 (RSV)
3 For though we live in the world we are not carrying on a worldly war, 4 for the weapons of our war-fare are not worldly but have divine power to destroy strongholds. 5 We destroy arguments and every proud obstacle to the knowledge of God, and take every thought captive to obey Christ,

Ephesians 6: 10 - 18 (NKJV)
10 Finally, my brethren, be strong in the Lord and in the power of His might. 11 Put on the whole armor of God, that you may be able to stand against the wiles of the devil. 12 For we do not wrestle

against flesh and blood, but against principalities, against powers, against the rulers of the darkness of this age, against spiritual hosts of wickedness in the heavenly places. 13 Therefore take up the whole armor of God, that you may be able to withstand in the evil day, and having done all, to stand. 14 Stand therefore, having girded your waist with truth, having put on the breastplate of righteous-ness, 15 and having shod your feet with the preparation of the gospel of peace; 16 above all, taking the shield of faith with which you will be able to quench all the fiery darts of the wicked one. 17 And take the helmet of salvation, and the sword of the Spirit, which is the word of God; 18 praying always with all prayer and supplication in the Spirit, being watchful to this end with all perseverance and supplication for all the saints—

2 Timothy 1: 7 (NCV)
7 God did not give us a spirit that makes us afraid but a spirit of power and love and self-control.

2 Timothy 2: 3 - 4 (MEV)
3 Endure hard times as a good soldier of Jesus Christ. 4 No soldier on active duty entangles himself with civilian affairs, that he may please the enlisting officer.

Hebrews 10: 35 - 36 (CEB)
35 So don't throw away your confidence— it brings a great reward. 36 You need to endure so that you can receive the promises after you do God's will.

James 4: 7 (DARBY)
7 Subject yourselves therefore to God. Resist the devil, and he will flee from you.

1 John 4: 17 (ASV)
17 Herein is love made perfect with us, that we may have boldness in the day of judgment; because as he is, even so are we in this world.

1 John 4: 4 (HCSB)
4 You are from God, little children, and you have conquered them, because the One who is in you is greater than the one who is in the world.

1 John 5: 4 (GNT)
4 because every child of God is able to defeat the world. And we win the victory over the world by means of our faith.

Revelation 12: 11 (GNT)
11 They won the victory over him by the blood of the Lamb and by the truth which they proclaimed;

WEARY

Genesis 28: 15 (NIV)
15 I am with you and will watch over you wherever you go, and I will bring you back to this land. I will not leave you until I have done what I have promised you.

Psalms 27: 14 (NKJV)
14 Wait on the Lord; Be of good courage, And He shall strengthen your heart; Wait, I say, on the Lord!

Psalms 30: 11 - 12 (NLT)
11 You have turned my mourning into joyful dancing. You have taken away my clothes of mourning and clothed me with joy, 12 that I might sing praises

to you and not be silent. O Lord my God, I will give you thanks forever!

Psalms 42: 11 (NKJV)
11 Why are you cast down, O my soul? And why are you disquieted within me? Hope in God; For I shall yet praise Him, The help of my countenance and my God.

Psalms 55: 22 (NLT)
22 Give your burdens to the Lord, and he will take care of you. He will not permit the godly to slip and fall.

Psalms 68: 9 (NIV)
9 You gave abundant showers, O God; you refreshed your weary inheritance.

Psalms 119: 28 (NKJV)
28 My soul melts from heaviness; Strengthen me according to Your word.

Psalms 121: 1 - 3 (ESV)
1 I lift up my eyes to the hills. From where does my help come? 2 My help comes from the Lord, who made heaven and earth. 3 He will not let your foot be moved; he who keeps you will not slumber.

Psalms 138: 7 - 8 (NASB)
7 Though I walk in the midst of trouble, You will revive me; You will stretch forth Your hand against the wrath of my enemies, And Your right hand will save me. 8 The Lord will accomplish what concerns me; Your lovingkindness, O Lord, is everlasting; Do not forsake the works of Your hands.

Proverbs 25: 25 (NIV)
25 Like cold water to a weary soul is good news from a distant land.

Isaiah 40: 29 - 30 (ESV)
29 He gives power to the faint, and to him who has no might he increases strength. 30 Even youths shall faint and be weary, and young men shall fall exhausted;

Isaiah 42: 16 (RSV)
16 And I will lead the blind in a way that they know not, in paths that they have not known I will guide them. I will turn the darkness before them into light, the rough places into level ground. These are the things I will do, and I will not forsake them.

Jeremiah 12: 5 (MEV)
5 If you have run with the footmen, and they have wearied you, then how can you contend with hors-es? And if in the land of peace in which you trusted, they wearied you, then how will you do in the thicket of the Jordan?

Jeremiah 31: 25 (ESV)
25 For I will satisfy the weary soul, and every languishing soul I will replenish.

Matthew 11: 28 - 29 (ESV)
28 "Come to me, all you who are weary and burdened, and I will give you rest. 29 Take my yoke upon you and learn from me, for I am gentle and humble in heart, and you will find rest for your souls.

Galatians 6: 9 (NET)
9 So we must not grow weary in doing good, for in due time we will reap, if we do not give up.

WIFE

Genesis 2: 18 (NLT)
18 Then the Lord God said, "It is not good for the man to be alone. I will make a helper who is just right for him."

Genesis 24: 40 (NKJV)
40 But he said to me, 'The Lord, before whom I walk, will send His angel with you and prosper your way; and you shall take a wife for my son from my family and from my father's house.

1 Samuel 25: 32 (AMP)
32 And David said to Abigail, Blessed be the Lord, the God of Israel, Who sent you this day to meet me.

Psalms 128: 3 - 4 (NIV)
3 Your wife will be like a fruitful vine within your house; your children will be like olive shoots around your table. 4 Yes, this will be the blessing for the man who fears the Lord.

Proverbs 5: 15 - 19 (NIV)
15 Drink water from your own cistern, running water from your own well.16 Should your springs overflow in the streets, your streams of water in the public squares? 17 Let them be yours alone, never to be shared with strangers. 18 May your fountain be blessed, and may you rejoice in the wife of your youth. 19 A loving doe, a graceful deer— may her breasts satisfy you always, may you ever be intoxicated with her love..

Proverbs 6: 29 (ESV)
29 So is he who goes in to his neighbor's wife; none who touches her will go unpunished.

Proverbs 12: 4 (NCV)
4 A good wife is like a crown for her husband, but a disgraceful wife is like a disease in his bones.

Proverbs 18: 22 (ESV)
22 He who finds a wife finds a good thing and obtains favor from the Lord.

Proverbs 19: 14 (AMP)
14 House and riches are the inheritance from fathers, but a wise, understanding, and prudent wife is from the Lord.

Proverbs 31: 10 (CEV)
10 A truly good wife is the most precious treasure a man can find!

Ecclesiastes 4: 9 - 12 (TLB)
9 Two can accomplish more than twice as much as one, for the results can be much better. 10 If one falls, the other pulls him up; but if a man falls when he is alone, he's in trouble. 11 Also, on a cold night, two under the same blanket gain warmth from each other, but how can one be warm alone? 12 And one standing alone can be attacked and defeated, but two can stand back-to-back and con-quer; three is even better, for a triple-braided cord is not easily broken.

Matthew 19: 4 - 6 (CEB)
4 Jesus answered, "Haven't you read that at the beginning the creator made them male and female? 5 And God said, 'Because of this a man should leave his father and mother and be joined together with his wife, and the two will be one flesh.' 6 So they are no longer two but one flesh. Therefore, humans must not pull apart what God has put together."

1 Corinthians 7: 9 - 11 (ESV)
9 But if they cannot exercise self-control, they should marry. For it is better to marry than to burn with passion. 10 To the married I give this charge (not I, but the Lord): the wife should not separate from her husband 11 (but if she does, she should remain unmarried or else be reconciled to her husband), and the husband should not divorce his wife.

1 Corinthians 11: 3 (GW)
3 However, I want you to realize that Christ has authority over every man, a husband has authority over his wife, and God has authority over Christ.

2 Corinthians 6: 14 (CEB)
14 Don't be tied up as equal partners with people who don't believe. What does righteousness share with that which is outside the Law? What relationship does light have with darkness?

Ephesians 5: 25 - 26 (NIV)
25 Husbands, love your wives, just as Christ loved the church and gave himself up for her 26 to make her holy, cleansing her by the washing with water through the word,

Ephesians 5: 33 (NOG)
33 But every husband must love his wife as he loves himself, and wives should respect their hus-bands.

1 Timothy 3: 11 (AMP)
11 Women must likewise be worthy of respect, not malicious gossips, but self-controlled, [thoroughly] trustworthy in all things.

1 Peter 3: 7 (GNT)
7 In the same way you husbands must live with your wives with the proper

understanding that they are more delicate than you. Treat them with respect, because they also will receive, together with you, God's gift of life. Do this so that nothing will interfere with your prayers.

WISDOM

Joshua 1: 8 (NLT)
8 Study this Book of Instruction continually. Meditate on it day and night so you will be sure to obey everything written in it. Only then will you prosper and succeed in all you do.

Psalms 19: 8 - 11 (NIV)
8 The precepts of the Lord are right, giving joy to the heart. The commands of the Lord are radiant, giving light to the eyes. 9 The fear of the Lord is pure, enduring forever. The decrees of the Lord are firm, and all of them are righteous. 10 They are more precious than gold, than much pure gold; they are sweeter than honey, than honey from the honeycomb. 11 By them your servant is warned; in keeping them there is great reward.

Psalms 32: 8 (MEV)
8 I will instruct you and teach you in the way you should go; I will counsel you with my eye on you.

Psalms 51: 6 (GNT)
6 Sincerity and truth are what you require; fill my mind with your wisdom.

Proverbs 1: 23 (NLT)
23 Come and listen to my counsel. I'll share my heart with you and make you wise.

Proverbs 2: 2 - 3, 5 - 8 (MEV)
2 so that you incline your ear to wisdom, and apply your heart to understanding; 3 yes, if you cry out for knowledge, and lift up your voice for understanding, 5 then you will understand the fear of the Lord, and find the knowledge of God. 6 For the Lord gives wisdom; out of His mouth come knowledge and understanding. 7 He lays up sound wisdom for the righteous; He is a shield to those who walk uprightly. 8 He keeps the paths of justice, and preserves the way of His saints.

Proverbs 3: 5 - 8 (NCV)
5 Trust the Lord with all your heart, and don't depend on your own understanding. 6 Remember the Lord in all you do, and he will give you success. 7 Don't depend on your own wisdom. Respect the Lord and refuse to do wrong. 8 Then your body will be healthy, and your bones will be strong.

Proverbs 3: 13 - 16 (NCV)
13 Happy is the person who finds wisdom, the one who gets understanding. 14 Wisdom is worth more than silver; it brings more profit than gold. 15 Wisdom is more precious than rubies; nothing you could want is equal to it. 16 With her right hand wisdom offers you a long life, and with her left hand she gives you riches and honor.

Proverbs 4: 5 - 7, 11 - 12 (NKJV)
5 Get wisdom! Get understanding! Do not forget, nor turn away from the words of my mouth. 6 Do not forsake her, and she will preserve you; Love her, and she will keep you. 7 Wisdom is the principal thing; Therefore get

wisdom. And in all your getting, get understanding. 11 I have taught you in the way of wisdom; I have led you in right paths. 12 When you walk, your steps will not be hindered, And when you run, you will not stumble.

Ecclesiastes 2: 26 (NIVUK)
26 To the person who pleases him, God gives wisdom, knowledge and happiness, but to the sinner he gives the task of gathering and storing up wealth to hand it over to the one who pleases God. This too is meaningless, a chasing after the wind.

Romans 8: 14 (WEB)
14 For as many as are led by the Spirit of God, these are children of God.

1 Corinthians 1: 21, 25 (NLT)
21 Since God in his wisdom saw to it that the world would never know him through human wisdom, he has used our foolish preaching to save those who believe. 25 This foolish plan of God is wiser than the wisest of human plans, and God's weakness is stronger than the greatest of human strength.

1 Corinthians 12: 8 (WEB)
8 For to one is given through the Spirit the word of wisdom, and to another the word of knowledge, according to the same Spirit;

Colossians 1: 9 - 10 (NOG)
9 For this reason we have not stopped praying for you since the day we heard about you. We ask God to fill you with the knowledge of his will through every kind of spiritual wisdom and insight. 10 We ask this so that you will live the kind of lives that prove you belong to the Lord. Then you will want

to please him in every way as you grow in producing every kind of good work by this knowledge about God.

2 Timothy 3: 16 - 17 (GNT)

16 All Scripture is inspired by God and is useful for teaching the truth, rebuking error, correcting faults, and giving instruction for right living, 17 so that the person who serves God may be fully qualified and equipped to do every kind of good deed.

James 1: 5 - 6 (NKJV)

5 If any of you lacks wisdom, let him ask of God, who gives to all liberally and without reproach, and it will be given to him. 6 But let him ask in faith, with no doubting, for he who doubts is like a wave of the sea driven and tossed by the wind.

James 3: 17 (NKJV)

17 But the wisdom that is from above is first pure, then peaceable, gentle, willing to yield, full of mercy and good fruits, without partiality and without hypocrisy.

1 John 4: 1 (WEB)

1 Beloved, do not believe every spirit, but test the spirits, whether they are of God; because many false prophets have gone out into the world.

WORD

1 Samuel 2: 3 (NKJV)

3 Talk no more so very proudly; Let no arrogance come from your mouth, For the Lord is the God of knowledge; And by Him actions are weighed.

Psalms 19: 14 (HCSB)

14 May the words of my mouthand the meditation of my heartbe acceptable to You, Lord, my rock and my Redeemer.

Proverbs 10: 19 (CJB)

19 When words are many, sin is not lacking; so he who controls his speech is wise.

Proverbs 12: 14 (NIV)

14 From the fruit of their lips people are filled with good things, and the work of their hands brings them reward.

Proverbs 12: 18 (NIV)

18 The words of the reckless pierce like swords, but the tongue of the wise brings healing.

Proverbs 12: 25 (NASB)

25 Anxiety weighs down the heart, but a kind word cheers it up.

Proverbs 15: 23 (ISV)

23 An appropriate answer brings joy to a person, and a well-timed word is a good thing.

Proverbs 16: 24 (ESV)

24 Gracious words are like a honeycomb, sweetness to the soul and health to the body.

Proverbs 17: 27 (VOICE)

27 Those with knowledge know when to be quiet, and those with understanding know how to remain calm.

Proverbs 18: 8 (NOG)

8 The words of a gossip are swallowed greedily, and they go down into a person's innermost being.

Proverbs 18: 21 (NKJV)
21 Death and life are in the power of the tongue, and those who love it will eat its fruit.

Proverbs 22: 12 (GNT)
12 The Lord sees to it that truth is kept safe by disproving the words of liars.

Proverbs 23: 9 (NRSV)
9 Do not speak in the hearing of a fool, who will only despise the wisdom of your words.

Proverbs 25: 11 (VOICE)
11 A well-spoken word at just the right moment is like golden apples in settings of silver.

Proverbs 25: 15 (NCV)
15 With patience you can convince a ruler, and a gentle word can get through to the hard-headed.

Ecclesiastes 5: 6 (ISV)
6 Never let your mouth cause you to sin and don't proclaim in the presence of the angel, "My promise was a mistake," for why should God be angry at your excuse and destroy what you've undertaken?

Jeremiah 23: 29 (NLT)
29 Does not my word burn like fire?" says the Lord. "Is it not like a mighty hammer that smashes a rock to pieces?

Matthew 10: 19 - 20 (WEB)
19 But when they deliver you up, don't be anxious how or what you will say, for it will be given you in that hour what you will say. 20 For it is not you who speak, but the Spirit of your Father who speaks in you.

Luke 6: 45 (RSV)
45 The good man out of the good treasure of his heart produces good, and the evil man out of his evil treasure produces evil; for out of the abundance of the heart his mouth speaks.

Luke 12: 12 (AMP)
12 For the Holy Spirit will teach you in that very hour and moment what [you] ought to say.

Ephesians 4: 29 (NIV)
29 Do not let any unwholesome talk come out of your mouths, but only what is helpful for building others up according to their needs, that it may benefit those who listen.

Hebrews 4: 12 (NOG)
12 God's word is living and active. It is sharper than any two-edged sword and cuts as deep as the place where soul and spirit meet, the place where joints and marrow meet. God's word judges a person's thoughts and intentions.

James 3: 4 - 5 (NIV)
4 Or take ships as an example. Although they are so large and are driven by strong winds, they are steered by a very small rudder wherever the pilot wants to go. 5 Likewise, the tongue is a small part of the body, but it makes great boasts. Consider what a great forest is set on fire by a small spark.

WORK

Genesis 2: 3 (NKJV)
3 Then God blessed the seventh day and sanctified it, because in it He

rested from all His work which God had created and made.

2 Chronicles 15: 7 (ISV)
7 Now as for you, be strong and never be discouraged, because there will be reward for your work."

Psalms 127: 1 (NIV)
1 Unless the Lord builds the house, the builders labor in vain. Unless the Lord watches over the city, the guards stand watch in vain.

Proverbs 14: 23 (CJB)
23 In all work there is profit, but mere talk produces only poverty.

Proverbs 20: 11 (JUB)
11 Even a child is known by his doings, whether his work is pure and whether it is right.

1 Corinthians 15: 58 (HCSB)
58 Therefore, my dear brothers, be steadfast, immovable, always excelling in the Lord's work, know-ing that your labor in the Lord is not in vain.

Ephesians 4: 28 (WEB)
28 Let him who stole steal no more; but rather let him labor, producing with his hands something that is good, that he may have something to give to him who has need.

Colossians 1: 10 (MEV)
10 that you may walk in a manner worthy of the Lord, pleasing to all, being fruitful in every good work, and increasing in the knowledge of God,

Colossians 3: 23 (RSV)
23 Whatever your task, work heartily, as serving the Lord and not men,

2 Thessalonians 3: 11 - 12 (TLB)
11 Yet we hear that some of you are living in laziness, refusing to work, and wasting your time in gos-siping. 12 In the name of the Lord Jesus Christ we appeal to such people—we command them—to quiet down, get to work, and earn their own living.

WORMANSHIP

Matthew 5: 14 - 16 (ESV)
14 "You are the light of the world. A city set on a hill cannot be hidden. 15 Nor do people light a lamp and put it under a basket, but on a stand, and it gives light to all in the house. 16 In the same way, let your light shine before others, so that they may see your good works and give glory to your Father who is in heaven.

Mark 16: 17 - 18, 20 (RSV)
17 And these signs will accompany those who believe: in my name they will cast out demons; they will speak in new tongues; 18 they will pick up serpents, and if they drink any deadly thing, it will not hurt them; they will lay their hands on the sick, and they will recover. 20 And they went forth and preached everywhere, while the Lord worked with them and confirmed the message by the signs that attended it. Amen.

Galatians 5: 22 - 23 (CEV)
22 God's Spirit makes us loving, happy, peaceful, patient, kind, good, faithful, 23 gentle, and self-con-trolled. There is no law against behaving in any of these ways.

Philippians 1: 6 (WEB)
6 being confident of this very thing, that he who began a good work in you will complete it until the day of Jesus Christ.

Philippians 2: 13 (ERV)
13 Yes, it is God who is working in you. He helps you want to do what pleases him, and he gives you the power to do it.

Colossians 3: 23 - 24 (NIRV)
23 Work at everything you do with all your heart. Work as if you were working for the Lord, not for human masters. 24 Work because you know that you will finally receive as a reward what the Lord wants you to have. You are slaves of the Lord Christ.

Titus 2: 7 (NCV)
7 In every way be an example of doing good deeds. When you teach, do it with honesty and serious-ness.

WORRY

Psalms 32: 7 (CEV)
7 You are my hiding place! You protect me from trouble, and you put songs in my heart because you have saved me.

Psalms 46: 1 - 3 (GW)
1 God is our refuge and strength, an ever-present help in times of trouble. 2 That is why we are not afraid even when the earth quakes or the mountains topple into the depths of the sea. 3 Water roars and foams, and mountains shake at the surging waves.

Psalms 91: 1 - 16 (NIVUK)
1 Whoever dwells in the shelter of the Most High will rest in the shadow of the Almighty. 2 I will say of the Lord, "He is my refuge and my fortress, my God, in whom I trust." 3 Surely he will save you from the fowler's snare and from the deadly pestilence. 4 He will cover you with his feathers, and under his wings you will find refuge; his faithfulness will be your shield and rampart. 5 You will not fear the terror of night, nor the arrow that flies by day, 6 nor the pestilence that stalks in the darkness, nor the plague that destroys at midday. 7 A thousand may fall at your side, ten thousand at your right hand, but it will not come near you. 8 You will only observe with your eyes and see the punishment of the wicked. 9 If you say, "The Lord is my refuge," and you make the Most High your dwelling, 10 no harm will overtake you, no disaster will come near your tent. 11 For he will command his angels con-cerning you to guard you in all your ways; 12 they will lift you up in their hands, so that you will not strike your foot against a stone. 13 You will tread on the lion and the cobra; you will trample the great lion and the serpent. 14 "Because he loves me," says the Lord, "I will rescue him; I will protect him, for he acknowledges my name. 15 He will call on me, and I will answer him; I will be with him in trou-ble, I will deliver him and honor him. 16 With long life I will satisfy him and show him my salvation."

Proverbs 12: 25 (NASB)
25 Anxiety in a man's heart weighs it down, But a good word makes it glad.

Jeremiah 17: 7 - 8 (ERV)
7 But those who trust in the Lord will be blessed. They know that the Lord will do what he says. 8 They will be strong like trees planted near a stream that send out roots to the water. They have noth-ing to fear when the days get hot. Their leaves are always green. They never worry, even in a year that has no rain. They always produce fruit.

Matthew 6: 25 - 34 (NCV)
25 "So I tell you, don't worry about the food or drink you need to live, or about the clothes you need for your body. Life is more than food, and the body is more than clothes. 26 Look at the birds in the air. They don't plant or harvest or store food in barns, but your heavenly Father feeds them. And you know that you are worth much more than the birds. 27 You cannot add any time to your life by wor-rying about it. 28 "And why do you worry about clothes? Look at how the lilies in the field grow. They don't work or make clothes for themselves. 29 But I tell you that even Solomon with his riches was not dressed as beautifully as one of these flowers. 30 God clothes the grass in the field, which is alive today but tomorrow is thrown into the fire. So you can be even more sure that God will clothe you. Don't have so little faith! 31 Don't worry and say, 'What will we eat?' or 'What will we drink?' or 'What will we wear?' 32 The people who don't know God keep trying to get these things, and your Father in heaven knows you need them. 33 Seek first God's kingdom and what God wants. Then all your other needs will be met as well. 34 So don't worry about tomorrow, because tomorrow will have its own worries. Each day has enough trouble of its own.

Romans 8: 37 (NIV)
37 No, in all these things we are more than conquerors through him who loved us.

Philippians 4: 6 - 7 (NLT)
6 Don't worry about anything; instead, pray about everything. Tell God what you need, and thank him for all he has done. 7 Then you will experience God's peace, which exceeds anything we can under-stand. His peace will guard your hearts and minds as you live in Christ Jesus.

2 Timothy 1: 7 (DLNT)
7 For God did not give us a spirit of fearfulness, but of power and love and a sound-mind.

1 John 4: 4 (WEB)
4 You are of God, little children, and have overcome them; because greater is he who is in you than he who is in the world.

WORSHIP

Psalms 29: 2 (NCV)
2 Praise the Lord for the glory of his name; worship the Lord because he is holy.

Psalms 66: 4 (NLT)
4 Everything on earth will worship you; they will sing your praises, shouting your name in glorious songs.

Psalms 95: 6 - 7 (NIV)
6 Come, let us bow down in worship, let us kneel before the Lord our Maker;
7 for he is our God and we are the people of his pasture, the flock under

his care. Today, if only you would hear his voice,

Psalms 99: 9 (NCV)
9 Praise the Lord our God, and worship at his holy mountain, because the Lord our God is holy.

Psalms 100: 2 (NIV)
2 Worship the Lord with gladness; come before him with joyful songs.

Psalms 109: 30 (NIV)
30 With my mouth I will greatly extol the Lord; in the great throng of worshipers I will praise him.

Luke 4: 5 - 8 (NIVUK)
5 The devil led him up to a high place and showed him in an instant all the kingdoms of the world. 6 And he said to him, 'I will give you all their authority and splendour; it has been given to me, and I can give it to anyone I want to. 7 If you worship me, it will all be yours. 8 Jesus answered, 'It is written: "Worship the Lord your God and serve him only."'

John 4: 23 - 24 (NOG)
23 Indeed, the time is coming, and it is now here, when the true worshipers will worship the Father in spirit and truth. The Father is looking for people like that to worship him. 24 God is a spirit. Those who worship him must worship in spirit and truth."

John 9: 31 (AMP)
31 We know that God does not listen to sinners; but if anyone is God-fearing and a worshiper of Him and does His will, He listens to him

Romans 12: 1 (NIV)
1 Therefore, I urge you, brothers and sisters, in view of God's mercy, to offer your bodies as a living sacrifice, holy and pleasing to God—this is your true and proper worship.

Hebrews 12: 28 (ISV)
28 Therefore, since we are receiving a kingdom that cannot be shaken, let us be thankful and worship God in reverence and fear in a way that pleases him.

Made in the USA
Las Vegas, NV
03 June 2022

49765028R00142